HOSTS AND CHAMPIONS

Popular Cultural Studies

Series editors: Justin O'Connor, Steve Redhead and Derek Wynne.

The Manchester Institute for Popular Culture was set up in order to promote theoretical and empirical research in the area of contemporary popular culture, both within the University and in conjunction with local, national and international agencies. The Institute is currently engaged in two major comparative research projects around aspects of consumption and popular culture in the City. The Institute also runs a number of post-graduate research programmes, with a particular emphasis on ethnographic work. The series intends to reflect all aspects of the Institute's activities. Current theoretical debates within the field of popular culture will be explored within an empirical context. Much of the research is undertaken by young researchers actively involved in their chosen fields of study, allowing an awareness of the issues and an attentiveness to actual developments often lacking in standard academic writings on the subject. The series will also reflect the working methods of the Institute, emphasising a collective research effort and the regular presentation of work-in-progress to the Institute's research seminars. The series hopes, therefore, both to push forward the debates around popular culture, urban regeneration and postmodern social theory whilst introducing an ethnographic and contextual basis for such debates.

Titles already published

Rave Off: Politics and Deviance in Contemporary Youth Culture

The Passion and the Fashion: Football Fandom in the New Europe

The Lads in Action: Social Process in an Urban Youth Subculture

Hosts and Champions: Soccer Cultures, National Identities and the USA World Cup

Game Without Frontiers: Football, Identity and Modernity

The Margins of the City: Gay Men's Urban Lives

Hosts and Champions

Soccer cultures, national identities and the USA World Cup

edited by

John Sugden
Alan Tomlinson

arena

Published by
Arena
Ashgate Publishing Limited
Gower House
Croft Road
Aldershot
Hants GU11 3HR
England

Ashgate Publishing Company
Old Post Road
Brookfield
Vermont 05036
USA

British Library Cataloguing in Publication Data:

Hosts and Champions: Soccer Cultures,
National Identities and the USA World
Cup — (Popular Cultural Studies)
    I. Sugden, John II. Tomlinson, Alan
    III. Series
    306.483

ISBN 1 85742 227 9 (Hardback)
ISBN 1 85742 228 7 (Paperback)

Cover image: Jac Depcyz

Printed and Bound in Great Britain by
Hartnolls Limited, Bodmin, Cornwall.

Contents

Acknowledgements

The editors would like to thank the North American Society for the Sociology of Sport (NASSS) and the Manchester Institute for Popular Culture for providing opportunities for the public discussion of the contents of this volume. We are particularly grateful for the encouragement given by Jean Harvey of the University of Ottawa and Steve Redhead from the Manchester Metropolitan University. Our final thanks go to Maggy Taylor in Manchester and Myrene McFee in Eastbourne who, between them, achieved the impossible by bringing order out of chaos in the final production of this text.

About the authors

Eduardo Archetti is at the University of Olso, Norway (Department of Anthropology).

Alan Bairner is at the University of Ulster, Jordanstown, Northern Ireland (Department of Philosophy and Politics).

Christian Bromberger is at the University of Provence, France (Laboratory for Mediterranean and Comparative Ethnography).

Chas Critcher is at Sheffield Hallam University, England (Department of Communication and Media Studies).

Bob Edelman is at the University of Berkeley, California, USA (Department of History).

Matti Goksøyr is at the Norwegian University of Sport and Physical Education, Oslo, Norway.

John Horne is at Heriot-Watt University, Edinburgh, Scotland (Leisure Studies, Moray House).

John Humphrey is at the Institute of Development Studies, University of Sussex, England.

David Jary is at Staffordshire University, Stoke-on-Trent, England (Faculty of Social Sciences).

Pierre Lanfranchi is at De Montfort University, Leicester, England (Faculty of History).

Udo Merkel is at the German Sports University, Cologne, Germany.

Steve Redhead is at the Manchester Metropolitan University, Manchester, England (Manchester Institute for Popular Culture).

Jim Riordan is at the University of Surrey, Guildford, England (Department of Linguistic and International Studies).

John Sugden is at the University of Ulster, Jordanstown, Northern Ireland (Division of Sport and Leisure Studies).

Alan Tomlinson is at the University of Brighton, Brighton, England (Chelsea School Research Centre).

Christopher Young is at Pembroke College, University of Cambridge, England (Department of German, Faculty of Mediaeval Languages).

Section I
Soccer culture, national identity and the growth of world soccer

1 Soccer culture, national identity and the World Cup

John Sugden and Alan Tomlinson

Sport is at once both trivial and serious, inconsequential yet of symbolic significance. A basketball or soccer defeat is not, in any sensible use of the word, tragic, yet it can have consequences which could be seen as tragic; there is always another time, in the cyclical epic of sporting contest, yet the emotionalism of a sporting encounter and result can embody deeply felt cultural values. Sport in many cases informs and refuels the popular memory of communities, and offers a source of collective identification and community expression for those who follow teams and individuals. Contemporary sport is also, more than ever before, a lucrative worldwide industry, often developing in tension with a model of sport which stresses (at either political or educational levels) essentially moral and character-forming aspects.

Soccer, in its multiple forms as played throughout the world, has all of these characteristics, and its features have made it the most widely played team sport in the world. With the World Cup Soccer tournament now contested every four years (neatly dovetailing with the calendar of the Summer Olympic Games), the spectacle of soccer delivers to television companies and channels the largest audiences in the history of broad-casting. This close to universal appeal is testimony to some of the inherent features of the sport: its unpredictability; its accessibility; and its physio-logically democratic premise.

It is unpredictable because goals are, in anything like an evenly matched contest, relatively hard to come by, as there is no guaranteed reward for territorial domination — unlike in basketball or American

3

football, where high-scoring is viewed instrumentally and incrementally as the expected reward or outcome for the talent and the work expended. Soccer's glorious unpredictability means that favourites rarely win with the ease anticipated; the soccer World Cup has never seen any team stroll to victory in the fashion of, say, the USA Olympic basketball "Dream Team" at the Barcelona Olympics in 1992. Perhaps Brazil came close to such a level of superiority in 1958, 1962 and 1970; but they could never be over-confident at the outcome of matches, and overwhelming favourites have often failed. Brazil in 1950, Hungary in 1954 and Holland in 1974 were widely seen as the most accomplished and outstanding sides of their day, yet all those sides failed to capture the title, Brazil losing to Uruguay and the other two to dogged and determined West German sides.

Soccer is accessible because it can be played in improvised fashion in just about any circumstances, and without the need for sophisticated or expensive equipment. It can flourish in small-sided spontaneous games on public parks, in confined spaces in the inner-city, in corners of school play areas, with balls of various sizes and clothes or other random objects for goal posts. Skills can be cultivated at this level and then honed in the setting of the full-scale game.

The physiologically democratic nature of soccer is one of the secrets of its worldwide impact. You do not have to be a particular shape, size or physique in order to excel at soccer. One of the joys of the game is to see the muscular Goliath outthought and outwitted by the unathletic looking David; and physiology does not determine, in any crudely predictable way, the position at which one will excel in soccer.* It obviously helps to be tall if you want to dominate "in the air", to win aerial balls with your heading prowess (for non-afficianados, this refers to the making of contact with the ball by the forehead, a skill particularly valuable for dominant defenders and goalscoring strikers). But some of the greatest and far from tallest players have been equally brilliant in the air as well as on the ground, and in a variety of playing roles rather than in any single specialist task-oriented position or role.

Those qualifying for the World Cup Finals in the USA in 1994 were the winners of qualifying groups in Europe (6 groups, 12 qualifiers); South

---

* The memory of the crippled Brazilian winger Garrincha torturing the physically perfect Northern European defender bears out this point on the democracy of physique in soccer.

America (2 groups, 3 qualifiers); Concacaf — a group covering Central America, the Caribbean and North America (1 qualifier); Africa (3 groups, 3 qualifiers); Asia (2 qualifiers); and a South America/Oceania (Oceania being Australia and South Seas nations) play-off (1 qualifier).

The holders of the trophy and the hosts qualified automatically. This process produced a line-up for USA '94 as follows:

Holders	Germany
Hosts	United States of America
European Qualifiers	Belgium
	Bulgaria
	Greece
	Holland
	Irish Republic
	Italy
	Norway
	Romania
	Russia
	Spain
	Sweden
	Switzerland
South American Qualifiers	Argentina [via Oceania play-off]
	Bolivia
	Brazil
	Columbia
Concacaf Qualifier	Mexico
Africa Qualifiers	Cameroon
	Morocco
	Nigeria
Asia Qualifiers	Saudi Arabia
	South Korea

These 24 sides qualified in 1993 to contest the fourteenth World Cup. The route to the finals was a relatively harmonious one, though there were tense expectations around the Asian qualifying group, which became known as the Group of Death when matches in Qatar on the Persian Gulf involved Iraq, Iran, the two Koreas and Japan. The chairman of the organizing committee of the Finals, Alan Rothenberg, was reported to be delighted at the outcome of the matches in this group, saying that the qualification of Iran and/or Iraq would have generated "logistical problems" in the organization of the Finals (BBC Radio 4, *Today* programme, November 18 1993). The Iraqi soccer manager, Adnan Dirjal, had said that: "If we qualify, it will be the biggest slap the monster America will get" (cited in *The Guardian*, December 28, 1993, p.13). Rothenberg's relief, on the qualification of Saudi Arabia and South Korea, was obvious. As reported in *USA Today,* using a thinly veiled reference to the USA's role, both in the Korean War and in the more recent Gulf conflict, Rothenberg said that the United States would be delighted to host teams from South Korea and Saudi Arabia just as, in the past, those nations had "hosted teams from the United States" (*USA Today,* October 30, 1993). He added a further sigh of relief that a third apparently unwelcome nation had not qualified. This was England, feared for the reputation of its football fans.

Few controversies marred the qualifying rounds leading into 1994 — unlike those for the 1990 World Cup in Italy, when many teams from Africa did not attempt to qualify, protesting at the small allocation of places to the continent; and the South American and Central American qualifiers were distorted by the misdemeanours of Chile and Mexico. Chile had walked off the field when losing to Brazil, and were disqualified from both the 1990 and 1994 tournaments. Mexico had been banned from the 1990 tournament, for cheating, having been caught playing over-age players in the World Youth Cup.

Chile was also involved in a controversy in 1974. Having qualified to play the Soviet Union in a play-off for a place in the finals in West Germany, and drawn 0-0 in Moscow, the Chileans scheduled their home game for the Estadio Nacional in Santiago. This stadium was infamous for its use as a political prison only one year before by the Pinochet military regime. Supporters of the democratically-elected President Allende had been rounded up and detained in the stadium, many summarily 'executed'. The Soviet Union refused to play in such a climate and venue, and were disqualified from the tournament after not turning up for the match.

Despite the representativeness of the process which produces the teams in the Finals, the thirteen titles from 1934-1990 were won by only six nations. The list of winners and venues makes interesting reading:

Date	Winner	Venue	Teams	Games
1930	Uruguay	Uruguay	13	18
1934	Italy	Italy	16	17
1938	Italy	France	15	18
1950	Uruguay	Brazil	13	22
1954	West Germany	Switzerland	16	26
1958	Brazil	Sweden	16	35
1962	Brazil	Chile	16	32
1966	England	England	16	32
1970	Brazil	Mexico	16	32
1974	West Germany	W. Germany	16	38
1978	Argentina	Argentina	16	38
1982	Italy	Spain	24	52
1986	Argentina	Mexico	24	52
1990	West Germany	Italy	24	52

Three nations have won the trophy three times — Brazil, Italy and West Germany. Argentina have won it twice, as has Uruguay. England is the only nation to have won the trophy to have won it only once. Host status is not an unambiguous advantage. The first two championships were won by host nations, but there was a relatively limited field of entrants, with little Atlantic crossover compared to later tournaments; and it was another thirty two years before a host nation won the title, when England did so, assisted by arranging home advantage for every game. Hosts also won the title in 1974 and 1978, and this garnered expectations for the Spanish in 1982 and the Italians in 1990. But 'Hosts and Champions' has not become a dominant feature of World Cup history. There have been some spectacular achievements by unfancied host nations — Sweden making it to the final to play Brazil, when the South American side became the first (and up to the 1990 tournament at least, the only side) to win the World Cup away from their own continent. Chile took third place in 1962. Mexico went as far as the quarter final in 1970 and 1986, as did Switzerland in 1954. In fact, in the first fourteen World Cup Final tournaments, the host nation never failed to progress beyond the initial first round stage. In 1994, at home and seeded as hosts, the USA were drawn to play Switzerland (in Detroit), and Columbia and Romania (both in Los Angeles). World opinion was clear that the hosts would do very well indeed to survive beyond the first round, so avoiding an ignominious 'first' in World Cup history. There have also been also some spectacular "home failures" — Brazil losing to Uruguay in what (though it was not actually a final) was the last and decisive game of the 1950 Finals; and the dazzling but temperamental Italian side of 1990 losing to the spoiling Maradona-inspired Argentina side in Italy in 1990. Brazil's spectacular failure of 1950 still festers in the national psyche: that magnificent soccer nation remains the only three-times winner of the Cup not to have won it on home soil.

The awarding of the 1994 Finals to the USA represented an irony of sorts, in that the world's most popular sport was to bring its biggest event to a sports-mad nation in which soccer had no embedded professional roots, and where soccer was far from a central concern of the sports public. In 1950 the inexperienced and multi-cultural footballers of the USA humbled England, the country that had given association football or soccer to the world, in the World Cup in Brazil. For the sports-mad American public this could have been the start of something big. The USA had also beaten Belgium and Paraguay in the first World Cup in Uruguay in 1930, losing 6-1 to Argentina in the semi-finals. So in a sense the 1950 victory — despite defeats by Spain and Chile — was a reminder of the past achievements as well as the potential of the USA in world soccer. Yet after the 1950 victory over England it was forty years before the USA qualified once more for this biggest of sporting spectacles. And in Italy in 1990, though playing spiritedly and winning many friends, the USA lost all its three games in the Finals, watched by only a reputed 2% of the domestic television audience back home. The response of other nations to the 1990 tournament was vastly different. Whilst the genuinely global world game remained a peripheral element in the consciousness of the American public, the fervour of national expression in countries across the world had never been so pronounced. From Cairo to Youande, Dublin to Dubrovnik, Madrid to Moscow, Seoul to Costa Rica, billions of enthusiasts — old, young, male, female, all the races of the world — followed the fluctuating fortunes of the "boys" over in Italy.

But things were different in the sports culture of the USA. There, the average fan in New York, Los Angeles or Dallas (three of the nine venues for the 1994 tournament, with the Rosebowl, Pasadena/Los Angeles selected to stage the final) was more interested in the build up to the USA's own "world-series", in its own sport of baseball. The USA's own big three team sports — baseball, basketball and American Football — still hold sway with the North American public. The American nation has created its own sports, and endowed them with a quintessential American-ness over and above the ethnic and cultural variations out of which contemporary America has been forged. But despite the claim that the development of characteristically American sports is testament to the success of the multi-cultural pluralist experiment, there remains a strong sense of ethnic identity in many aspects of institutional and everyday life. Pride over ethnic identity remains strong in the American experience. Half of the population of California will, it is confidently forecast, soon be of Hispanic origin. Some estimates claim that close to 1 in 5 of the USA population has Irish roots. When Columbia drew with West Germany in the 1990 Finals in Italy, so qualifying for the second stages where they lost 2-1 in extra-time to Cameroon in front of a 50,000 crowd in Naples, expatriate Colombians filled the streets of New York in an extravagant celebration of national pride, until rudely interrupted by the party poopers of the New York Police Department.

Whereas, in many countries of the world, soccer's roots lie in the urban, impoverished working-class areas of the big city — from Belfast to Buenos Aires — in the USA the game has blossomed most in the respectable suburbs, schools and colleges of the white middle class. The tension between this sphere of its growth and the commitment of ethnic communities to soccer in its traditional centres of strength was a fascinating one in the build-up to the 1994 Finals. The USA has been a prolific exporter of culture — from McDonalds, Budweiser, Pepsi and Coke through to popular music, film and the Superbowl and not without controversy, as French responses to Hollywood hegemony showed during the 1993 GATT talks. But as a nation, it has often appeared reluctant to import cultural forms which might highlight its own cultural and ethnic diffuseness. The response of the USA to the arrival of the biggest event in the world game's calendar was a precarious blend of respect for global tradition and desire to show how innovations could be drawn on to put on a great show. 1994 was the year when the USA, for the first time, hosted the Real World Series.

Many Americans remained either indifferent or hostile to the very idea of soccer. Just prior to the draw for the tournament, in December 1993, the *USA Today* columumnist Tom Weir reminded his compatriots that American sports do not respect the art of the foot, that US spectators are most thrilled by action from the waist up:

> all arms and hands, things that happen from the waist up.... The World Cup draw is Sunday and admit it, you don't care. And no matter how much this event gets crammed down your throat... you still won't care. But don't feel guilty about it. There's a good reason why you don't care about soccer, even if it is the national passion in Cameroon, Uruguay and Madagascar. It's because you are an American, and hating soccer is more American than mom's apple pie, driving a pickup or spending Saturday afternoon channel-surfing with the remote control (John Weir, *USA Today*, December 17, 1993, p. 3C).

Nevertheless, the World Cup was by now a USA commitment, and was destined for success on the level of show and spectacle, whatever the response of a broadly passive general American public.

Understanding the significance of this event involves evaluating the contribution of sport not just to the making of separate national identities, but to the trans-national forms of interaction and communication which give expression to the intermingling of distinctive cultural forms of life, which are symbiotically linked to the flow of cultural commodities in the marketplace (Houlihan, 1994: Chapter 8). These themes have been developed by theorists in the form of debates concerning the nature of globalization, and the sociologist Anthony Giddens notes that:

> processes of change engendered by modernity are intrinsically connected to globalizing influences, and the sheer sense of being caught up in massive waves of global transformation is perturbing (Giddens, 1991: 183-184).

Global sporting events express this very paradox — the exhilaration of following events of worldwide interest, of involving oneself in matters of cosmopolitan modernity, sits alongside a recurrent sense of unease concerning who one really is. Rooting for the nation, in the context of a global discourse of competitive sport, is both an expression and a resolution of this paradox.

In this book experts from around the world reflect upon the nature of soccer, as a source of cultural expression and national identity. The case-studies include essays on nine of the 1994 qualifying nations, and on two nations — England and Japan, symbolising perhaps past and future glories — which did not qualify; and on the expanding global base of soccer, its cultural hold on the passions of populations, and its relation to intensifying forms of mediated spectacle. Consideration is given to the formula that has produced champions, the ups and downs of hosting the event, and recurrently, to the deep meanings that soccer has had and continues to have in all corners of the globe. The writers are not just academics; they are committed sportspeople. Their contributions deal not just with the academic and analytical side of the culture and politics of soccer, but also with the spirit and style of the game in different times, places and cultures; and with the drama and passion that have characterised the game in so many cultures and for so long.

The seductive irrationality of the sports fan is captured in the Irish novelist Roddy Doyle's evocation of an early evening in a Dublin bar, following the Irish Republic's heroic endeavours in the World Cup Finals of 1994:

> They tried. They rattled the Italians. They hounded them and bit their arses. They ran and slid after them and got in their way. They never let us think it was all over. They charged and ran back, and charged again. The second half. Schillachi hit the bar. Schillachi scored but he was offside. But the Irish kept at it, kept running and bullying. They were great and I loved them.
> Then it was over.
> We said nothing.
> The fans in Rome were still waving the flags, still singing. People in the pub were doing the same. I told Belinda I loved her.
> It was over.
> It was one of the great times of my life, when I loved being from

Dublin and I loved being Irish. Three years later, it still fills me. The joy and the fun and the pride. Adults behaving like children. Packie gritting his teeth. Being able to cry in public. Getting drunk in daylight. The T-shirts, the colour. Mick McCarthy's long throw. The songs. The players. Paul McGrath. The excitement and madness and love. It's all still in me and I'm starting to cry again.

They came home the next day. Nelson Mandela was in town as well, picking up his freedom of the city (Doyle, 1993: 20-21).

There lies the power of soccer, its capacity to compel, to express national identity and sentiment in far more than trivial or peripheral ways. In the build up to the Finals of 1994, there were millions of Roddy Doyles around the world, and in the United States itself, anticipating such evenings and memories to come.

References

Doyle, Roddy (1993), 'Republic Is a Beautiful Word — Republic of Ireland 1990', in Nick Hornby (ed.), *My Favourite Year — a collection of new football writing*, London: H.F. & G. Witherby, pp. 7-21.

Giddens, Anthony (1991), *Modernity and Self-Identity — Self and Society in the Late Modern Age*, Cambridge: Polity Press.

Houlihan, Barrie (1994), *Sport and International Politics*, London: Harvester Wheatsheaf.

2 FIFA and the World Cup: The expanding football family

Alan Tomlinson

The Fédération Internationale de Football Association (FIFA) was founded by seven European footballing nations in 1904. Ninety years on, FIFA could boast 179 member nations, and 44 further affiliated but non-member nations. The story of its growth is testimony to its remarkable impact on international sport and upon cultural relations around the world. The growth of soccer itself (and many other modern sports) was coterminous with the rise of nation-states; sport was an ideal vehicle through which individual nations could organise internal communities (Hobsbawm, 1969: 308), and symbolize their prowess and world superiority (Riordan, 1993: 261). The power of soccer to express national identity in both internal and external forms has propelled the game to the status of the world's most popular sport. International sport, in its turn, has contributed to the making of societies, through the symbolic expression of the sense of national identity. The nation, "imagined ... as a community, conceived as deep, horizontal comradeship" (Anderson, 1983: 16) has found its fullest expression in two spheres: tragically, in conflict and war; less harmfully, in competition and sport. From its roots in a Eurocentric initiative, world soccer has come to represent a global passion, capable of mobilising national sentiment and pride in unprecedentedly dramatic and, more recently, sophisticatedly mediated forms.

The founding nations of FIFA were Belgium, Denmark, France, the Netherlands, Spain, Sweden and Switzerland. In some cases, these nations were looking for guidance from the longer-established British associations. Robert Guérin, of the French USFSA (l'Union des Sociétés françaises des sports athlétiques) actually approached Frederick Wall, the Secretary of the English Football Association. The Englishman offered a diplomatic, but uncooperative, response: "The Council of the Football Association cannot see the advantages of such a Federation, but on all such matters upon which joint action was desirable they would be prepared to confer" (Tomlinson, 1986: 85). As a French commentator puts it, Guérin became the first President of FIFA, helped by the phlegmatic and haughty English response, "for lack of interest of the British" (Wahl, 1986: 12). In the founding moments of the world body's history, the British — and the English in particular — displayed an indifference and insularity that was to be debated over and over again during the next 90 years, particularly when the British game was revealed to be lacking in comparison with that of other more progressive nations. But England and the British did become a major force in FIFA, at certain strategic points in its history. The seven Presidents of FIFA have included three Englishmen, who between them have presided over the organisation for thirty years, a third of its existence. The Presidents have been as follows:

Robert Guérin	France	1904–1906
Daniel Woolfall	England	1906–1918
Jules Rimet	France	1921–1954
Rodolfe Seeldrayers	Belgium	1954–1955
Arthur Drewry	England	1956–1961
Stanley Rous	England	1961–1974
João Havelange	Brazil	1974–

For the first seventy years of its life, FIFA was controlled by Northern European administrators, and in its earliest days the major recurrent tensions and controversies concerned the amateur/professional status of players. England soon joined the fledgling organisation, for it was clear that the experience of the game's founders would be valued. The English FA (Football Association) had been approached by Belgium in the late 1890s and by the Netherlands in 1902, both suggesting that the formation of an international association would benefit the European game: it was seen, then, as an obvious leader of such developments. Even when FIFA was formed without England, it was clear that its experience would offer benefits: for France had played its first international match a mere three weeks before the meeting at which FIFA was formed; Denmark was not to play an international until 1908, at the Olympics in London, the same year in which Switzerland played its first international match. Three of FIFA's founding nations (Sweden, France and Spain) had not actually formed a Football Association in their own country at the time at which the international body was founded. Paradoxically, in these cases, the international initiative was the spur to the founding of national associations. In France's case this leads to the bizarre entry, in one encyclopaedic source: "Fédération Francaise de Football ... Year of Formation: 1918 ... Affiliation to FIFA: 1904" (Oliver, 1992: 278).

FIFA's founding fathers were novices, then, and so it was unsurprising that the English Football Association (founded in 1863) was drawn into the leadership role. It joined in 1905, stayed until 1920, joined again from 1924-1928 (leaving over disputes concerning payments to amateurs) and then rejoined in 1946. For the first three World Cups, in the 1930s, the world's oldest footballing nation was not actually a member of FIFA. What brought the English in during the first decade of the century was a sense of leadership and duty. Robert Guérin, the French President of FIFA, resigned when his efforts to organize an international competition came to nothing, with no entries coming in by the deadline. Daniel (D.B.) Woolfall took over as President, with a clear mandate from the English to "regulate football on the Continent as a pure sport" (Tomlinson, 1986: 87). Woolfall was a civil servant from the northern English town of Blackburn, and had been a contributor to Blackburn Rovers' domination of the English FA Cup competition in the 1880s. He led FIFA through a period of steady growth up until the end of the First World War, but disputes over sporting relations between "former enemy nations" led to ostracisms, resignations, the temporary dissolution of FIFA, and the setting up (by Denmark, Finland, Norway, Sweden and Italy) of a new Federation of National Football Associations. FIFA emerged from this challenge at the turn of the decade, with Jules Rimet, the French lawyer, taking the position of provisional head of FIFA in 1920 before becoming official President in 1921, a post he was to hold for 33 years, during which his name was given to the World Cup trophy, which was won outright by Brazil on becoming World Champions for the third time in 1970. During the Presidency of Rimet the number of member-associations grew from twenty to eighty five, and five World Cup tournaments and finals took place.

This dramatic growth was consolidated during the Presidencies of the Belgian Seeldrayers and the Englishmen Arthur Drewry and Stanley Rous. But in 1974 the politics of international sport began to work against this Eurocentric domination of the administration of the international game. In that year Havelange won the presidency in a vote against Sir Stanley Rous. It was a power change of seismic significance not just for soccer, but for the global political economy of sport. The saga of Havelange's ousting of Rous is revealing, and the nature of the protagonists in the saga warrants further attention — not from any "great man" theory of history, but from the recognition that

> men make their own history, but they do not make it just as they please; they do not make it under circumstances chosen by themselves, but under circumstances directly encountered, given and transmitted from the past (Marx, 1979: 103).

Rous, Havelange and the social and political relationships in which they have been embedded are indicative of the distinctive globalizing forces which have driven the world game in the second half of the twentieth century.

An amateur affair

Before taking the FIFA post (in his mid-sixties) Sir Stanley Rous (knighted for his services to the staging of the first post-World War II Olympics in London in 1948) had been Secretary of the English Football Association from 1934 to 1962, leading the British Associations back into FIFA in 1946. England's first national team manager, Walter Winterbottom, recognised Rous' achievements:

> ... in our own country he took us out of being an insular Association Football league and got us back into world football and this was tremendous (BBC Radio, 1984).

But Rous was no modernist. He ran the world game with the concerned air of the reforming patrician schoolmaster. When his pupils got out of hand he hardly knew what had hit him, or what had undermined his authority.

Rous was not a stereotypical colonial type. He was a child of the lower middle-classes (both his elder sisters became schoolteachers) and studied physical education at St. Luke's College, Exeter, before going on to teach at a grammar school near London. He was part of a socially mobile class, entering a professional cum service career, no inheritor of established privileges. He was a highly influential figure in the administration of the English game, modernising its bureaucracy and introducing teaching schemes for all levels of coaching, playing and refereeing.

His code of sport was classically amateurist in spirit, his career embodying the principles of "fair play", from his teaching to his amateur playing days and his time as a respected international referee. Commentators conjure up a romantic picture of Rous on the world soccer stage:

> As far back as 1933 Rous could be found in the great football capitals of the world, in huge boots and baggy shorts, refereeing international matches. He was a big man, dedicated to the concept of fair play (Simson and Jennings, 1991: 38).

In developing a basis for coaches to be trained and prepared for spreading a contemporary gospel of sport and soccer, Rous provided post-colonial missionaries of the body who could ensure that sporting links at least could be retained with former British colonies, and with other nations.

Looking at Rous' playing days helps reaffirm the dynamic of the old versus the new which is characteristic of his contribution to the development of the world game. Interviewed for his 90th birthday, Rous recollected his own playing days:

> I started as a centre-half but I gave away so many penalties they told me to go in goal and try to stop them. I was a very average amateur player. I played at St. Luke's College, I was captain down there. In the army I played in the first war. I didn't play for very long because I broke my wrist twice and I had to give up playing. I still remember those days ... even if I can't remember what happened last week. We used to look upon it as a sport, as a recreation, we had very little regard of points and league positions and cup competitions. We used to play friendly matches mostly. There was always such a sporting attitude and the winners always clapped the others off the field and so on ... that's all changed of course (BBC Radio, 1984).

Rous' commitment to the classical amateur game is also revealed in a

17

forward written for a book on the World Cup in 1978, in which he cited the author's public school soccer education, Oxbridge soccer blue and playing experience with Pegasus (the Combined [Oxford and Cambridge] Universities amateur club) as ideal qualifications "to write a detailed report of the FIFA World Cup in 1978" (Miller, 1978). As he became involved in the game worldwide, he mourned the loss of a form of sporting innocence. As early as the 1962 World Cup in Chile, he bemoaned the loss of the 1930s when international tours were "free and easy affairs".

A set of crucially revealing tensions is expressed in these responses; the old world versus the new; a quiet life versus a frenetic cosmopolitanism; archaic amateur values versus a rigorous professionalism; and character-building participation versus win-at-all-costs approaches. Rous could be both innovative and orthodox; adventurous yet crabbily cautious; resonant of modernity yet steeped in traditional values. A world figure in sport, he carried with him into the sporting arena the inherent contradictions of a period in British history of very uncertain remaking. Claimed as a modern world figure within the game, Rous looked comfortable hobnobbing with the Queen at English Cup Finals, yet could publicly rebuke the British Prime Minister Harold Wilson for posing with the victorious English team after its 1966 World Cup victory.

In the early 1970s Rous was confident that England was still a dominant influence on the game, and he was widely respected. As Harry Cavan, who was to become a confidant of Havelange in the new regime, said: Rous was:

> probably the most travelled man in football in the world in those days. He had the right connections, the right influence and above all he had the ability and the skill to do the job. And of course he was clever. He was generally one or two moves ahead of most of the others (BBC Radio, 1984).

But Rous was not immune from challenge. Third World countries were becoming impatient with the Northern European domination of the world game; they wanted more opportunity to shine on the world stage. For such countries, Rous' European-based patrician style did not promise fulfilment of the potential of the world's most popular sport. In 1974 João Havelange mounted a successful challenge to Rous' presidency, defeating the incumbent in a second ballot.

Rous seemed stunned by this defeat. The English sports journalist, Brian Butler, recalls the moment of truth in conversation with Rous himself:

> I remember just before the second ballot was taken you sat down and had an orange squash, quietly in one corner. João Havelange did so much lobbying he was really such a blur and that was where you lost (BBC Radio, 1984).

Rous did claim to have been aware of the challenge — "because I know what activity was being practised by my successor, the appeals that he'd made to countries". Rous, parvenu member of the cricketing fraternity of Lords/MCC (the Marylebone Cricket Club), of Wimbledon's All England Club (tennis), and of Hurlingham (polo), made "appeals ... to countries" sound like a nasty disease. His reflective response to the memory of defeat identified the loss of his power base in the contemporary politics of world football:

> Yes I think an Indian spoke against and I was surprised at that. People like Indonesia spoke against me ... their officers have changed so much in those countries you know. There were quite a few then who didn't really know me and they were persuaded to vote for Havelange (BBC Radio, 1984).

Arousal and ascendancy

Who was it who actually emerged from the Third World to assume power in FIFA? Havelange spent his early boyhood in Belgium, and trained as a lawyer before making several fortunes in ventures in the chemical, insurance and transport industries. As an amateur sportsman — a double Olympian, swimming for Brazil in the 1936 Berlin Olympics, and a member of the water-polo team at the 1952 Helsinki Games — he gained a high profile in the Brazilian sports establishment. Moving into sports administration he became President of the Brazilian sports federation, and supremo of Brazilian football. He reshaped Brazilian football by the 1970s, forming a national championship out of the various regional and inter-regional championships. This initiative — at times involving up to nearly a hundred clubs travelling across a country of 8.5 million square kilometres — was based, in World Cup fashion, upon groups playing each other. Big clubs had to play small ones, and all clubs had to travel all over the vast country. Not surprisingly, crowds were small, and the travel expenses for the clubs were punitive. Not a few Brazilian commentators have seen this initiative, in tandem with

> the diaspora of mature Brazilian talent to Europe, as the beginning of the end of Brazil's dominance of world football, on the playing side. But such controversy was not to hold Havelange back; it was only the end of the beginning of his worldwide dominance of the sport.

Havelange's base was a strong one indeed from which to launch his campaign for the FIFA Presidency. He had got onto the Brazilian Olympic Committee in 1955, and in 1963 he was elected to the International Olympic Committee, where he worked closely, from 1966 onwards, with the Franco appointee from Spain, Juan Antonio Samaranch. During the golden years of Brazil's international soccer success, Havelange was at the helm of Brazilian sport, and could claim in his:

> own promotional literature ... that while in charge of Brazilian sport he 'became Brazil's most successful football manager' and that he was 'the architect of Brazil's success at the World Cups in 1958, 1962 and 1970 (Simson and Jennings, 1992: 39).

There are several Brazilian coaches and team managers — maybe some players too — who would no doubt dispute this inflection in the Havelange curriculum vitae.

But the base was certainly there, and in 1970 Havelange launched his campaign for the controlling position of world soccer — backed, on an anti-European ticket, by soccer officials from the Argentine and Uruguay. This broadened his base, and his candidature was a widely representative one, harnessing simultaneously the resentments and aspirations of South American, Southern European, African and Asian footballing nations. He spent the first few years of the 1970s on a worldwide canvassing campaign. In the build-up to the 1974 election (to be held just prior to the World Cup Finals in West Germany) Havelange visited eightysix FIFA countries, concentrating most of all on Africa and Asia (Interview in *Playboy*, Brazilian edition, 1985). It is little wonder that Sir Stanley Rous sat quietly in a corner in Frankfurt in 1974 during the polling; clearly, there were few delegates who could feel comfortable enough to speak to him.

Patrick Nally, former business intimate of the late Horst Dassler of

Adidas, captures the flavour of Havelange's wooing of the world of international soccer:

> There had never been an election campaign like it for a sports presidency ... Sir Stanley Rous hadn't travelled to all the countries throughout Asia and Africa and certainly not to all the little islands. It was such a radical change to suddenly have this dynamic, glamorous South American character, brimming with *bonhomie*, travelling the world with his wife, meeting people, pressing the flesh, bringing over the Brazilian team, travelling with the likes of Pele. It was Brazilian carnival time ... Havelange had spent a fortune going round the world with the Brazilian team and had canvassed every single member of FIFA. It was unheard of. No sports president had ever gone round the world glad handing and campaigning (Simson and Jennings, 1992: 39-40).

Havelange's campaign was also based upon commitment to reform and expansion, in response to the Asian and African constituencies. He pledged to increase the number of nations competing in the World Cup Finals from sixteen to twenty four; and to raise Third World footballing standards generally. This latter goal was to be achieved by promoting coaching seminars, rather grandly framed as an International Academy, throughout Africa and Asia; and by introducing a World Youth Championship, to be hosted regularly by Third World nations. He committed himself to cash subsidies for the development of facilities and stadia in Third World countries, and for the provision of courses for soccer professionals and the establishing of more club competitions in the different countries.

Whilst campaigning, and on winning, there was little evidence that he had any economic basis for the realisation of these ambitious plans. For this, Havelange needed sponsorship on an unprecedented scale:

> Under Havelange, FIFA strode into the modern world of sponsorship; Coca-Cola culture, one of the most advanced and sophisticated multi-national strategies, provided the economic base for Havelange's ambitions (Tomlinson, 1986: 96).

An appreciation of the way in which this economic base was secured is fundamental to any adequate grasp of the character of the contemporary political economy of sport; and it involves two key players in the multinational corporate game — Adidas and Coca-Cola — as well as touching upon the powerbroking of world sport in associated spheres such as the Olympic Games.

When it dawned upon Sir Stanley Rous that the old rules of the game (patrician concern and reciprocal loyalty) were no longer appropriate, he did make a last-ditch effort to rally support. This brought Horst Dassler, of the German multinational sports company Adidas, into the script of the unfolding drama of world soccer politics. Some of Rous' German friends recommended Dassler, who then organised a lobby of the delegates, and almost turned the election back Rous' way.

Havelange himself was so impressed at Dassler's style that, when he needed to raise the funds for implementing his commitments, it was Dassler to whom he turned. Dassler and Adidas were given deals with FIFA and with national federations, for adoption of Adidas kit and equipment, in exchange for a commitment to find the funding for the manifesto which had got Havelange elected. Patrick Nally claims the credit for finding the appropriate deal, by working for Dassler in developing a marketing programme which would attract adequate sums into world soccer. Coca-Cola was already involved in the Olympics, and sport was obviously a prime association for a product which "sells itself on purity, youthfulness, energy and zest" (Simson and Jennings, 1992: 43). For Nally the challenge was clear. Coca-Cola had a track record second to none, and if soccer could get an association established with Coca-Cola, "you're into the biggest blue chip company on a global basis". What was new about the deal struck by FIFA was its global, worldwide scope. Nally claims that no country in the world had, in the early to mid 1970s, an international marketing budget, and Coca-Cola was no exception.

Where Havelange had travelled the world to canvass the votes for election, Nally now travelled the world for eighteen months to convince nationally-based Coca-Cola management to direct marketing budgets towards backing Havelange's commitment to developments for world soccer. Clinching Coca-Cola's decision to centralise a worldwide marketing initiative around soccer provided the economic basis for Havelange's programmes. In the implementation of them, FIFA, at the time with no full-time personnel, was a marginal contributor. The new infrastructure for world football was laid out by Adidas' boss and his marketing partner who, as Simson and Jennings starkly put it:

> were taking over world soccer ... The way that Nally and Dassler
> brought the Coca-Cola company into sponsoring soccer became a
> blueprint for the development of other sports federations (Simson
> and Jennings, 1992: 45 and 46).

Havelange's success represents a superb irony in the FIFA story. The
challenge of the developing world to the advanced world was led by a
glamorous figure resonant of the modern, and consolidated economically
by money from the capitalist centres of mid-Europe and North America.
The Third World had been aroused and in footballing terms was on the
ascendancy; in power terms, the alliances within FIFA combined the
political and cultural interests of emergent nations with the market
aspirations of multi-national and trans-national economic interests still
based firmly in the first world of capitalism.

Third World first

There is no doubt that Havelange has fulfilled his pledges, and "since the
Coke money tap was turned on", he "has remained the unchallenged
president of FIFA" (Simson and Jennings, 1992: 47). And his activities have
continued beyond just football; as an International Olympic Committee
member he worked on other committee members to influence the vote
which landed the Olympic Games for Barcelona, and he had been
influential in the candidacy of Samaranch for the Presidency of the IOC.

He has been resented. Tommy Keller, from Switzerland, and President
of the International Rowing Federation, spoke out against the new order in
world sport, alleging that it "was dominated by a Latin American and
Latino-European Mafia" (Simson and Jennings, 1992: 53). Artemio Franchi,
a former President of UEFA, the European Football Union, was scathing
about FIFA's new administrative building when it opened at the end of the
1970s: "It's ostentation ... and *South American* ostentation" (*World Soccer*,
October 1984, p.14). Brian Glanville, the English football journalist to whom
Franchi expressed this view, has been outspoken in his criticisms of
Havelange and his regime: "I very much ... believe that Havelange has
ruined the World Cup, has sold it down the river to the Afro-Asians and
their ilk ..." (*World Soccer*, October 1984, p.14); "... I deeply dislike what FIFA

has become under the ineffable Havelange and ... I as deeply despise the European countries which have truckled to him ..." (*World Soccer*, November 1985, p.18).

These brazenly Eurocentric criticisms romanticize the earlier history of FIFA, and assume a superiority in an old order which feels itself unaccountable to the rest of the world. But the nations which Glanville appears to be so contemptuous of have, for many, enriched the flavour of the World Cup Finals, helping justify the grandiose label, "World".

In fact, Third World nations have shared the winning of the trophy with Western nations, with Uruguay, Argentina and Brazil accounting for seven World Cup triumphs between 1930 and 1990; and Italy, West Germany and England accounting for the other seven victories. Beyond the performances of Latin America's "big three", there have been other memorable performances by Asian and African nations.

One of the most memorable World Cup runs of the more recent television era was that by the unfancied North Koreans in 1966, well before Havelange's ascendancy. The North Koreans were unfancied not least because they had not had to prove themselves in the qualifying phases; as, at that time, only one place was allocated to African and Asian nations, there was a mass withdrawal, with North Korea the only remaining candidate from those regions/continents. So although North Korea strolled to the Finals with 6-1 and 3-1 victories over Australia, they were not really taken seriously. In their first match in the Finals they were casually dismissed by the Soviet Union in an easy 3-0 victory. But then they drew with Chile and went on to beat the mighty Italian team 1-0. The shamed Italians flew home early to Italy to a riotous reception of catcalls and rotten tomatoes, whilst the North Korean unknowns prepared to meet the splendid Portugal side. In a legendary quarter-final match the Koreans played a dazzling passing game, a form of precise pin-ball soccer, and raced into a remarkable three goal lead after just twenty two minutes of the match. For those lucky enough to be at Goodison Park, Liverpool, this was an unforgettable sporting moment. The predominantly Northern English crowd rallied behind the tiny Koreans, respecting their audacious attacking football, yet simultaneously urged on the great Portuguese player Eusebio, who responded with four goals inside just over a half hour of play. The 51,000 crowd — the vast majority of which was non-partisan — cheered

and applauded both sides at the end of an encounter which repre-sented a memorable celebration of sporting excellence and reciprocal respect. If North Korea had matched its dazzling attack with a more robust and less naive defensive game, 1966 could easily have seen the first appearance of an Asian side in the semi-finals of the World Cup.

1966 was no fluke in terms of the impact of Asian sides. For the 1970 tournament, separate Asia-Oceania and Africa groups had been estab-lished. North Korea withdrew from one of the groups, and Israel pipped Australia to appear in the Finals, going on to draw with Italy and Sweden and to lose only one match, to Uruguay. Although hardly a third world nation, Israel carried the banner for an important principle. Clearly the small, unfancied or traditionally weak sides were capable now of compet-ing with the very best. Understandably, the Third World and Asia in par-ticular wanted more guaranteed representation. For 1974, Australia at last made it. South Korea had beaten Hong Kong, and then Japan's conquerors Israel. Australia had triumphed over Iran as well as, still earlier, Iraq and Indonesia. Level after two matches, Australia and South Korea met in a play off match in Hong Kong, the Australians winning by the odd goal.

This then was the climate in which Havelange gained power. Australia lost two out of three games in the Finals (to East Germany 2-0, and West Germany 3-0), but not heavily, and also gained a goalless draw with Chile. It was clear that in terms not just of global equity, but also of standards and comparability of high-level performance, the third world nations should be more fairly represented in the final stages. At the 1978 World Cup Iran gained a draw with the ancient footballing power of Scotland. By 1982, at the World Cup Finals in Spain, Havelange's reforms had come to fruition and there were 24 nations in the final stages, with two sides now qualifying from each of the Asia-Oceania and Africa groups. New Zealand and Kuwait were the qualifiers from the Asia-Oceania group. Kuwait lost quite heavily to the splendid French side, caused eyebrows to be raised by losing to the only goal of the match against England, and gained a draw against Czechoslovakia. If in initial appearances in the Finals, the good results gained by the unknown sides from Asia-Oceania were dismissed as one-offs or flukes, by now it was clear that these nations were not there merely to make up the numbers. At the 1986 Finals Iraq and South Korea, qualifiers from the now separate Asia group, wrote no giantkilling

headlines — but neither were they outclassed, and Iraq's three defeats were by the narrow margins of 1-0, 1-0, and 2-1.

In 1990 in Italy the United Arab Emirates side was outclassed, but South Korea again competed well. It was at this tournament that a non-Latin American Third World side might have won the World Cup,dramatically embodying Africa's emergence on the world footballing stage. The respectable and improving performances of sides from Asia and other areas beyond the power bases of world football gave lie to those critical voices from the centres of authority and privilege. The sneer in the remark by the journalist Glanville — "sold ... down the river to the Afro-Asians and their ilk" — is indefensible. Unless all sides were conspiring to fabricate a sense of contest and level competition, the inventory of performances by the emergent footballing nations was beginning to suggest that Western (and in some senses smug Latin American) assumptions about the innate superiority of their game were ill-founded.

The African scene

It has been a hard struggle for African nations to gain recognition, and though the allocation of two in 1982 was increased to three for the 1994 Finals, "with over 40 countries taking an active interest in the game, this falls way short of a fair system" (Oliver, 1992: 692). The first African nation to compete in the World Cup was Egypt in 1934 (losing 4-2 to Hungary), and then it was not until 1970 that the continent was represented again, by Morocco. Zaire in 1974, and Tunisia in 1978, carried the African hopes in Mexico in 1970. Morocco lost by only 2-1 to the powerful West Germans; Zaire's 1974 performance was a blip in the improving profile of the African game — they conceded fourteen goals against Yugoslavia, Brazil and Scotland, and scored none; Tunisia, in Argentina in 1978, defeated Mexico, drew with West Germany and lost by only 1-0 to the group winners, Poland. Without doubt, the African continent deserved more than the measly single allocation for the Finals.

By the 1982 Finals FIFA had allocated two places to Africa (though Europe's representation had gone up from 9 to 13), and Algeria and Cameroon had a dramatic impact. Neither qualified for the second round in the Finals, but the Cameroon left Spain undefeated, drawing all three games, including a 1-1 result against the eventual Champions Italy. Algeria

defeated Germany 2-1, and Chile 3-2, but did not get through to the next round: in a crucial game in the group West Germany and Austria, knowing that a 1-0 victory for the Germans would see both European sides through from the group at the expense of Algeria (who had already completed their fixtures), played a notoriously uncompetitive match that has been labelled the "Great Gijon Swindle" or Anschluss, and which finished with the mutually desirable 1-0 scoreline. FIFA all but ignored a furious protest from the outraged Algerians. Their performance, and that of Cameroon, was an assertive reminder of the established strength of the African challenge.

1986 was a reminder that at that stage in the continent's soccer development the strengths within Africa lay in the Northern part of the continent. As Oliver puts it, "such was the supremacy of that part of Africa that all five nations north of the Sahara made it to the quarter finals of the qualifying competition and only Egypt missed out on the semi-finals" (Oliver, 1992: 46). Algeria and Morocco were the northern African teams to qualify. Although the former fought a tight 0-1 defeat at the hands of Brazil and drew with Northern Ireland, it was the Moroccan side which served warning of the seriousness of the African challenge. Up against the might of Western, Northern and Eastern Europe, Morocco rudely awoke what had become known as the Group of Sleep, finishing ahead of England, Portugal and Poland and going on to meet West Germany in the second round. The great Lothar Matthaus saved German blushes with the only goal of the match in the last minute.

In 1990 at the Italia '90 tournament Cameroon went one better than the Moroccans of 1986, outplaying the bemused English for much of a two hour match, and being only eight minutes away from the semi-finals when England scored the equalizing goal in normal time. In the qualifying rounds for this tournament a combination of economic recession and resentment at FIFA's allocation of the two places produced the lowest number of competing teams in the Africa group since 1970. But the ebullient performances of the "Indomitable Lions" of Cameroon produced some of the most abiding memories of the 1990 Finals, from their magnificent nine-man defeat (two were sent off for foul play) of the Argentinian holders in the opening match of the Finals, through to the epic encounter with England, when their naively scything physical challenges in defence handed England a lifeline and then victory. The Cameroon side

provided the celebrity of the tournament, in the veteran flair of Roger Milla, scorer of several memorable goals and recipient of what is really the personality award for the World Cup: "Picking up the Adidas Franz Beckenbauer Prize from the man who held up the world cup to the roars of the faithful in Munich twenty years ago, was Cameroon's thirty-nine year old, lambada-dancing forward, Roger Milla" (Simson and Jennings, 1992: 41). The Cameroon run still took some blinkered pundits by surprise — despite the unbeaten record of two tournaments earlier — but after it FIFA had to recognise the African scene more fully. For the 1994 tournament Africa was handed three places.

Family fortunes

FIFA's official history notes the restricted financial base upon which Rous operated during his period as President, with funds coming from just the one source of profits from the World Cup. So though Rous presided over an expanding family of FIFA members, and ushered the world game into the age of television transmission, Rous' FIFA could be seen, in retrospect, as "rather conservative ... and reserved in its decisions... It hardly seemed possible to accomplish more without taking risks" (FIFA, 1984: 82). Thus, in the making and writing of its own history, does FIFA set the stage for the entry of Havelange into the FIFA story. He is hailed as a risk-taking entrepreneur rather than a necessarily cautious patrician. Under him, FIFA is said to have followed "another direction, that of universality", applying "methods in football which were long known in social, economic and political life" (FIFA, 1984: 26). The implication here is clear. Honourable though Rous may have been, he was out of touch with the modern, unable to exploit the potential of "long known" methods for the good and development of the game.

The ambitious Havelange moved quickly, noted the body's official history, giving "FIFA truly international and universal dimensions. His first concern was a comprehensive, worldwide football development programme, which was pursued with the International Academies. As FIFA did not have the necessary financial means, the FIFA President implemented his vast experience and fantasy as a businessman, in order to materialize these ambitious plans. With their great involvement in sports and their worldwide business interests, the Coca-Cola Company were very

positive towards this idea and assumed the sponsorship of these projects" (FIFA, 1984: 82). As in all patriarchal families, the telling of the family history reaffirms the status of the incumbent patriarch. But with new members of the family hostile to the ideals of earlier generations, earlier patriarchal figures can be re-evaluated unsympathetically, in the light of more modern developments.

In the glossy internal history of FIFA, the new-found wealth and fortunes of the world footballing family made possible the development of a truly global base to the game. Havelange could accomplish this in style, running up expenses of £100,000 a year by 1979, and annual running costs for his Rio office of £250,000 in 1986. When "FIFA officials flew into Spain for the World Cup in 1982 their expenses were nearly £2 million — almost as much as it cost to transport and accommodate the twenty-four teams. Their new-found wealth was dazzling. In the next two years FIFA splashed out £650,000 on international travel and gifts" (Simson and Jennings, 1992: 47). FIFA had travelled a long way since the British soccer federations could withdraw just over half a century earlier, in the purity of protest at "broken-time" payments to amateurs.

Made in America

The construction, expression and maintenance of forms of national identity is a complex process, and identities can be fragile, the reactions to the expression of them unpredictable (Arbena, 1993: 153). Global forces marginalize more culturally distinctive sports: Guttmann concludes an erudite review of sports' diffusion with the comment that "the international dominance of Western sports continues and resistance to this form of cultural imperialism remains weak" (Guttmann, 1993: 134). But in the case of soccer a difference process is at work — not merely the either or of the domination of the imperialist or the resistance of the oppressed. Rather, in the FIFA story and the way in which nations have expressed the imaginings of their own community and national identities, the story has been one of appropriation. The form of soccer has been taken and remoulded into the style and the culture of the recipient; soccer has been appropriated and remade in these ways, to the extent that the traditional centres of power in the world game have lost their "natural" dominance.

There were still anomalies in the power structures at the time of the run-in to the USA '94 finals. No British side qualified for these final stages, and on confirmation of the non-qualification of all of the four British sides the German Sepp Blatter, general secretary of FIFA, launched an attack on British soccer as '30 years behind the times', and on the continued British "domination of the world game's law-making body, the International Football Association Board", suggesting that "football's mother country ... exerts an influence out of all proportion to its current standing in the game" (Malam, 1993: 20). This Board was still made up of 20 seats, of which "16 were reserved permanently for the four British Associations", with "the four remaining seats filled by election for a fixed term from amongst other FIFA members" (Oliver, 1992: 3).

Blatter, widely seen at the time as the successor to Havelange, was well-equipped to sustain the global programme so effectively established by the Brazilian: "Completely approachable, he manages to combine the skills of the practised diplomat and natural communicator with the zeal of the idealist and the modernist" (Malam, 1993: 20). A German succession would not swing any pendulum of power back to any traditional North European alliance, for Blatter was an appointee of Adidas' Horst Dassler, "trained at the Adidas headquarters ... before he went off to FIFA" (Simson and Jennings, 1992: 46). The expanding world base of soccer would not be diminished by such a succession.

This is not to say that the Third World footballing family has no problems. The legendary Brazilian player Pele — certainly the biggest star of the USA's own soccer initiatives in the 1970s — was not present at the Las Vegas draw in December 1993. Embroiled in a row with Havelange's son-in-law Ricardo Teixeira (President of Brazil's Football Federation), Pele held his own press conference in Las Vegas. "Already facing a law suit for defamation, he was not prepared to be specific, but said: 'I cannot accept corruption, and football has a big problem with that in Brazil ...'. For speaking out, he had been given no part in the draw" (Lovejoy, 1993:32). Clearly, the structure of Brazilian football and Havelange's "means of gaining unassailable power" (Tomlinson, 1986:97) in the game might have left some legacy of resentment. After almost two decades in power at FIFA, though, Havalange clearly felt little dependence upon a former player, of whatever stature.

But despite instances and allegations of corruption in the higher economic levels of the game, part of soccer's global appeal has been that it does not demand expensive or extensive equipment. It has gained footholds not just in the stadia of the modern world, but did so on the cobbled streets of condensed working-class communities in Britain, on the beaches of Brazil and the plains of the African continent. It guaranteed mass sport at its cheapest and most cheerful, and the possibility of gaining international profiles in top-level performance, and so contributing to the political agenda of a nation through the expression — and sometimes manipulation — of national sentiment. By any criterion of global represen-tation, soccer became the world's greatest game, and FIFA — one of the earliest organisations operating as what Sklair has called a "trans-national practice", more recently operating on combined 'economic' and 'cultural-ideological' levels (Sklair, 1991: 6) — has created, in the World Cup, the world's greatest showcase for its most popular game.

It is a great irony — yet at the same time a truism of a globalizing world based upon the driving forces of a capitalist political economy and the search for new worldwide consumer markets — that the increased representation of Third World nations will be celebrated in the heart of the First World capitalist system. But this is hardly an accident. FIFA's deal with Coca-Cola was hammered out in the mid-1970s at the company's headquarters in Atlanta, Georgia. That deal can be seen as a pivotal moment in the history of modern soccer, and from the moment that deal was struck it became likely — regardless of the state of the game within its own sports culture — that the USA would host the biggest soccer event in the world. With the World Soccer Cup in the USA in 1994, and the cen-tenary Summer Olympic Games in Atlanta in 1996, modern sport's, and soccer's, impact and appeal beyond their Western roots can be seen to be premised upon the patronage of the trans-national political economy.

The story of FIFA's expanded football family is one of alliances between emerging cultural and political interests in the developing world, and entrenched economic interests in the developed capitalist world. Yet throughout the turbulent family rows and break-ups in this story, soccer has continued to provide gripping drama and sporting spectacle. FIFA, for all its contradictions and limitations, has made much of this possible, in ways and initiatives that would not have been undertaken or embraced by the traditional old guard of the Eurocentric founding fathers.

References

Anderson, Benedict (1983), *Imagined Communities — Reflections on the Origins and Spread of Nationalism*, London: Verso.

Arbena, Joseph. L. (1993), 'International Aspects of Sport in Latin America: Perceptions, Prospects, and Proposals', in Eric G. Dunning, Joseph A. Maguire and Robert E. Pearton (eds.), *The Sports Process — A Comparative and Developmental Approach*, Champaign, IL: Human Kinetics Publishers, pp. 151-167.

FIFA (1984), *History of FIFA*, Fédération Internationale de Football Association, Official History, Zurich.

Glanville, Brian (1984), 'FIFA knows how to blow its own trumpet', *World Soccer*, October, pp. 14-15.

Glanville, Brian (1984), 'World Cup at Risk', *World Soccer*, November, pp. 18-19.

Guttman, Allen (1993), 'The Diffusion of Sports and the Problem of Cultural Imperialism', in Eric G. Dunning, Joseph A. Maguire and Robert E. Pearton (eds.), *The Sports Process — A Comparative and Developmental Approach*, Champaign, IL: Human Kinetics Publishers, pp. 125-137.

Hobsbawm, Eric (1968), *Industry and Empire*, Harmondsworth: Penguin.

Lovejoy, Joe (1993), 'World Cup 1994...', *The Independent* (II), Monday December 20: p.32.

Malam, Colin (1993), 'Mother is alone now children have grown up', *The Daily Telegraph*, Saturday, November 13 1993, p.20.

Marx, Karl (1979), 'The Eighteenth Brumaire of Louis Bonaparte' [1852], in Karl Marx and Frederick Engels, *Collected Works Volume II, Marx and Engels 1851-1853*, London: Lawrence and Wishart, pp. 99-197.

Oliver, Guy (1992),*The Guinness Record of World Soccer — The History of the Game in Over 150 Countries*, Enfield: Guinness Publishing.

Riordan, James (1993), 'Sport in Capitalist and Socialist Countries: A Western Perspective', in Eric G. Dunning, Joseph A. Maguire, and Robert E. Pearton (eds.), *The Sports Process — A Comparative and Developmental Approach*, Champaign, IL: Human Kinetics Publishers, pp. 245-264.

Simson, Vyv & Jennings, Andrew (1992), *The Lords of the Rings — Power, Money and Drugs in the Modern Olympics*, London: Simon & Schuster.

Sklair, Leslie (1991), *Sociology of the Global System*, London: Harvester Wheatsheaf.

Tomlinson, Alan (1986), 'Going Global: the FIFA Story', in Alan Tomlinson and Garry Whannel (eds.), *Off The Ball — The Football World Cup*, London: Pluto Press, pp. 83-98.

Wahl, Alfred (1986), 'Le footballer français: de l'amateurisme au salariat (1890-1926)', *Le Mouvement social*, No. 135, avril-juin, pp. 7-30.

Section II
Case studies in soccer culture and national identity

3 Argentina and the World Cup: In search of national identity*

Eduardo Archetti

In this chapter I will present some general ideas on how a particular discourse on the character of the Argentinean style of playing football developed in this century. It is an attempt to depict a social and historical process wherein the identification of a framework of meaning, values and symbols makes possible the construction of a "self-identity" (for whatever moral, economic, cognitive, or political purpose). I will operate with two notions of identity: one "essentialist", with identity as "something" (an attribute, entity, thing) which an individual or a group has in and of itself, an identity that is subject to growth and decline, to continuity and change, to health and sickness (Chapman, McDonald and Tonkin, 1989:17). Obviously, this perspective adopted by the actors themselves is also built up in a context of oppositions and relativities.[1] However, in social anthropology a relativist position perceives identity as positional and very strategic: a group has no *one* identity, but a variety (and in theory a potentially very large variety) of possibilities. The main point to be stressed is that in both the essentialist and the contextual framework there is a possibility of change and variation. But, in the essentialist perspective changes can be accepted only if key values and meanings are somehow maintained. Therefore, the essentialists are more concerned with continuity and with the rhetorics of decline and crisis.

The search for identity in football is tied to style, both in the sense of individual and collective style. This implies the achievement of a difficult balance between individual characteristics and communal belonging in a game that is basically collective. The great players can transcend the style of given teams, but, nevertheless, in the quest for identity the great heroes are always mixed with the success of teams, they need each other. I will argue that the Argentinean discourse and practice of football has developed in two directions: one essentialist, characterised by the search for the "typical" style represented by "mythical teams" and "model players", and another contextual in which oppositions of styles open for a relativist representation. In the relativist representation it is common to accept that Argentineans play a kind of "Latin American style", close to the way Uruguayans play, or that the Argentinean contemporary style is an attempt to combine European discipline with Latin American improvisation.

Since its beginning Argentinean football has been a part, and a very important one, of a kind of general history of football uniting the periphery (new nations) and the centre (Europe). This general history is not only related to the growing internationalization of competitions but, in the specific case of Argentina, to the permanent "foot-drain", since the middle twenties, to Europe. This history has created a two-fold process: a reinforcement of the ideal model symbolized by the success in Europe of Cesarini, Orsi, Di Stéfano, Sivori, Kempes, Ardiles, and, more recently, Maradona (the "typical" players representing the "essential" style); but, at the same time, a relative picture of the conditions for success (the necessity of physical strength and continuity, and team discipline). In the Argentinean mythology Di Stéfano represents the "universal player" combining some essential aspects of Argentinean style (technical skill and the creation of unexpected events) with some properties of European style (tactical discipline, courage, leadership and a winning mentality). Maradona, on the contrary, is closer to the "essential" style based on technical virtuosity.[2]

In the following, I will describe a historical process that creates a stock of values, events and meanings. This symbolic capital constitutes the core of the representations and in this sense is very close to the essentialist perspective. These key elements permit:

(a) a process of *self definition* that includes players, managers, journalists and public in general;
(b) a specific way of registering given events that will constitute "crucial events" (victories, teams, players);
(c) a rethinking of past events from the perspective of the present; and, finally,

(d) the production of a narrative that is a mixture of "real" history, pseudo-
histories and mythologies (Ardener, 1989).

However, both the history and the narrative are open and, therefore, allow
for the growth of oppositions and alternative readings. The contemporary
scene of Argentinean football is represented by the "conflict" of the two
"schools": one identified with Menotti and the other with Bilardo. Both
coaches reached a world-wide recognition and prestige through Argentinean World Cup victories in 1978 and 1986. However, Menotti's victory
was achieved at home, in the World Cup of 1978 celebrated in Argentina,
while Bilardo's victory was in Mexico in 1986. In the world of football the
victory of Bilardo is much more prestigious because his team did not have
the "home advantage" of 1978. Menotti's second attempt, in the World Cup
of 1982 in Spain, was not a success: Argentina did not pass the quarter-
finals. Bilardo's second World Cup, in 1990 in Italy, brought Argentina to
the final and the silver medal after losing against Germany. Menotti,
explicitly and in a very articulate form, defends the essentialist position
while Bilardo represents a kind of "bastard" product in which discipline
and tactical dispositions are considered of extreme importance.[3]

The origin

The spread of football was due to Britain's world power status and her
active presence in commerce, industrial production, territorial control and
financial international connections (Mason, 1989). In the case of Argentina,
the rapid expansion of the game and its internationalization was also
related to the importance of the British colony in the last half of the 19th
century. By 1890 there were 45,000 British nationals living in Buenos Aires
and small cities close to the capital. The Buenos Aires Football Club, a
division of the Buenos Aires Cricket Club, was founded in 1867. The first
recorded match was played that year by two teams of the same club; the
"Reds" had as captain Tomas Hogg and the "Whites" William Held. Many
clubs were founded after 1880 and the majority of them sprang out of
British schools. In the period 1890-1900 the Lomas Athletic Club gained five
titles. All the players had been students in the Lomas de Zamora School, a
prestigious British boarding school. Alumni, the great Argentinean club of
the beginning of this century, was originally the Buenos Aires Higher

School. After 1900 it was decided that the clubs change their English names, for Spanish ones. However, the first association had an English name: the Argentine Football Association. This association kept English as the official meeting language until 1906. In 1912 the Association was divided and for the first time Spanish was partially used: Federación Argentina de Football and Asociación Argentina de Football. Not until 1934 was "football" replaced by the Spanish "fútbol" when the new and definitive association was created: Asociación de Fútbol Argentino (Scher and Palomino,1988:25).

Not only was the game a British export but so too were the standards and the quality of play. In the first decade of the 20th century Argentinean football grew under the influence of the accomplished teams that came to play in Buenos Aires and in Rosario. Southampton arrived in 1904 and won all the matches (3-0 against Alumni, the Argentinean champions). In 1905, Nottingham Forest played several matches and returned to England undefeated. The first home victory in 1906 was over a team of British nationals living in South Africa. It was celebrated in Buenos Aires as a glorious event. The winner was Alumni and this success consolidated the image of Alumni as a great team. Before the first World War, Everton and Tottenham visited Argentina with great success. In 1923 Chelsea played several matches and won all of them. The myth of the invincibility of British football was then created. This myth was intelligently manipulated by the British themselves and not only in relation to the Argentineans. Tony Mason writes:

> The British belief that their football was best remained a plant of sturdy growth despite unpredictable frosts...Defeat in the World Cup of 1950 by the United States could also be forgotten in a pre-television era as an inexplicable aberration. Even the famous defeat at Wembley in 1953 by Puskas's Hungarians, whose manager turned the knife by insisting that not only were they amateurs but the players had given up their annual holidays to come over and play the match, seemed to matter less than the home victories under the new floodlights and on BBC Television, of Wolverhampton Wanderers over Moscow's Spartak and Budapest's Honved. British claims to superiority at club level provoked *L'Equipe* into initiating the moves which led to the establishment of

the European Cup in 1955. It was twelve years before a British club won it (Mason,1989:177-8).

Argentineans waited almost a century, from the establishing of the game in their country, before defeating England in a tournament in Rio de Janeiro in 1964.

From 1895 onwards football spread all over the country. By 1910 there were clubs and provincial leagues as far as Santiago del Estero, up in the Northern part of the vast territory. However, Buenos Aires, Rosario and La Plata remained the main centres of the new game. The rapid growth of Buenos Aires due to the arrival of one million immigrants from Europe in the beginning of this century determined the character of the national league. Buenos Aires and small industrial cities close to the capital, like Avellaneda (with the great teams of Racing Club and Independiente), Quilmes, Banfield and Lanus dominated organized football. At the same time, the close contact with Montevideo and the regular games between Argentinean and Uruguayan teams since 1902 (a trophy donated by the world famous "tea baron" Sir Thomas Lipton) created a core of football in the Rio de la Plata basin. In addition, the success of Uruguay and Argentina in the Olympic Games of 1928 and in the first World Cup in 1930, where the two teams played in the finals, made possible the creation of the concept of "fútbol rioplatense" (football from the river, Rio de la Plata, which separates Argentina from Uruguay). This style was based on a superb technique, keeping, with endless touches, the ball in the team, and on rapid changes of rhythms in the attack. With the main aim of surprising enemies, Argentineans and Uruguayans played the game at different speeds: very slow in the middle of the field and very fast in the last metres when they approached the goal. It is, perhaps, necessary to remind the reader that the national teams of Argentina and Uruguay dominated the South American Cup from its first year, 1916, until the late fifties. During this period, Argentina won 12 titles, Uruguay 8 and Brazil only 3.

It is possible to imagine that the "original" style of Argentinean football was British, a kind of kick and run way of playing where physical strength and continuity dominated. However, in the early twenties some teams from Central Europe played in Buenos Aires. The Argentinean mythology recorded especially the visit of the Hungarian Ferencvaros in 1922. No kick-and-run is remembered. The Hungarian players were liked due to

41

their technical skills and the ability to dribble. In the twenties and thirties the myth of a "typical Central European style" was created in Argentina. Argentineans believed that their style of playing was very much like the football played in Austria and Hungary (Lorenzo and Castelli, 1977:37).

For Argentinean football the "foundation myth" (i.e. the emergence of a style of its own) is located in the 1920s and is associated with the following aspects: the cult of "dribbling", the appearance of "pairs" of players in a team (insider and wing) and the crystallization of a style defined as elegant, skilful, cheeky and lively. It is interesting to note that the development of stunts was related to "founder players": the "bicycle" with Pedro Calomino; the "marianella" with Juan Evaristo; and the "flying heading" with Pablo Bartolucci. Only in an essentialist recreation of history is it possible to imagine that these stunts, registered as key events, were an original creation of Argentinean players. However, a style must be seen and perceived in opposition to others. The turning point of international (European) recognition was for Argentinean football the final in the Olympics in Amsterdam in 1928. Nevertheless, history has recorded the famous tour of Europe of Boca Juniors in 1925 as the founding myth. Boca's way of playing, the elegant and easy movements of the players, absolute control of the ball, skill in dribbling and a move to a sort of circus-like style, spectacular and artistic, astonished Europeans. In addition, it is said that Argentineans demonstrated that it was possible to play and to win with less physical effort and strength. In contrast to kick-and-run football, this style was associated with two qualities: play at different speeds, as I mentioned above; and to keep control of the ball, even if it was necessary to hold possession by playing back. What the game lost in intensity and continuity, it gained in precision. At the same time, and closely related to the two defeats against Uruguay in 1928 and 1930, the essentialists created the myth of the generosity of Argentinean football, as opposed to tactical considerations that could guarantee a victory. Victories are ephemeral, everything is style. Brera comments on the final of the World Cup in 1930:

> Argentine plays a football with a lot of phantasy and elegance but the technical superiority can not compensate the abandonment of tactics. Between the two "rioplatense" national teams, the ants are the Uruguayans, the cicadas are the Argentineans [own translation] (Brera, 1978:98).

42

The history of records registered the two victories of Uruguay; the mythology immortalised the superiority of the Argentinean way of playing. The myth was transformed into history when, after the final, the Italians bought the most skilful "cicada" of the Argentineans: the left-winger Raimundo "Comet" Orsi. Juventus offered him what constituted at that time a privileged contract: 8,000 lire per month, a beautiful house and a car with chauffeur. The Argentineans considered the purchase an outrageous action against national dignity: heroes were not for sale. It took one year before Orsi could leave Argentina. His emigration was the beginning of the permanent exodus of "Rioplatense" and Brazilian players to Italian football. The "periphery" was suddenly integrated as a part of European football history. Moreover, the internationalization of the player market provoked a rapid change in Argentinean football. In the years 1930-31, professionalism was introduced in the Argentinean League as a measure, among other things, to stop the emigration of the great stars.

The Argentinean defeats of 1928 and 1930 were dramatic. Against the background of these two important international failures the rationalized myth of the generosity of Argentinean players and style was reinforced. In this process the unity of the "rioplatense style" was condemned to disappear. Uruguayans were perceived as rude, almost enraged players. The myth of the "Charrua (Uruguayan Indian) grip" was born as opposed to the "Argentinean (non-Indian) aristocratic elegance". The metaphor of the ants against the cicadas makes sense: this was undoubtedly the way Argentinean defeated males preferred to be perceived and to imagine themselves.

In the Argentinean football of the thirties there was a lot of space between defenders and forwards. The forwards had not only plenty of space for their movements but also quite a lot of time for thinking about what to do with the ball. The defenders never tried to reduce the space by using collective movements and never practised man to man marking. This kind of football invited an ambitious, attacking offensive way of playing. The greatest Argentinean players of this epoch were forwards. The Italians knew it, and, consequently, bought insiders, wingers and centre-forwards. The only exception in the case of Argentinean star players was Luis Monti, a centre-half, who joined Juventus in 1931. This movement constituted a kind of "world market" of players in which the attacking

43

offensive and creative players came from the periphery. This historical fact permitted the crystallization of the essentialist image of the Argentinean football. Both Europeans and Argentineans created a mythology around these exceptional players.

In 1934 Italy won the World Cup, with three Argentinean stars playing an outstanding role in the Italian national team: Luis Monti and the two brilliant wingers, Guaita and Orsi. They qualified on the basis of Italian descent.(4) It is believed in Argentina that the Italian "revolution" was made possible by the combination of great physical strength (a typical English attribute) with a renewed technical skill (the Argentinean contribution). The athletic power of the Italians was fed by the talent of Monti, Guaita and Orsi, and due to them, Argentinean football was considered a decisive component of this change (Lorenzo and Castelli,1977:36-7). Hence, the Italian victory was also an Argentinean victory. Again, in the history of records Argentineans felt dispossessed. Earlier, the main cause was the tactical ability and rudeness of Uruguayans, now it was the existence of a world market of players and rules that permitted the sons of Italians to play in the Italian national team. It is important to keep in mind that the consolidation of an Argentinean style occurred in a context of international defeat for the national team. The myth of the Argentinean superiority was never history. The history of Argentinean victories was related to something abstract, "a style", "a way of doing", "a way of playing", or to concrete names, the great players in exile. Thus, the exile and the existence of a world market of players contributed to the isolation of the Argentinean national team: Argentina decided to stay away from international competitions. The country's return to the World Cup in 1958 in Sweden represented the most traumatic moment in Argentinean football history.

From the end of the thirties until the second half of the fifties, Argentineans chose to stay in South America. In addition, the Second World War interrupted the expatriation of great players. During these years great national and club teams were constantly produced and many of them dominated the South American arena. The Brazilians and the Uruguayans developed a kind of 4-2-4 system in order to counteract the extreme ability of the Argentinean insiders. The insiders were players occupying the right or left in the middle of the field but also very offensive, helping the wingers and the centre forward in their attempts to score goals. They were the key players in a team, a combination of tactical intelligence with a good scoring capacity. In the forties the Uruguayans discovered that the left-insider should play a more defensive role, and they began to play with four backs (Lorenzo and Castelli,1977:38). Both insiders represented in this period the creativity of the team and, at the same time, the capacity for scoring. They were offensive players, never occupied with the boring task of regaining the ball for the team. They were perceived, and they behaved in the field, as the most eccentric aristocrats. The "essence" of the Argentinean style was then associated with the names of great insiders: Nolo Ferreira, De la Mata, Méndez, Labruna, Simes, Martino, Moreno, Farro, Baéz and Grillo. The contribution of Argentina to the Italian national teams, in the thirties and later in the sixties, consisted mostly of insiders: Cesarini, Maschio, Sivori, Lojacono and Montuori. Even Angelillo, a classical centre-forward, played in the sixties on the Italian national team as an insider.

It is interesting to note that Juan Carlos Lorenzo and César Luis Menotti, whom in theory and in practice, represent two different ideologies in Argentinean football history, agree on the fact that this period and the style related to it can be defined as "typical Argentinean". Lorenzo writes that during this epoch the Argentinean way of playing was characterised by a general attitude that praised a great offensive vitality and an incredible lack of discipline in defence (Lorenzo and Castelli,1977:41). According to Menotti this style has produced an innumerable quantity of great players that over time consolidated a kind of ethos that it is necessary to protect (Menotti,1986:63). Lorenzo will argue that this great advantage was, at the same time, a negative factor that hindered the changes that were needed in Argentinean football before the World Cup of 1958 in Sweden. Menotti, on the contrary, points out, from an essentialist perspective, that this style should be preserved, and, in this sense, any change is a sign of decay and, therefore, loss of self-identity.

The Argentinean football ethos was maintained and reproduced as a myth after San Lorenzo de Almagro's famous tour of Europe in 1946. This great team had a "small chamber orchestra" in the attack composed of a violin (Ferro), a viola (Pontoni) and a cello (Martino) (Lucero,1975:140). On the 15th of January 1947 they defeated the Spanish national team by six goals to one in Madrid. This tour, that included some matches in the

Basque country, is still remembered in Spain. Panizo, the great left-insider of Athletic Bilbao, said:

> When I started as football player you could do marvellous things but if you did not score enough goals or continued to run in spite of the fact that a defender took your shirt, everyone said that you were slow. I was very happy, therefore, when the Argentineans of San Lorenzo de Almagro, that by that time was one of the best teams of the world, visited the San Mames stadium. The people were astonished to see them play, and they commented: "Look, all of them play like Panizo" ... I never understood that some fans preferred you to send the ball to nowhere instead of playing back and safe... Now it is different, but then the people did not understand, they said that I was slow, that my way of playing stopped the team [own translation] (Unzueta, 1986:39).

So strong is the myth of the Argentinean football that Segurola, a Spanish journalist, writes in an article on Panizo:

> But then arrived San Lorenzo de Almagro ... a team that was able to play as equals with the "machine" River Plate, then the best team of the world. And everyone played like Panizo. Never again was his quality in the San Mames stadium questioned ... There was a general agreement among the fans that Panizo, so much criticized during his first times with the Athletic shirt, offered a revolutionary proposal to Spanish football after the Second World War, developing the idea that San Lorenzo masterfully showed, where every player played like him [own translation] (*El País Deportes*, 19/2, 1990:7).

I would like to add two remarks: first, San Lorenzo de Almagro was revolutionary because the high tempo was replaced by the search for empty spaces through keeping the ball under team control until an opportunity for attacking was created. Second, it is accepted in Spain, even today without discussion, that San Lorenzo de Almagro and River Plate were the two best teams in the world.

Between 1938 and this key point in the forties international contacts with European football almost disappeared. In this period, Argentineans developed, in isolation from Europe, the idea that they played the best football in the world. This idea was confirmed by the team's success in the South American competitions. From 1941 to 1947, the National League was dominated by River Plate with the famous team "la máquina" (the machine). This team still belongs to the imaginary world of beauty, excellence and superiority, to the epics of an Argentinean "golden age", a time that will never come back. It is a kind of unchallenged mythology because River Plate never played in Europe against the best teams and, therefore, they vanished from history undefeated. Every Argentinean fan will still remember the name of the five in the attack: Muñoz, Moreno, Pedernera, Labruna and Loustau. River Plate lost its best players after a strike in 1948 when most of them, in a search for better wages, left Argentina for Colombia. Among the travellers was a player who never had the opportunity to play regularly in the first team, Alfredo "the Blond Dart" Di Stéfano.

It is precisely the great success of Di Stéfano in the successful Real Madrid of the fifties which reaffirmed the myth of the superiority of Argentinean football: the best player of the best European team was an Argentinean. Even more, during his time as player in River Plate he was ignored, eclipsed by the other stars. Hence, Argentineans could say with self-confidence that if a "second class star" became the best player in the world, then what if Moreno, Pedernera or Labruna could have had the same opportunity that he had had?

Argentineans continued to believe in their superiority. The South American Cup of 1957 confirmed it. Argentina won easily in Peru, defeating the Brazilians in the final by 3 goals to 1. In this team a new "small chamber orchestra" was presented: the teenagers Maschio (20), Angelillo (17) and Sivori (19), "los ángeles con la cara sucia" (angels with a dirty face). After the victory, all of them were bought by Italian clubs: Maschio to Bologna, Angelillo to Inter and Sivori to Juventus. They became great players and, due to their Italian ancestors, they also played in the different Italian national teams of the sixties. Again, as in 1930, Argentineans felt both dispossession and pride at the same time. They lost successful players, young players in their best age, to a better life in Europe. The opening of the world market, after the interruption due to the difficult times in Europe during and after the Second World War, again put Argentinean football in the position of a periphery providing rich European teams with young talented players.

47

The crisis of 1950

In 1958, the Argentineans decided to take part in the World Cup in Stockholm. This date was considered as a privileged opportunity to transform the myth of superiority into real history. "The encounter with history" developed into the most traumatic and tragic event in Argentinean football history, only comparable in intensity with the national frustration of Brazilians after the defeat in Maracaná in the final of the World Cup in 1950.(5) The humiliation suffered against Czechoslovakia, a clear 6-1 defeat, put the whole nation into a state of psychological shock and transformed the players from heroes into a bunch of traitors. The team was supposed to represent the typical style with slow tempo and great technical ability. At the symbolic level, the presence of the great left-insider Labruna, a survivor of the great "máquina" of River Plate, close to his forties, was a guarantee of confidence and historical continuity. The debacle was rapidly rationalized by the coach Guillermo Stábile, top scorer in the Argentinean team in the World Cup of 1930 in Montevideo and later professional player in Italy: the best Argentinean players, "los angéles con la cara sucia", were robbed by "our bad brothers of Italy" and "the best centre-forward of the world is playing at Milan and his name is Angelillo" (Brera,1978:280-86). Brera comments on Stábile's rationalization in the following way:

> ...the Argentineans were presumptious in a masochist way: they believed that they were superior to all, they did not take the time to study a tactical scheme adapted to their real means: moreover, the Italian and Spaniard bad brothers have always robbed their best players" [own translation] (Brera,1978:286).

Symbolically, for the makers of public opinion this crisis was a reflection of a general decadence of Argentinean football in a national context of deep economic crisis. A model of growth, based on the substitution of imports, on isolation from the world market, went into crisis. This metaphor was used in order to understand the defeat of 1958: the isolationism of Argentinean football ought to be changed. The political and socio-economic decay of Argentina after 1955 was related to football: the everlasting true style could no longer be taken as invincible. The "golden age" of football was associated with a continuous growth of the economy since the general crisis of the thirties. New inputs coming from European football were needed. It is interesting to note that the victory of Brazil in the Cup also conditioned changes in the way football was perceived. From Europe it was necessary to import physical strength, from Brazil the famous system 4-2-4. Argentina began to buy defenders from Brazil — the great players Orlando and Dino arrived at the beginning of the sixties — so that the Argentineans could learn to play with four defenders adopting the style of zonal marking.

During these years Argentinean football began a long march in the desert, with very few successes at the international level. Our national heroes were playing in Spain (Di Stéfano) and in Italy (Sivori). They symbolized the victories that our national team never achieved. Real Madrid and Juventus were suddenly transformed into "national teams". In the case of Real Madrid this was even more understandable because, in addition to Di Stéfano, there were two other Argentineans on the team: Dominguez and Rial. By this tour de force, characteristic of crises of national identities, the essentialists defined Di Stéfano as the "typical" Argentinean player. Menotti writes:

> I sustain that Argentina has been the owner of a style at international level that always was dependent on great talented players. Due to different reasons we never realized this at the team level ... But it is fantastic to realize that it was Di Stéfano that showed Europe that there was another style, another way of playing football. When he travelled, Di Stéfano, in his suitcase, had a great heritage, the heritage of "la máquina" of River Plate ... To this he added his temperament, and his dynamics, but it must be clear that he did not win just because of these ... He had a great capacity, he imposed his style [own translation] (Menotti,1986:63).

However, from an European perspective, Di Stéfano represented a new type of player, the synthesis of "two styles": the Argentinean and the European. In 1990 he was chosen the "all time best European player":

> (In Paris)...journalists of all countries and players of all origins, chose Di Stéfano the all time best European player ... The winner, a man with a threatening glance, descendant of three stocks of immigrants and educated in the liquid fields of River Plate, had proved that football is a *nationless* emotion and a plural force in

which both ability and impetus can coexist. In the spirit of the old blond gaucho ... the Muses and the Devils were powerfully reunited. Such a powerful coalition provided him with a mixed style: he added to a cold nordic inspiration a refined Southern maliciousness [own translation] (J.C.Iglesias, El País Deportes, 8/1-1990:24).

In search of a new identity

In the sixties Juan Carlos Lorenzo represented the "European revolution" in Argentinean football. He had an active career as player in Italy (Sampdoria), France (Nancy) and Spain (Atlético Madrid and Rayo Vallecano). He successfully worked as coach in Spain and Italy (Lazio and Roma) and was in charge of the Argentinean national team in the World Cups of 1962 and 1966. He was strongly opposed to the "typical Argentinean style" that he characterised as very slow, without discipline in defence and with an extreme preoccupation for jugglery. He defined this style as "anachronistic traditionalism producing stagnation" (Lorenzo and Castelli,1977:31). He emphasized that this ideology produced, at the same time, excellent jugglers and very incomplete football players. He tried to combine ability with speed and tactical discipline. His model was the German team of 1954. They lost in the preliminaries against Hungary but, at the end, in the final they defeated them. According to Lorenzo, the Germans understood that "art" could be destroyed with physical power and they did it in the final: "Germany won due to its physical capacity, spirit of sacrifice ... and a strong and intelligent tactical discipline" [own translation] (Lorenzo & Castelli, 1977:44). Moreover, he argued that the Brazilian victory of 1958 was closely related to an ideal combination of ability with speed and tactical discipline in defence. His philosophy was summarized in a slogan: "before we played football, now we run football" [own translation] (Lorenzo and Castelli, 1977:49).

It is easy to understand that in the sixties, after the catastrophe of Sweden, Lorenzo was a charismatic "pioneer" of a "needed revolution" in Argentinean football. He was considered, and he became, a national figure, enjoying, for a long period, the total support of the Argentinean Football Association. However, he did not succeed as coach and Argentine did very poorly in the World Cups of 1962 and 1966. His most important contribution was, without doubt, to question the traditional style. He emphasized that the model players were the Argentineans that triumphed in Europe: Orsi, Monti, Guaita, Di Stéfano, Sivori and Angelillo. They were, in a way, jugglers but, above all, they were real, disciplined professionals. The national teams that he coached symbolized the transitional years, a period of a deep identity crisis: they abandoned the "rioplatense" slow tempo, and the tactical discipline was interpreted not only as running faster but also as tackling harder and without mercy. The image of Rattin, the captain, sent off in the quarter-finals against England in 1966, proudly leaving Wembley, walking slowly on the Royal red carpet, and provoking one hundred thousand English fans is still remembered as the symbol of his epoch. After the match the English coach, Sir Alf Ramsey, defined Argentinean players as "animals, just animals".

Argentinean teams did not get the recognition that, they strongly believed, they deserved. At club level, the sixties produced Estudiantes de la Plata, where Carlos Bilardo was a player, one of the "hardest" teams in the Argentinean football history. The coach, Zubeldia, represented the victory of machiavelism and speculation. The matches against English, Scottish and Italian teams in the finals of the Intercontinental Cup were "violent struggles", football became war. For the essentialists, Estudiantes de la Plata and Lorenzo were the denaturalization of a style based on generosity, ability, art, inspiration, beauty and individualism. In this perspective, the success of the great players in Europe was related to these values. Orsi, Di Stéfano and Sivori were always perceived as great jugglers who imposed their art against collective discipline and physical destruction. It was the time of H. Herrera and Inter in Europe. The essentialists saw Lorenzo, Zubeldia and H. Herrera as the "enemies", as representing greediness, force, work, boredom and collective discipline. They accused them of teaching players pragmatic amoral standards: any means is valid if victory is achieved. In addition, they argued that proper behaviour on the field could only be obtained by maintaining the values of generosity and beauty. This was the "real and everlasting Argentinean style".

The debate in Argentinean football was related to a concrete historical crisis: neither the typical way of playing nor the "modern" Argentina gained a World Cup. For Argentineans the lack of victories in a period where they believed they had produced the most outstanding players in the world was experienced as a source of profound frustration. Some essentialists never understood that the best players always play in the best teams. The relativists in their turn, like Lorenzo and Zubeldia, put Argentinean players in a difficult position telling them that what counts is discipline, speculation and "smart tricks". These two approaches divided the cultural world of football, reproducing over time the same identity crisis that they tried to solve. Argentineans generally are now as divided as they were in the sixties.

The age of national success

Football and sport in general are exceptional in being a privileged area as far as patriotism is concerned. I have tried to show that Argentinean football created a symbolic and practical male arena for national pride and disappointment, happiness and sorrow. In this field of discourses and practices women were excluded. The question of national identity in sport and politics seems to be a domain reserved for the male imagination. In this process, the image of a national identity is chosen from a manifold reality, it is a kind of arbitrary selection and, therefore, it is always open. The debate between essentialists and relativists illustrates this problem: a national identity, independently of the perspective assumed, is always "imagined" (Anderson, 1983:11). For the essentialists, it is continuity that counts, the defence of the "essence" of a style; for the relativists, it is the relation to other styles, the adaptation to a moving international context, that matters. The essentialists, however, accept changes, as I have pointed out before, but always functional and "tactical" changes that help to keep the imagined football traditions alive.

The World Cup of 1978, in Argentina, was the ideal occasion for confronting history, for transforming the myth into reality: Argentineans were the best in the world in football. The political context invited a revival of traditions. Since 1976, the military Junta was trying "to extirpate the cancer of revolutionary guerrilla infiltrated in the body of Argentinean society". The nationalist language of the military, fighting against "the influence of foreign ideas and communism", created a positive atmosphere for an essentialist discourse in football. History produces unexpected coincidences in this case, the presence within the same symbolic field of the reactionary generals with a "progressive" essentialist: César Luis Menotti.

This coincidence in turn produced paradoxes that Argentineans are used to: the victory of a style in football was transformed into "the victory of the race" against foreign influences and powers. This was not the language but the tragedy of Menotti.

Menotti was a talented left-insider: slow, tall, elegant, very technical, visionary and a great scorer. He began his career in Rosario Central with great success. Later, he played in two of the five "great" teams of Argentina: Racing Club in 1964 and Boca Juniors in 1965. His stay in Boca Juniors was very problematic. His style based on slow tempo and elegant touches did not fit very well with the kick and run playing that has always characterised Boca Juniors. Like many Argentinean players he too emigrated. In 1967, as a pioneer, he played in New York in The Generals and in 1969 in the famous Santos of Brazil (Gasperino and Ponsico, 1983.)[6]

He was always known as a very articulate person, with contacts in radical university milieus, and sympathetic to left-wing ideas. At the end of his playing career, he began a short career as journalist and in 1973 was appointed coach of Huracán, a prestigious club of Buenos Aires but without a single League title. During this year, he built up a great team that at the end of the season, easily, won the title. After the latest failure in the World Cup of 1974, he was appointed coach of the national team for the next Cup of 1978 in Argentina. The Argentinean victory of 1978, followed by the success of the Juniors (Maradona, Diaz, Barbas, Simon and Calderón among others) in the World Club Championship in Tokyo the following year, converted him into a national hero. It is easy to imagine that for Argentineans these victories were the realization of a national dream, nurtured since the beginnings of organized football. It was the historical confirmation of an "imagined" and elusive superiority.

For the Junta it was clear: the victories demonstrated the excellence of the "race" and the importance of staying together, like the national team, against all types of enemies. Menotti desperately tried to rationalize the success, searching in the history of football and not in current political history, for categories and concepts to interpret the happy events. He developed a simple ideological theory: society and politics is based on hypocrisy and tricks; "his philosophy of football" tries to demonstrate the importance of playing with generosity, creativity and honesty, without tricks. Football, then, in a difficult period of Argentinean history could be seen as an arena dominated by "permanent" values of decency. He says:

> Many people could say that I have coached teams during the time
> of dictatorships, in an epoch when Argentina had governments
> with which I had nothing in common and, even more, they
> contradicted my way of life. And I ask, what ought I to do ? To
> coach teams that played badly, that based everything on tricks, that
> betrayed the feelings of the people? No, of course not ... We were
> conscious and we knew all the time that we played for the people.
> A people, that in this moment in Argentina, needed a new point of
> departure for doing together something different ... We tried to play
> in the best way because we understood that we were obliged to
> give back the spectacle of football to the people. To give it back
> through victory, if this was possible, but, after all, in the pleasure of
> playing honest football. Each of us had an order when we entered
> the field the day of the final: to look at the people in the stand. We
> are not going to look to the stage-box of the authorities, I said to the
> players, we are going to look to the stand, to all the people, where
> perhaps sits the father of each of us, because there we will find the
> metal workers, the butchers, the bakers and the taxi drivers [own
> translation] (Menotti, 1986:27).

Menotti recreates a history of purity through an explicit cult of the
ancestors, the great players of Argentina, many of them named in the
paper, that pursued success without tricks. He is opposing these qualities
against the pollution coming from other ways of interpreting football.
Menotti tell us that tricks are matter out of place in his essentialist
perspective. In this way he contraposes the "pure" Argentineans against
the "impures", the polluted and, therefore, the polluters of the essential
Argentinean identity. In his discourse on football "the real enemy" is the
Estudiantes de la Plata of the coach Zubeldia where, accidentally, Carlos
Bilardo played during his active period as football player. According to
Menotti, Zubeldia and his team developed a football based on the
systematic use of tricks and, therefore, represented the "other football", a
way of playing that must be combatted (Menotti, 1986:29-30). In this kind
of discourse, the Argentinean "real style and identity" is always threatened
and, therefore, in spite of the importance of tradition, is also perceived as
ephemeral. To be Argentinean in football, following Menotti, then, is to feel
vulnerable and at risk, for one has defined oneself in terms of a national

style and/or a set of qualities that can never be regarded as fully secure. In this perspective, Argentineanness is the very opposite of Brazilianness or Englishness which are defined as stable and solid. It is said in Argentina that the Brazilians and the English have maintained the purity of the style despite tragedies and failures. If we follow this logic we can conclude by saying that from an essentialist perspective the fragility of identity needs support and requires a permanent re-creation.

Neither in 1978 nor in 1986, did the Argentineans play in a such a way that they could eclipse the mythical Brazilian teams of 1958, 1970 or 1982, the Hungarian team of 1954, the Dutch team of 1974 or the French team of 1982. Some of the outstanding players of 1978, like Passarella, Ardiles or Kempes, or Maradona in 1986, who later succeeded in European football, will always be remembered. Argentina entered into the history of records but not the mythology of football. Even the victory of 1978 was obtained at home, in a terrible political context, with some players practicing a very hard style of football and with a dubious victory against Peru in the quarter-finals. Argentina needed to score five goals against Peru in order to get into the finals. What, before the match, seemed almost impossible they did with surprising ease. Later, Argentinean football authorities were accused of paying some of the key Peruvian players for letting Argentina win the match. This accusation was never proved but the suspicion remained. Nevertheless, Menotti insisted that he recreated in 1978 a team based on a tradition. Bilardo will never argue in such a way, for him football is a game, it is not a privileged arena for discovering national qualities. In this direction what matters is victory and not philosophy or the proof of moral qualities.

The problem, I believe, is that for most Argentineans national feeling is always a matter of contrast, it presupposes other countries and other styles. The "imagined" community, the "imagined" style is always thought of as unique. In this sense, football appeals to a sense of collective belonging: nations need traditions, great teams and great heroes. And in addition they need their qualities to be recognized by others. Menotti repeated, over and over again, that his two victorious teams, the senior in 1978 and the junior in 1979, generated a considerable quantity of players that achieved great success in European football. This fact was a measure of his triumph as a coach and as defender of the "great tradition" of the ancestors. He ironically commented:

I laughed when one day I listened to the coach of the national team, Bilardo, saying that we did not leave anything. He must travel around in Europe, he must ask, and he will find out what was Argentinean football before Menotti and his team work, and what it was after us...I wish that he could reach only twenty percent of the achievements of our epoch [own translation] (*El Gráfico*, 7/4-1988).[7]

Bilardo's team of 1986 did not enter the imagination of millions of fans as a marvellous team. Even in Argentina it was said, after the victory in Mexico, that the team was dependent on one genius (Maradona), two excellent players (Burruchaga and Valdano) and eight disciplined "Japanese" that, all the time, worked and worked for the others . What entered then in the mythological world of football ? The vision of Maradona, the man that in Mexico "won alone", "a hero", "the creator of luck", "the intrepid robber", "the omnipresent", "strong as a bull", "fast like a missile", "the star of the century", "in his blood doctors will not find blood but fuel for missiles", "passing like the air in narrow spaces", annihilates the image of a team with a different style (Darwish, 1986:15). The style is a man, a lonely individual like Orsi, Di Stéfano and Sivori in the past. In this sense, the great heroes are appropriated by others, they do not awake national feelings among neutral spectators, because "they elevate football to the level of a musical abstraction, to the most absolute purity" (Darwish, 1986:15). They have the capacity to recreate and to re-actualize the beauty of the game. A French journalist wrote:

> Diego Maradona, in one month of reason and some seconds of madness, has resuscitated a glorious and old epoch when the dribbling and the dribblers were an essential element in the game and the spectacle of football ... Over time, football become collectivized, normalized, close and defensive, in such a way that the individual was sacrificed for the benefit of the team ... It is good, securing, amusing to see that football will never stop to be nourished and enriched by the individual talent of the men ... [own translation] (Rethacker, 1986:9).

The problem, from the Argentinean point of view, is not only the fact that heroes are universalized in a context where football belongs to a kind of "world global culture", but that they are perceived as "historical accidents", as "products of an arbitrary nature". Maradona, in this kind of interpretation, is not associated to a tradition, to a national style, he is himself, he is unique, and, therefore, his nationality is a random event. It was said, after Mexico, that any team could have won if they had had Maradona. Any national Brazilian team will always be defined as "the team to beat", as "the favourite" before each World Cup, and, consequently, they are treated with an almost religious respect and consideration. The same could be said of the German national team. This has not been and will not be the case with Argentinean teams. Maradona, however, understood this very well. He does not perceive himself as the continuation of a great national tradition; rather, as he put it himself, his talent is a "divine gift":

> My faith helps me in each moment of my life. God is with me and my family, with my parents, my sisters, my brothers, with every one. I always say that God plays with me. I realize this when I am in the football field and when I am out, in the street, or in my house [own translation] (*Corriere della Sera*, 11/11-1985:1).

Therefore, his explanation of the first goal against England in Mexico, "I scored with the hand of God and the head of Maradona", is logical. He is touched by the magic of God and not by the power of his football ancestors. He is not the continuation of a great tradition. He is himself, he is simply Maradona alone in front of God. He must not be compared with other human beings. He is not the product of a cultural heritage, he has been created as a divine, religious subject.(8)

The Argentina of Bilardo's epoch reached another final in the World Cup of 1990 in Italy. The team was built up around Maradona, a tired and injured man, a pale shadow of the marvellous player of 1986. Even more disciplined and physical than in 1986, the Argentineans of 1990 were able to beat better teams, like Brazil and Italy, on their way to the finals. In some matches the "magic" of Maradona paralysed defenders but his poor overall performance anticipated the broken man of 1991 when for consuming cocaine he was suspended from the Italian League for a year. The happy marriage or, perhaps better, the historical coincidence of the careers of Bilardo and Maradona was over, and with them an important period in the history of football in Argentina culminated in a kind of operatic finale: Maradona's tears of impotence during the closing ceremony.

In February 1993 the Argentine Football Association celebrated its centenary with two rituals. The first was logical: a football match between Argentina and Brazil with the expected come back of Maradona to the national team. The second was also expected but highly polemical: Maradona was given the title of "all time best Argentinean player". The other name was Alfredo Di Stéfano. Di Stéfano left during the player's strike of 1948, never returned, never played with the national team, and ended up playing for Spain. His glory and success is identified with Real Madrid, a Spanish club. Maradona was World champion twice: Junior in 1978 and Senior in 1986. It is normal in a nationalist mood that the "all time best Argentinean player" was also World champion with the national team.

Conclusion

In this chapter I have developed two main ideas. The first one is related to the question of how national identity is represented as "an ideological construct" where given qualities are associated with a "typical Argentinean way" of playing football. In the search for essential features, given teams and players are recorded and their characteristics are transformed into "a-historical traits". Football is used as a symbolic arena for producing discourses about an "imagined and limited" national belonging. However, I have tried to demonstrate that Argentineans believed for a long period of time, until the crisis of the World Cup of 1958, that they practiced the most creative and beautiful football in the world. This could be interpreted in different ways, as a deep complex of superiority, as a very provincial perspective or as a manifestation of insecurity. I have insisted that this "image" was reinforced by the presence of international stars who achieved great success in European football. In this direction, a national identity was heavily dependent on the role played by outstanding individuals. If a style depends so much on given heroes, who are also mortal human beings, my argument has been that identity is then transformed into something ephemeral and problematic. History, then, is not only made of continuity, like the essentialists sustain, but of lucky accidents and unexpected events. I believe, without having the space to present fully this idea, that it is possible to find the same logic in the Argentinean interpretation of a stormy and difficult history as an unrealized modern nation in the periphery of the world. This history is dominated by two "unique" parties, the Radical and the Peronist, unlike the others that exist in the modern world, whose ideologies are related to the cult of the dead ancestors (Irigoyen and Perón). A diffuse tradition permits then the legitimation of beliefs through the exceptional role of unusual individuals. The Argentinean football tradition is, in the end, a subsidiary of individual heroes and their marvellous performances. The style is, then, a myth; the individuals are the real history. You can invent a tradition but never concrete individual lives.

My second idea is very simple: football is an arena dominated by the conflict of interpretations. It is a kind of theatre in the world, it is a field made of "realities and masks", it is a stage dominated by dissimilar meanings, it is a beautiful game that invites us to think about reality as the product of different skills and tactics. The actual division between Menottists and Bilardists illustrates this remark and permits us to see identity, values and meaning as a complex field of analysis, articulating in complex and myriad ways with conceptions of national identity.

*   This paper was originally presented in the conference "Le football et l'Europe" organized by the European Culture Research Centre, European University Institute, Florence, Italy, 3-5 May 1990 with the title "In search of national identity: Argentinean football and Europe". The original draft has been considerably changed and hopefully improved. I would like to thank for their critical comments Pierre Lanfranchi, Tony Mason, Richard Holt, and, especially, Alan Tomlinson.

Notes

1   In an analysis of Brazilian football carried out by Da Matta and other anthropologists it is postulated that football is a privileged arena that permits a discussion of identities and dramas in social life (see Da Matta et al. (1982)).

2   For Argentinean football history see Olivera (1932), Ramírez (1977), and Scher and Palomino (1988).

3   The contemporary division between "menottistas" and "bilardistas" is still relevant for understanding the "war of styles" in the Argentinean football. It is said that A. Basile, the present coach of the Argentinean team, is "menottista" and a "personal enemy" of C. Bilardo since his time as active

football player in Racing Club, a team traditionally opposed to Bilardo's Estudiantes de la Plata. Bilardo, coach of Sevilla of Spain in the season 1992-93, was regularly presented in the Spanish press as strongly opposed to Jorge Valdano, the Argentinean coach of Tenerife, who declared himself closer to the philosophy of football represented by Menotti. The matches between Sevilla and Tenerife were often presented as the "war between two Argentinean styles and traditions of playing football" (*El País Deportes*, 3/1-1993:31).

4   Argentina could be considered a typical immigrant country. From 1857 until 1916, a total of 4,758,729 immigrants entered Argentina with a net immigration of 2,575,021. The majority of immigrants were Europeans, with the Italians steadily increasing in ascendancy. One of the main consequence of this flow of population was the rapid growth of Buenos Aires, from 187,00 inhabitants in 1896 to 1,576,000 in 1914. By 1930 Buenos Aires had almost 3,000,000, one third of them being of European origin (Cornblit,1969) .

5   Obdulio Varela, the mythical centre-half and captain of the Uruguayan team, remembered this day in the following way:

> ... after the match I went out with the masseur to a friend's bar. We did not have a single penny and we asked for a credit. We sat in a corner and saw all the people. All of them were crying. It was like a lie: everyone had tears in their eyes ... We had ruined everything and what had we got ? We got a title, but what was it in relation to this sadness ? I thought about Uruguay. There, perhaps, the people were happy. But I was here, in Rio de Janeiro, in the middle of so many unhappy people ... If now I had to play the final again, I will score against us, yes, Sir, against us [own translation] (Soriano,1984:78).

The memory of a fan present this day at Maracaná reinforces Varela's remark:

> At times of sadness all the people were united. It is like the moments of happiness. The same happened in a moment of sadness. Everyone was suddenly a Brazilian, it was Brazil which lost, it was our country which was defeated [own translation] (Vogel,1982:90).

6   Gasparini and Ponsico (1983) have written the most militant pamphlet against Menotti. They described him as a very ambitious person with double moral standards and as a political opportunist. The title of the book indicates their message: Menotti was "the coach of the 'process'". In the military Junta jargon the dictatorship they installed was baptized as "the 'process' of national reorganization".

7   Bilardo thinks differently. For him the exile of Argentinean players is a signal of a deep crisis and not of success. He asks himself:

> Which football nation in the world could stand the fact that 150 players of first level had left the country the last two years ? If this happens in Italy, they must put in their teams players of the second division ... Under these conditions the existence of Argentinean football is a miracle [own translation] (*El Pais Deportes*, 8/1- 1990: 9).

8   The Italian journalists and Napoli's fans have understood this "religious dimension" in Maradona. They can write and think about miracles and magic. The day after the victory of Napoli against Juventus, Gregori writes:

> This is a field of miracle, a chest which not anyone can open: Maradona yesterday has shown diamonds, rubies, emeralds, sapphires. With a simple gesture, a simple movement of his muscles, he has resuscitated a moment of enchantment ... The two goals were the product of magic ... Maradona is like yesterday: unbelievable, untouchable, untrustworthy, superb and arrogant when he is in possession of Beauty, killing all the other stars who, by accident, are close to him [own translation] (*La Gazzetta dello Sport*, 26/3-1990: 3).

Paolo Forcolin is even more enthusiastic:

> Half an hour of the game, two goals, two magic inventions of "Bambin Gesú" (Young Jesus Christ), him, Diego. This was the end of the match [own translation] (*La Gazzetta dello Sport*, 26/3-1990: 5).

Can we imagine that Spanish journalists or Barcelona's fans could call him "Niño Jesús"? Belmonte, in a passionate monograph on a small neighborhood in the slums of Naples, found out that Neapolitans preserve a Catholic ritual facade but prefer their many Saints and Madonna-goddesses to Christ and maintain an active belief in myriad local house-spirits (Belmonte,1979). In this context then, quite different from the bourgeois spirit of Barcelona and Catalonian society, it is unlikely to expect Maradona to become "Bambin Gesú". Could Maradona, a small "sudaca" (a discriminatory word used against South Americans), product of a slum family of Buenos Aires, representing "bad taste" and exaggeration, replace the magical image of the "blond" tall heroes of Barcelona: Kubala, Cruyff and Schuster?

References

Anderson, Benedict (1983), *Imagined communities. Reflections on the origin and spread of nationalism*, London: Verso.

Ardener, Edwin (1989), 'The construction of history: "vestiges of creation"' in M. Chapman, M. McDonald and E. Tonkin (eds.), *History and Ethnicity*, London: Routledge.

Belmonte, Thomas (1979), *The Broken Fountain*, New York: Columbia University Press.

Brera, Gianni (1978), *Storia critica del calcio italiano*, Milano: Tascabili Bompiani.

Chapman, Malcom, McDonald, Maryon and Tonkin, Elizabeth (1989), 'Introduction: History and Social Anthropology' in M. Chapman, M. McDonald and E.Tonkin (eds.), *History and Ethnicity*, London: Routledge.

Cornblit, Oscar, (1969), 'Inmigrantes y empresarios en la política argentina' in T. Di Tella and T .Halperín Donghi (eds.), *Los fragmentos del poder*, Buenos Aires: Editorial Jorge Alvarez.

Da Matta, Roberto et al. (1982), *Universo do futebol: esporte e sociedade brasileira*, Rio de Janeiro: Edicoes Pinakotheke.

Darwish, Mahmund (1986), 'Maradona. Plegarias al héroe nuestro de cada tarde',*El País Domingo*, (14/12):15-8.

De Marinas, Horacio (1981) 'La pasión futbolística', *La vida de nuestro pueblo,* 33 (CEDLA, Buenos Aires).

Escobar Bavio, Ernesto (1923), *Historia del fútbol en el Rio de la Plata*, Buenos Aires: Sports.

Gasparini and Ponsico, (1983), *El director técnico del proceso*, Buenos Aires: El Cid Editor.

Lorenzo, Juan Carlos and Castelli, Jorge (1977), *El fútbol en un mundo de cambios*, Buenos Aires: Editorial Freeland.

Lucero, Diego (1975), *Siento ruido de pelota. Crónicas de medio siglo*, Buenos Aires: Editorial Freeland.

Mason, Tony (1989), 'Football' in T. Mason (ed), *Sport in Britain,* Cambridge: Cambridge University Press.

Menotti, César Luis (1986), *Fútbol sin trampas*, Barcelona: Muchnik Editoros.

Olivera, Eduardo (1932), *Orígenes de los deportes británicos en el Rio de la Plata*, Buenos Aires.

Ramirez, Pablo (1977), *Historia del fútbol profesional*, Buenos Aires: Perfil.

Rethacker, Jean-Philippe (1986), 'Le dribble magique de Diego', *France Football*,1/7:9.

Scher, Ariel and Palomino, Héctor (1988), *Fútbol: pasión de multitudes y de elites*, Buenos Aires: CISEA.

Soriano, Osvaldo (1984), *Artistas, locos y criminales*, Buenos Aires: Bruguera.

Vogel, Arno (1982), 'O momento feliz. Reflexoes sobre o futebol e o ethos nacional' in Roberto Da Matta et al., *Universo do futebol: esporte e sociedade brasileira*, Rio de Janeiro: Edicoes Pinakotheke, 63.

Unzueta, Patxo (1986), *A mi el pelotón*, San Sebastián: Baroja.

4 Brazil and the World Cup: Triumph and despair

John Humphrey

Brazil is the team most people around the world associate with the World Cup. It was not only the first team to gain the Jules Rimet Trophy outright when winning the 1970 final; it has also been a team which has won, and sometimes lost, in style. In an epoch of goalless dramas and penalty shoot-outs, the best Brazilian teams have always scored many goals and, on occasion, conceded a few as well. The 1970 team, winners in Mexico, scored 19 goals in just six matches. In 1958, the Brazilian team scored eleven goals in three games from the quarter-final stage. In 1990, the West Germans scored four goals in their last three games to become the current holders of the Jules Rimet trophy. Unlike Holland, in 1974 and 1978, and Hungary in 1954, Brazil showed that artistry could win. Beauty could be effective.

Brazil is well-known for being the only team to win a world cup played outside of its own hemisphere — in Sweden in 1958. Less well-known is the fact that Brazil is the only world cup winner *not to* have won the cup on its home territory. Four other winners of the World Cup — Uruguay, Italy, England and Argentina — all won the cup first at home. Three of them went on to win the cup abroad at a later date, while the only other team to win the Cup, West Germany, triumphed in Munich in 1974, 20 years after defeating Hungary in the 1954 final.

Hungary's defeat in 1954 remains one of the great World Cup upsets, but for Brazilians, the 1950 final remains an even greater misfortune. Brazil's chance to win the World Cup at home, in the newly-built Maracanã stadium in Rio de Janeiro, came on 16 July, 1950. 200,000 people went to celebrate a great victory but witnessed a 2-1 defeat, described later by Pelé as "a sadness so great, so profound that it seemed like the end of a war, with Brazil the loser and many people dead" (cited in Perdigão, 1986: 37).

Hope, despair and involvement — the Brazilian people and the World Cup

Football is Brazil's national sport. It was the first professional team sport to take root in the country, and, in both the amateur and professional arenas, is still far and away the most important sport. But this fact alone does not explain the distinctiveness of the Brazilian obsession with the World Cup. At club level, the passions aroused by the big teams in Rio de Janeiro and São Paulo would not appear out of place in Liverpool or Manchester. Active soccer fans in Brazil, as elsewhere, are male and a minority of the population, even though leading football clubs often have extensive social and sporting facilities which attract a much broader range of participants (Allen, 1986).

When the national squad takes the field in the World Cup, however, the picture changes completely. The Brazilians believe that their team and footballing tradition are peculiarly Brazilian. They regard their country's black and latin roots as having given rise to a style of football based on individual flair, agility, artistry (as well as artfulness and trickery) and all-out attack. As such, football proclaims the value of popular characteristics and virtues, and it is as deeply rooted in popular culture as samba and carnival.

During the 1982 World Cup Final normal life in Brazil was suspended when the national team took the pitch. For the second-round matches, played at 1.15 p.m. local time, factories remained shut for the whole day, the banks closed their doors at 11 a.m. and huge traffic jams formed around midday as millions of Brazilians hurried home to watch their team on television. Families and friends — of both sexes and all ages — gathered around their sets, and the city of São Paulo became quieter than on a Sunday morning. Intermittently, this unnatural afternoon calm was shattered by the burst of thundercrackers released by fans in their gardens and backyards to celebrate the nation's goals.

On four consecutive occasions — against the Soviet Union, Scotland, New Zealand and Argentina — the team's victory was followed by wild celebrations. People flocked to the streets in cars and on foot to mark the victories with dancing, singing and drinking. São Paolo's main avenue, the Avenida Paulista, was given over entirely to music and dance. After defeat in the game against Italy, the Paulista was deserted. The only people to be seen were the street-traders packing up the flags, banners, drink and food that no one had come to buy. The unthinkable had happened. The Brazilian team with the best midfield trio in the world had lost to Italy, a team which had only managed to draw with Poland, Peru and Cameroon.

In 1950, the sense of national defeat was even greater. The Brazilian team had taken third place in the 1938 World Cup, played in France in 1938, and since then the effects of professionalisation of football, begun in 1933 in response to the professionalisation in neighbouring Argentina and Uruguay (Levine, 1980: 238), had taken effect. Tactically, Brazilian football had matured, and the team's manager, Flávio Costa, used a version of Herbert Chapman's WM system, which he had earlier used to great effect when manager of Flamengo (Perdigão, 1986: 83-85). Brazil had already won the South American Championship in 1949 (for the first time in over 25 years), and the whole nation confidently expected a victory. With the spread of radio, the whole nation could accompany the victory.

This was the problem. In 1938, a strong Brazilian side had lost to Italy in the semi-finals in large measure because of over-confidence. Two of the best players were 'rested' in anticipation of the final, and the team's management had allowed advanced celebrations (Isto É, 1982: 29). In 1950, both the pressures on the team and the anticipation of victory were enormous.

Many explanations have been given for the traumatic loss to Uruguay in the final. They vary from racist criticisms of the team's black players (Da Matta, 1982: 73)[1], to putting responsibility on the politicians and celebrities who clamoured to participate in the glory. Flávio Costa, the manager, argues that, in the end, the team lost on the pitch, partly because of failures in its tactical system which allowed Ghiggia to make one goal and score another for Uruguay, and partly because the team thought it had won before even starting the game (preface to Perigão, 1986: 12).

The optimism of the Brazilian team was not out of place. The finals of the 1950 competition were disputed by 13 teams in four groups. The winners in each group — Brazil, Spain, Sweden and Uruguay — moved to the second and final phase, disputed not by knock-out but on a league basis. The Brazilian sports confederation, the CBD, insisted on this arrangement in order to maximise its revenues, doubling the number of games in the final phase (Isto É, 1982: 35). The Brazilian side won its first two games of this phase with ease, scoring seven times against Sweden and six times against Spain. According to Brian Glanville:

> Brazil now played the football of the future, an almost surrealist game, tactically unexceptional but technically superb, in which ball players of genius while abrogating none of their own right to virtuosity and spectacle, found an exhilarating *modus vivendi'* (1980: 53).

Uruguay, meanwhile, had drawn 2-2 with Spain with a second-half equaliser, and just managed to beat Sweden 3-2, scoring two goals in the last 15 minutes. The last match of the second phase, Brazil against Uruguay, was in effect the final — but with one difference; a draw would be enough to give Brazil the championship. No-one expected a draw — an annihilating victory was on the cards. The newspaper *O Mundo* had already published a picture of the team under the caption "Here Are The World Champions" on the day before the final (Perdigão, 1986: 68).

In the first half, Brazil attacked strongly, forcing 19 corners, but no goals were scored. Brazil did finally score early in the second half, but this provoked a reaction from the Uruguayans who went on the offensive, scoring the equaliser in the twentieth minute of the second half and the winner 13 minutes later.

This was not part of the plan. Jules Rimet has recounted the scene at the end of the game in his *La Histoire Merveilleuse de la Coupe du Monde*. He was to hand over the trophy to the winning team (Brazil) in the centre of the pitch once the national anthem had been played. He left the VIP box when the match was at 1-1, sufficient to give Brazil the Cup. By the time he had got to the pitch, the match was over and the crowd in silence. There was no guard of honour, no national anthem, no speeches. Eventually, amidst the crowds milling on the pitch, he came across the Uruguayan captain and handed over the trophy without saying a word (Perdigão, 1986: 163-164).

Robert De Matta has observed that in Brazil the term football is always put together with game, as in *Jogo de futebol*, a game of football. Unlike in English, game in this context has connotations not only of competition, but also of luck and destiny:

The teams do not only play against time and their opponents, but also against destiny, and it is this which must be altered or corrected for victory to smile on them (Da Matta, 1982: 69).

Defeat implies not only a failure to win the match, but the impossibility of winning in the face of fate. In this case, the optimism prior to the match — a constant feature of Brazilian attitudes to World Cup teams since 1938 — quickly transmutes into a deep and lasting sense of gloom. The defeat on 16 July 1950 created a deep scar which is still visible today. The manager and the team are still remembered as the team that lost to Uruguay and in so doing revealed significant aspects of the Brazilian character. In popular mythology, the defeat cannot be interpreted merely as the result of a tactical failure to close up the right side of the Uruguayan attack.

The decline of Brazilian football

Memories of the 1950 defeat were assuaged, but by no means eradicated, by the victories in 1958, 1962 and 1970. The great teams of those years won, and won in style. They scored a lot of goals and conceded very few. But it is now over 20 years since the 4-1 victory against Italy in the Aztec stadium in 1970. During this period, Brazil has played in five world cups, never again reaching a final.

Many reasons can be advanced for this period of failure, from the most structural and basic to the most conjunctural — from the decline in spaces for football in Brazilian cities to dark suspicions over the 6-0 victory of Argentina over Peru in 1978, which put Brazil out of the competition. Neither seem satisfactory. On the one hand, Brazil continues to produce talented players, exporting many of them to the leagues of Europe — particularly Italy, Portugal and Germany. On occasions, Brazilian teams contain a plethora of brilliant players. The 1982 team, in particular, had a surfeit of stars. On the other hand, repeated failure points to something more than mere misfortune.

One can attribute the successes in 1958 and 1962 to the skills of Garrincha and Pelé. Indeed, until the team included both, it lacked lustre. The teams incorporated the virtues of Brazilian soccer, as encapsulated in the figure of Mané Garrincha. Garrincha was the great dribbler of the 1958 team. While anyone could admire his football, Brazilians saw in his play the affirmation of Brazilian values over European, and also popular values over those of the elite. For many people in Brazil there was no better sight than a six-foot, blond, superbly-coached and tactically-trained European defender on a rigid calorie-controlled diet being made to look like a fool by the devastating artistry of an undernourished, anarchic black winger with two twisted legs who would never have got past the medical exam in European soccer. In class terms, Garrincha was the semi-literate who could get by on his wits and cunning, able to put one over on the rich and the more powerful (or perhaps the police). His football and his style had a quality which today might be called 'street-wise'. He was one of the boys: clever, artful and cunning.

The 1958 team, then, was the embodiment of a certain Brazilian way of playing football which finally proved itself superior to the European style. It had the individual genius of players like Pelé, Garrincha and Didi, combined with a commitment to all-out attack. In the four games which Garrincha and Pelé played together, the team scored 13 goals. In Brazilian eyes, this was a triumph over the European 'strength football', a game based on physical fitness, strong (possibly violent) challenges and subordination to the tactical plan.

But behind this success lay other factors. Following the professional-isation of the game in the 1930s and 1940s, the best of Brazilian football was concentrated in Rio and São Paulo. With the emerging strength of teams such as Flamengo in Rio and Corinthians and Santos in São Paulo, the recruitment of talented youth was systematised and junior teams developed to nurture talent (Levine, 1980: 241). At the top level, an intense rivalry between São Paulo and Rio was channelled into an annual competition between the best clubs in the two states. This was the nearest the country had to a national competition at the time[2], and it had a number of advantages — particularly the concentration of competition into a limited number of highly attractive games between the five top clubs of each state (Savoy and Garcia, 1984: 220). It provided high-level, limited competition.

Since the late 1960s, however, the organization of football in Brazil has been increasingly defective. The Rio-São Paulo competition was extended to include clubs from other leading states in the late 1960s, and in 1971 the first Brazilian championship was organised, with 20 clubs, still concentrated in Rio and São Paulo. This competition was quickly expanded, and it became part of the military regime's strategy of national integration. Representatives from all the states in the Federation were entitled to participate. By 1976, there were 54 clubs in the competition, and by 1979 ninety two teams were involved (Savoy and Garcia, 1984: 220).

This expansion had two motive forces — the politics of the political system and the internal politics of football. In the course of the 1970s, the administration of football became increasingly politicised by a regime anxious to obtain electoral support. When João Havelange moved from presiding over Brazilian football to the top job at FIFA, his place was taken by Hélio Nunes, who was not only an Admiral but the President of the political party, ARENA, in Rio de Janeiro (Levine, 1980: 246). In the late 1960s, the military government had banned existing parties and created two new parties — a majority government party and a minority opposition. While elections did not provide access to executive power (the President, State governors and city mayors were appointed by the military), winning elections was important for the government and for its legitimacy. From 1974 onwards, winning elections in cities became increasingly difficult for the regime, and it resorted to various different means to obtain electorial success.

Participation in the national championship was one strategy for obtaining votes. It is said that Nunes' administration was characterised by the slogan "Where ARENA is doing badly, put a team in the national championship" (Savoy and Garcia, 1984: 220-221). In some cases, teams not qualifying for the championship were given places for short-term electoral reasons. The Government at state level invested heavily in building large football stadiums, often much larger than required by the local population. Between 1969 and 1975, thirteen stadiums with an average capacity of 63,000 spectators were built in Brazil, nine of them in the backward North and Northeast of the country (Savoy and Garcia, 1984: 222). This provided both football arenas and kick-backs for local political interests. Local politicians were often involved in football, and those involved in football often used this as a platform for political careers (Levine, 1980: 247).

However, the tendency to expand football has deeper roots. It has continued after the end of the military regime in 1985. Brazilian football, like many other institutions in Brazilian life, is organised on the basis of state-level federations and a national-level Confederation (since 1979 the Brazilian Football Confederation, CBF). All the eligible teams have one vote in the State federations and each State has one vote in the national confederation. Size counts for nothing at either level. Leaders at each level tend to use a strategy of promoting the interests of the smaller clubs as a means of maintaining power. Resources are used as patronage to assure the allegiance of smaller clubs and States. The money collected by central bodies is not divided between the clubs as of right; it is distributed by the heads of each body, who have a large degree of discretion.

The advantages and disadvantages of this system in terms of who controls football and the flows of resources between different units will not be discussed here. But the effects on the game are serious. The larger Brazilian teams play in two main competitions — their State championship and the National Championship. In both competitions, the tendency is to maintain a large number of teams. The smaller teams pressure for a big competition (the rules are not fixed year after year) so that they can play against the big teams, who will earn them money — particularly when the income from games goes disproportionately to the home team. A team like Corinthians will attract large crowds in a small town in the Interior of the State. Corinthians, however, will earn little from the away game and the home game will not be attractive for the home fans. Large numbers of games without meaning (for example, first rounds of tournaments where well over half the teams qualify for the next round) generate little money for the teams with the best players. The administrative structures of Brazilian sport as a whole, may be transformed as a result of the 'Zico' Law. Zico, one of the stars of the 1982 World Cup team, was Minister for Sport briefly in the early 1990s. He introduced a law to modernise the administration of the sport. However, in July 1993, Pelé was still complaining of corruption and maladministration in the CBF.

The result of the current system is that the big teams play too many competitive matches, but still have to play friendlies and other tournaments — such as the one between past champions of the Libertadores Cup, the Latin American equivalent of the European Cup. São Paulo Football Club, for example, played 54 games in just 123 days in the period February-May 1993. Top players were playing three times a week in May — twice in the semi-final stages of the São Paulo State Championship and once in the Libertadores Cup. After this marathon effort, the team was to have one week's rest before going to Spain to play friendlies (Folha de S. Paulo, 30/5/93). Some players went to the USA for the quadrangular tournament between Brazil, Germany, England and the United States and shortly after that Brazil would face eight games in the South American World Cup qualifying competitions in a period of just three months. The second half of the year would see yet more championship football in Brazil.

In these circumstances, it is hardly surprising that top players are not at their best. Raí, the captain of São Paulo and Brazil, had a disappointing start to the South American qualifiers. Raí might play better in the 1994 Finals after a relatively relaxing year playing for Paris St. Germain. Over-playing means that players are not only physically exhausted, but lack the capacity to concentrate too. In the context of overplaying in the domestic game, the export of the best players to Europe could be an advantage rather than a source of disunity and weakness in the national side.

Prospects for 1994

After the 1970 triumph, the Brazilian team went into decline. Much reference has been made to the influence of the military. It has been suggested that the militarisation and politicisation of football in the 1970s at all levels — from national administration, to club management, to the running of the national squad — deprived Brazilian football of its distinctive artistry, freedom of expression and essentially popular character.

Claudio Coutinho the national team manager in 1978 has been accused of trying to impose an alien European style, based on physical fitness and discipline, on the Brazilian team. He has been quoted as saying that there are a lot of similarities between a football team and a platoon or regiment (Savoy and Garcia, 1984: 220). However, Coutinho went on to be manager of the great Flamengo team of the early 1980s, which won the Libertadores Cup and many other titles. A more convincing explanation, offered by Isto É, is that the 1978 team lacked the players required to emulate the Dutch team of 1974.

Having talented players and a talented manager is not enough, however, to win the World Cup. In 1982, Telê Santana's side was crammed with talented players — particularly the midfield of Falcão, Zico and Socrates. It could score lots of goals. Between June 1980, when Telê Santana managed Brazil for the first time, and the finals of the World Cup in 1982, the team played 31 times, winning 23 times, drawing 6 and losing just twice, scoring 75 goals and conceding 18 (Oliver, 1992: 636). In the finals, Brazil outscored their opponents by 13 goals to 3 in their first four matches, but needing only to draw against Italy to reach the semi-finals, the fragility of their team was revealed when Paulo Rossi scored a hat-trick of goals largely gifted to him by an uncertain defence. Junior, the attacking left-back and star of the Flamengo side which had won the Libertadores Cup, had said before the Cup that Flamengo did not mind conceding goals because they could always score more than their opponents. Against Scirrea, Collovati and Gentile this proved not to be the case, and the inability of the team to go on the defensive after equalising in the 68th minute told against them.

In 1994, the team could not be discarded. A Brazilian team will always have individuals capable of bringing a game to light and technical skills sufficient to delight any fan. But the team was likely as not to prove unpredictable. The various aspects of the team were shown clearly in the Americas Cup competition in June 1992. Three goals against Germany in an overwhelming first-half display, but three goals then conceded in the second-half. Against England — a team in total disarray following defeat by the USA — an altogether more tentative display saw Brazil draw 1-1 and England end up feeling they could have won a game they had entered hoping merely to avoid a heavy defeat. The São Paulo team, whose captain Raí also captained Brazil, was more consistent, but subject to the same weakness. In the first leg of the final of the Libertadores Cup they annihilated a good Universidad Católica side from Chile. At 5-0 up in the second-half, São Paulo played majestic football. In the return leg, things were different. Having been given a late and doubtful penalty in the opening leg, La Católica needed a 4-0 victory to take the match to penalties (the 'away goal counts double' rule is not used in the Libertadores Cup), and São Paulo looked decidedly shaky after conceding two goals in the first 20 minutes. São Paulo held on, but not convincingly.

Brazil would do well to emulate the consistency of the São Paulo team. They started the qualifying competition for the 1994 Finals badly, winning one and drawing two of their first four matches. Convincing wins later on calmed the nerves, but the team still played poorly. In 1993, the manager tried to subordinate the players to the system, refusing to put individualistic players in the side. The poor early performance in the qualifiers forced some change in this policy. More daring and more license for brilliant individuals was necessary if Brazil were to play to their traditional strengths. But this would leave them open to the dangers of

1950 and 1982. Indeed, many Brazilians were clamouring for the the 1982 manager, Telê Santana, to lead Brazil into the 1994 World Cup. With the right management, Brazil would be likely to provide entertainment in 1994, but remained unlikely to win.

Notes

[1] Football is a good starting point for a critique of Brazil's ideology of racial democracy. Labour market analysis is statistically more convincing, but not as entertaining.

[2] A truly national competition could only be developed when extensive air travel was possible. Brazil is bigger than Europe.

References

Allen, Elizabeth (1986), '"Flamengo, Flamengo" The Club Means More Than Football in Brazil', *Scottish Journal of Physical Education*, Volume 14, Number 2, Autumn: pp. 36-42.

Da Matta, Roberto (1982) 'Notes sur le futebol brésilien', *Le Débat*, Number 19, February: pp. 68-76.

Glanville, Brian (1980), *The History of the World Cup*, London: Faber and Faber.

Isto, É. (1982), *Espanha 82: o brasil e as copas do mundo*, São Paulo: Caminho Editorial.

Levine, Robert (1980), 'Sport and Society: the case of Brazilian futebol', *Luso-Brazilian Review*, Volume 17, Number 2: pp. 233-252.

Oliver, Guy (1992), *The Guinness Record of World Soccer*, Enfield: Guinness Publishing.

Perdigao, Paulo (1986), *Anatomia de uma Derrota*, São Paulo: L&PM.

Savoy, Isney and Garcia Júlio Cezar (1984), 'No País do Futebol', *Retrato do Brasil*, Volume 1: pp. 217-222.

5 England and the World Cup: World Cup willies, English football and the myth of 1966

Chas Critcher

England failed to qualify for the 1994 World Cup. Not for the first time, the world's premier football tournament was to take place without a team to represent the nation where the game began and where it still remains the most popular team sport. England's exit from the tournament at the qualifying stage came about finally because they lost vital games away to Norway and Holland, with whom they had only drawn in their home ties. Thus these two went through. The final match, bar a pointless exercise against San Marino, was away to Holland.

The match was not without its controversy. The Dutch defender Ronald Koeman committed a blatant professional foul, for which he should quite clearly have been sent off. Instead, he was only cautioned, remained on the field and scored Holland's opening goal from a free kick. The British popular press was much taken with this apparent injustice, conveniently overlooking the fact that Holland had been incorrectly disallowed an early goal for supposed offside. More thoughtful media commentators admitted that the result merely confirmed the abject state of English football. The management team (chosen for its public relations face rather than any proven expertise) lacked tactical vision. Quality players were simply not coming through, the average English professional lacking basic skills expected in the rest of Europe. For all the hype and promise of the new Premier League, English football was declining rather than improving. Those who argued, on the basis of past evidence, that the strength remained at club level were disillusioned when a few weeks after Enland's defeat, the best club in England, Manchester United, were defeated over defeated over two legs in the European Club championship by the Turkish team Galatasary.

For those with a knowledge of recent footballing history, there was a sense of déja vu. We had been here before, not only in 1973, when England had also failed to qualify, but even earlier. Just over forty years before the defeat by Holland, an English national side, who had never lost to a foreign nation from beyond the British Isles at home, met Hungary at Wembley. They were routed 6-3 by a rampant Hungarian team, probably at the time the best in the world and certainly in Europe. For the more perspicacious observer, the defeat demonstrated the fundamental flaws in the unchanging English tradition of how to play the game. An editorial in *The Times* pointed to the lessons:

> British footballers have a four-point programme to master if they are to survive. They must become athletes, 100 per cent fit; they must become gymnasts; they must make the ball a slave, answering every command; and they must start thinking intelligently ahead of the pass. We must reshape our whole outlook.

Written in 1953, this applies equally to 1993. At the national representative level, English teams are simply not good enough. There is an unwillingness or inability to improve the skill foundations of the game. The reasons for this failure are many and varied. There are problems with the structure of the game, from top to bottom, where skill loses out to speed and strength. There is lack of tactical awareness in coaching and management, ex-players being promoted without experience, training or expertise. Clubs show a wanton disregard for the fortunes of the national side, being more obsessed with how many replica shirts they can sell to gullible supporters. The expulsion of English teams from European club competition following the Heysel crowd tragedy of 1985, denied clubs and players the experience of playing against more sophisticated continental sides. It will be argued here that there is also an unacknowledged problem of culture. The game in England remains rooted in the skilled working class. The values it expresses are those of a heightened masculinity in which toughness and aggression are valued above skill and forethought. Rooting out these problems would have been and remains a stiff challenge, even if the problems were recognised and the will to resolve them existed — which is largely not the case.

In part, the magnitude and nature of the crisis has been disguised. One way of denying the problem has been to emphasise the success of British club sides, especially Liverpool. In the 1970s and early 1980s, they were consistently the most successful club side in Europe. Overlooking their long-term dependence on British players who were not English, Liverpool's success at international level has been interpreted as an indication that there could not be anything fundamentally wrong with the game, only with the management of the international side. This convenient explanation has helped sustain a vitriolic campaign of personal abuse in the popular press against successive England managers, as if a simple change of personnel would rectify the problem.

The other factor which helped to mystify the nature of the problem was that we had once won the World Cup. Thus there was no good reason why we could not win it again. That nobody under thirty could actually remember this event did not prevent it assuming mythical status. England's victory when the World Cup was played in England in 1966 helped sustain the notion of a golden age of English football. Thus the national past rather than the international present, has become the yardstick by which to measure success and the model to emulate. The 'myth of 1966' has become the dead weight of history.

Route 66

It is said, and was much repeated on the thirtieth anniversary in November 1993, that most people alive at the time can remember where they were and what they were doing the day that President Kennedy died. Equally inscribed in English popular memory is the day that England won the World Cup on July 30th 1966. It is a series of television images which formulate the memory: England manager Ramsey's determined walk across the turf to confer with his team before they entered extra time; the linesman flagging that the ball had crossed the line for what proved the winning goal; England's anti-hero, Nobby Stiles doing a jig, Cup in hand, at the end. Most of all we remember the words of television commentator Kenneth Wolstenholme in the dying seconds as England scored their fourth and clinching goal: 'There are people coming on the pitch, they think it's all over; it is now!' Even those for whom this is a received memory will know at least some of the names of the winning team: Banks,

Cohen, Wilson, Stiles, Charlton, Moore, Ball, Hunt, Charlton, Hurst, Peters.

Not since 1953, the year of the Coronation, the conquest of Everest and the Stanley Matthews Cup Final (and despite the Hungarian defeat) had a year seemed to symbolise the preeminence of the English nation. The English football team's victory seemed to set the seal on the resurgence of Britain in the 1960s. Some even thought it contributed to the subsequent return in a re-election of the Labour government of Harold Wilson. What observers at the time and since have forgotten is that it was a close-run thing. As hosts, England qualified automatically for the final stage. Perhaps this was just as well, since twelve months before start of the tournament, scheduled for July 1966, England lacked a settled team or tactical formation.

Leatherdale (1984) has provided an excellent account of England's build-up to and progress through the tournament. The national team manager was Alf Ramsey, appointed early in 1963. He had played in the defeat by Hungary in 1953 and in that by the United States in the 1950 World Cup. He then became an outstanding manager, taking the small town club of Ipswich to the league championship. Ramsey used his status to insist on the abandonment of an anachronistic selection committee and became the first England team manager to have full autonomy. He did not have the most auspicious of starts when England were eliminated from the European Nations Championship, losing 5-2 away to France. Further defeats followed: a 5-1 hiding in Rio and the third home defeat against continental opposition when beaten 3-2 by Austria at Wembley. By December 1965 Ramsey had rung the changes and a reformed side, containing nine players who would eventually play in the World Cup final and playing a new 4-3-3 formation, won 2-0 in Spain. Extraordinarily, England embarked on a European tour just two weeks before the World Cup was due to start. Against admittedly minor nations, England won all four matches, scoring twelve goals and conceding just one. This was to set a pattern, for the strength of the England team was to prove to be in defence, with Banks in goal and Moore as sweeper the dominant figures.

In the World Cup tournament, England were drawn in Group One against Uruguay, Mexico and France with the considerable advantage of playing all their games at Wembley Stadium, the home ground of the English national side. In their opening game against Uruguay, a

ENGLAND and the WORLD CUP

bad-tempered stalemate ensued which revealed deficiencies in the English side with a long history:

> At half time it was a familiar story. England had huffed and puffed to win the greater share of possession, but the ball had been used more effectively when in the care of the Uruguayans. Neutral observers could delight in the way the former World Cup holders shielded the ball, caressed it as if it were a thing of beauty, whereas the England players chased, kicked and thumped the ball all over the place with no more loving care than would be lavished on a punchbag (Leatherdale, 1984: 131).

The outcome was a goalless draw. In their next match, against Mexico, England won comfortably 2-0 but still failed to impress:

> England had managed to win only their fourth match out of sixteen in the World Cup Finals since 1950, but had displayed so little initiative that few (apart from Ramsey) could view the future with any optimism (Leatherdale, 1984:135).

Nor did the subsequent display against France instil much optimism. Stiles, who had punched a Uruguayan in the opening match, now flattened a French player off the ball. Immediately afterwards, England scored the second of two scrappy goals which were enough to see them through to a quarter final tie against Argentina.

A rough game was expected and produced. The entire Argentine team and manager had been warned about 'unethical tackling' by FIFA and Stiles had also been admonished for his conduct. Ten minutes before half-time, the Argentine captain Rattin, who had already been booked, was sent off following another foul and an altercation with the referee. England eventually scored the only goal of the game in the 77th minute, a header from Hurst, who had been brought in to replace the injured Greaves. Subsequent attempts to blame the Argentineans by Ramsey, whose characterisation of the Argentineans as 'animals' was echoed in the popular press, ignored the foul count: nineteen against Argentina, thirty three against England. England, it was clear, were a tough team to encounter and even tougher to beat. They had so far only scored five goals but had yet to concede any. They were now in the World Cup semi-final and would face Portugal.

This was the match in which the English team appeared to have showed itself to be especially skillful as well as hard. Only ten fouls were committed in the whole match. The game was won by two virtuoso goals from Bobby Charlton, who until then had had an indifferent tournament. Portugal did become the first team to score against the English defence, but they could manage no more.

England's opponents in the Final were West Germany, criticised in some quarters for an austere style of play and a tendency to histrionic display when tackled but containing many fine players, including Franz Beckenbauer. The details of that match, for English soccer fans the most famous of all, have been recounted too often to justify detailed commentary here. Germany took an early lead, only for England to equalise before half-time. When England scored with thirteen minutes left, they looked set for victory but Germany equalised in the final minute to take the game into extra time. The deciding goal was one of the most discussed and analysed of any World Cup. A shot from Hurst hit the bar and came down in an ambiguous relationship to the goal line. The linesman signalled a goal which the referee accepted. In the closing stages, Hurst scored again. England had won the game and the World Cup 4-2.

Winning way

In the delirium that followed, the still, small voice of reason asking just how good England were, was unlikely to be heard. For the nation, it was enough that they had won. And they continued to win for the next five years. Ramsey won 63 and drew 23 of his first 100 international matches. His finest hour was, for some, to come in the World Cup of 1970, when England showed themselves to be as good as Brazil:

> Whatever the other performances of the England team in Mexico that match — England lost by 1-0 — was the one by which Ramsey ought to be judged. In it his players justified the modern British approach to football — great physical resource, collective responsibility and personal excellence (Hopcraft, 1971: 121).

Only well into the 1970s did it become evident that Ramsey had become the victim of the rigidities of his own thinking and the inflexible nature of English football:

His uncompromising functionalism won a World Cup and set a trend that was copied throughout our national game. Since then Ramsey has been a victim of his own success, the emphasis on sweat and versatility inimical to the development of gifted individualism. He can only select as he finds and it is the hard and fast who abound in English football (Pawson, 1973: 53).

After England's failure to qualify for the 1974 World Cup Ramsey was re-placed. He had single-handedly transformed the role of the national team manager but the total authority he had assumed was to expose subsequent managers to the assumption that they alone were responsible for the failures of the side.

An unkind verdict on his success in 1966 was delivered by an English coach working abroad, George Raynor, who observed that the main objec-tive of the manager was to find a substitute for skill 'and Ramsey obviously found one'. In retrospect, England were not memorable world champions:

> ...an objective verdict would be that England's team spirit and magnificent defence (a total of three goals conceded equalled the record in the World Cup), allied to moments of individual goal-scoring virtuosity (Charlton against Portugal, Hurst against Germany) won them the Cup. That these attributes should be to the fore was, perhaps, inevitable. As England could not hope to win on skill and flair, it was natural that their triumph should be based on functionalism: fitness, determination and organisation (Leather-dale, 1984: 157).

This detached assessment is unusual because otherwise England's World Cup win of 1966 has achieved the status of a myth. Like all myths it has served to disguise reality. For thirty years, the events of the July afternoon have been recalled and reinterpreted as The Golden Age of English Football. Instead of looking forwards to what English football needs to become to compete successfully at international level, the tedency has been to look backwards at what we once achieved. For much of the time, the myth remains hidden, a piece of folklore recalled increasingly by the older generation. But every now and then, it resurfaces. Thus happened quite recently when England's captain in that World Cup triumph died prematurely.

Mything in action

In February 1993, Bobby Moore died of cancer at the age of 52. This provoked the British press to reflect upon his achievements as a player and those of the teams he had been part of, especially that of 1966. Even the quality press could not resist the temptation to eulogise Moore and place him in the context of another myth — Britain in the 1960s:

> Bobby Moore's afternoon of glory seemed merely the natural culmination of Britain's new standing as the fount of means to achieve the post-war urge to chuck away the ration books and the school books. In the summer of 1966, Moore and the England team took their place in the pantheon of a new pop culture that included musicians, poets, painters, photographers and clothes designers (Richard Williams, *Independent on Sunday*, 28.2.93).

The same article admitted that we now could see that the country was then teetering on the brink of economic bankruptcy and had unresolved political tensions about its failure to establish a meaningful relationship with Europe in the aftermath of decline of Empire. There was even an admission that the victory had not had a beneficial effect upon the development of English football:

> That Saturday turned into a mixed blessing for English football. It was given an imperishable achievement but one that cast a long and lasting shadow.

For the most transparent expression of myth, however, we must turn to the popular press. The tabloid *Daily Mirror* devoted its front page and much of its inside to a sustained eulogy, including an editorial where the myth of the man and the moment was evoked:

> Bobby Moore was a great footballer and a true gentleman. He was as much an ambassador for his country off the pitch as he was a supreme artist on it. His death is a loss not just to football but to Britain. For he represented a past which the nation desperately needs to recover. Bobby symbolised the greatest triumph of this country's national sport. But he was the ultimate symbol of an age where there was true pride in pulling on an England shirt. There will never be another Bobby Moore. And that is as great a tragedy as his death.

Here in condensed form we can find the myth of '66 and the elements which comprise it. First there is quite clearly the element of nationalism: an ambassador for his country, symbol of the nation's triumph, loss to Britain. But there is no continuity here, for 'we' have lost the pride in our country which we 'need desperately to recover' though apparently and paradoxically we cannot, for there will never be another like him. We look to the past for guidance but then admit we cannot reproduce it; nationalism is rooted in past glories which we should like to emulate but cannot. The myth of national identity is situated in the past with which the present is unfavourably compared. Less obvious is the appeal to a particular kind of masculinity. A 'true gentleman', a consciously archaic phrase, embodies ideals of how a man should carry himself on and off the field. (Much of the biographical material in the same paper is taken up with Moore's dignified reaction to being accused of stealing a bracelet in Bogota immediately before the 1970 World Cup tournament.) The 'pride in pulling on an England shirt' has by implication been lost, it being a familiar complaint in the popular press that today's players, cosseted and overpaid, lack real passion when playing for England.

Absent from the editorial is the third main element in the myth, alongside those of nationalism and masculinity. That is class. It is, however, available elsewhere in reflections on '66. Here, for example, is an extract from a book on the Charlton brothers, published in 1971:

> Bobby and Jack played in all of England's World Cup matches; the two Charltons could be observed by the whole nation as brothers of vivid footballing character and self-portraiture — so dissimilar, yet each, in his own way expressing Englishness. Bobby graceful, cultured, creative, conveying some sort of artistic instinct; and in the English tradition, a sense of restrained emotion, a faint air of diffidence overlying his talents and endeavour. And Jack the honest artisan, straight as a gun barrel, stiff as a sentry, solid, stout-hearted, dependable. Foreigners must have seen it too (Harris, 1971: 86).

More florid than the *Daily Mirror*, this still evokes the same myths. The two players are taken as signs of nationhood, present in the moment of victory, observable by the whole nation, embodying Englishness. Even non-English people, 'foreigners', would have recognised it. Yet, lest it be thought the English are boring, they are unalike, one uneasily admitted to be creative with 'some sort of artistic instinct', the other immovable and implacable. The latter is also given a coded class identity as artisan and sentry. Again the language is peculiarly anachronistic: artisan is a nineteenth century term, even sentry is an image of military service. What they do is to offer us a displaced image of class. Whatever else he is, this man is clearly not from the mercantile or the officer class.

Thus around England's one and only World Cup victory, there has been woven a myth: the myth of 1966. Its main elements are those of nostalgic nationalism, an unequivocal masculinity and a submerged reference to class. Like all myths, it depends not on the accumulation of themes but the complex way in which they are entwined. It becomes not one interpretation but the unchallengeable meaning of 1966. None of this may seem to matter very much. Every nation will develop its own myths around hero figures. For people and events to symbolise, someone has to work at the symbolisation. The question is less whether myths and symbols are good or bad in themselves, than what their consequences are. The myth of 1966 does not comprise accidental or incidental elements. It draws on and confirms base themes in English culture which have had and continue to have ramifications in English life and culture.

England, your England

The connections between success in an international football competition and the life of the nation are not best caught by simply inserting the event into contemporaneous happenings. Knowing, for example, that the Beatles were at the height of their fame in 1966, that demonstrations took place in Northern Ireland against a royal visit and London against the Vietnam war, or that a child murderer was convicted (Leatherdale, 1984: 128), may provoke memory but does not make connections. Nor would it help to situate the event in Britain of the 1960s for that decade has itself assumed mythical status; we should merely compound one myth with another. Rather, the need is to demystify the event and its context, to try to identify what the event was taken to mean and how that meaning has subsequently shaped developments inside and outside the game.

What above all, victory in the World Cup was taken to mean was a triumph of traditional English virtues. We did not, at least so we pretended, triumph by trying to play the opposition at their own game; we played it our way, to our traditional strengths: pride, determination, organisation. We did not, so we like to believe, resort to the underhand tactics of lesser nations; even our brutality was honest. The very ordinariness of the English team itself became a kind of virtue; it could have been any one of us, had we been blessed with the talent.

The English pride themselves that they flourish in adversity, declining to ask how they got into such a situation in the first place. They also prefer, given the option, to stand alone and face the enemy, then wonder why they have so few allies. They are suspicious of fancy ideas and prefer the established home truths, surprised to find the rest of the world has moved on. All these characteristics were evoked to explain the World Cup victory. The consequence is that English football, its politics and culture have become and remain insular and conservative. It is observable in our attitudes to European Union. With the decline of Empire, we have no choice but to join a new economic bloc but we wish to do so on our own terms which will preserve our own autonomy. Thus in the English political debate about the Maastricht treaty we have reproduced precisely the same ideas about our own uniqueness which for years kept the English national football side out of the World Cup and our club sides out of Europe.

The reference point for much of our thinking about economics, politics and culture, including football, is not what others do but what we used to do. We look for models not in the present international context but in our past national history. In 1993, this harkening back to a golden age became a political slogan. Faced with a burgeoning crime-wave and related signs of apparent moral collapse, the Conservative government called for a return to 'basic values' rooted in the past. It was suggested that the family, schooling and the Church had been failing society and that the solution was to go back to the way we once were: a mythical Britain of social harmony and moral rectitude. Parallel appeals to the past were made in the aftermath of our exit from the World Cup: where was the spirit of 1966 — the pride and the passion? Why could we no longer produce a Bobby or a Jack Charlton, much less a Bobby Moore?

Whatever happened to British football becomes as much of a conundrum as whatever happened to the English nuclear family. Both are unanswerable in the terms in which they are posed. The only answer has to be that you can't turn the clock back, the world has moved on. The problem is not how to reverse the motor of history but how to adjust to its new and different rhythms. In politics and football, this has not been the predominant response. Instead, the tendency is to find someone or something to blame and to punish them for their failures.

In football, the scapegoat for the failure of 1993 became England manager Graham Taylor. His was originally a safe appointment. A modest success in domestic club management with no experience of international competition as player or manager, he was selected as much for his moral and personal qualities as his footballing expertise. It was thought, as it turned out inaccurately, that he would handle the demands of the media more successfully than the previous manager Bobby Robson. Taylor's selection policy was inconsistent and his tactical understanding naive. This invited the accusation that he was the main problem and that his replacement would solve it, the stance adopted by most of the popular press. More thoughtful commentators, however, pointed out that Taylor was the symptom not the cause of the malaise in English football.

In the aftermath of the exit from the World Cup, a post mortem was conducted on the body of English football. The antiquity of its organisational structures were revealed, not least in the average age (67) and the amateur composition of the committee due to appoint Taylor's successor. The incessant demands of domestic football on players from a young age were stressed, as were the apparent contradictions between the priorities of the Premier League and those of the national side.

More interesting for our present purposes was the discussion about the obvious deficiencies of skill evident in English footballers, when confronted by even quite modest international sides. The philosophy of FA coaches in particular came in for much criticism. Charles Hughes, head coach, is a disciple of the Position of Maximum Opportunity. This stems from the apparently reasonable belief that the faster and more often the ball is projected into the opposing penalty area, the more frequently scoring opportunities will occur. The problem with this approach is that it is rooted in the way the British play the game and takes little account of the more complex rhythms of the game as it is played elsewhere. It is, in short, an insular philosophy, which assumes that we can find our own solutions to our problems instead of seeking answers in the philosophies and practices of those nations who succeed where we fail, often (as in the case of Norway, who finished top of England's World Cup qualifying group for the 1994 Finals) from a much slimmer resource base.

This reluctance to learn from abroad stems in part from the suspicion that new coaching approaches would prove, metaphorically and literally, alien to the English game. And so they would, for the English game is steeped in tradition. This applies not only to organisational structures, where key decisions are taken by bureaucratic time-servers from the administration of the amateur game and club directors appointed for their riches, but to the culture of the game: what it is required to express and the forms such expression takes. Here we find, in enduring and apparently immovable form, those influences which contributed to and were confirmed by the myth of '66. For our beliefs about football are indeed based on a traditional sense of national identity, masculinity and class. That is why English football continues to express ideals which seem idiosyncratic to the rest of the world. It places a premium on physical strength, on quick movement of the ball, on a constant and unremitting pace. Conversely, it sets its face against ball control, measured passing and varying rhythms. When confronted with those who practice the latter skills, English football simply becomes more frantic, opting for long high centres slung in hopefully for a big centre forward, a tendency epitomised in Taylor substituting a big Arsenal forward for Gary Lineker as England went out of the 1992 European championship. Hence English football followers are puzzled when players who look exceptional in domestic competition prove to be ordinary at international level, the most recent example being the Arsenal striker Ian Wright. The answer is that in international football they are denied both the time and the space so often conceded in the domestic game. James Walvin has observed that:

> In may respects English international football might appear to be distinct and isolated from the game's social roots. In fact it tends to reflect both the strengths and the weaknesses of the national game (Walvin 1975: 154).

More recently has come the observation that we produce:

> a style of domestic football that is hugely popular, ironically in places like Scandinavia, because by comparison with most other areas of the world it is a hugely popular freak show; a blood and guts sport unrivalled in its masochism (Norman Fox, *Independent on Sunday* 6.6.93).

Elsewhere I have tried to explore how the tactical and skill deficiencies of English football can be understood in terms of an enduring cultural tradition — a 'style' of playing the game:

> What is embodied in English football, even or especially in the style in which the game is played, is more than mere technical expertise. For what constitutes excellence in the English game — the direct approach, the constant effort, the unremitting pace — is not merely a sporting but a cultural definition. In endorsing the English or British way of playing, as opposed to that of continental Europe, South America and now Africa, it also appeals to a wider sense of Englishness: belief in effort, an aversion to theory or fancy ways ... it stands for a kind of national culture, an ideal of manliness and a class identification which can no longer inform the game with the confidence they once had (Critcher, 1991: 82-3).

Past tense, future imperfect

We have now come full circle and can trace the relationships between the myth of '66, the contemporary crisis in the English game and even some insights into the moral and political discourse of the nation. The ideals which the triumph of '66 confirmed are precisely those which now stand in the way of the needed transformation of the game — and indeed the inability of British society more generally to adjust itself to the modern world. As long as there is a sustained belief that foreigners have little or nothing to teach us, that sport is an arena for the realisation of a recalcitrant sense of masculinity and that football should express the values of a class once nurtured on the experience of hard manual labour, then English football will not be able to take what should be its rightful place amongst the top nations of the world, and the competition between them held every four years.

It seems churlish now to deny due credit to the English team of 1966. It is, after all, quite usual for the World Cup to be won by a team playing in their own country or at least continent. Yet on balance that victory served to disguise the deep-rooted problems in the English game, to perpetuate the belief that success on the international stage could be achieved without radically altering our ways. The victory of 1966 had negative consequences for the development of the game in part because of how it was achieved, in part because of how it was interpreted. For in fact Ramsey was a tactical innovator, though he and those who followed him did not always realise that the quest for a successful system or style was a permanent one, since others would learn to combat previous systems. The success of a particular system and style was understood; the need for constant innovation was not. But also the style was interpreted as a validation rather than a reformulation of traditional virtues, on and off the pitch. Hence the tendency when faced with current failures to invoke the successes of the past, to assume that if we could rediscover what we had then (the pride, the players, the manager) then things would be put right.

There is some small cause for optimism. The failures of the national side are now so obvious that their deep-rooted nature and the remedies required may become visible. There simply has to be introduced into English football, however gradually, a different definition of the game, more in tune with the realities of contemporary international competition than the myths of past national supremacy. This would involve a minor cultural revolution, from the game's administration at the top, through the coaching structure to the way the game is played in the park on a Sunday morning. This will not happen overnight. Because, as hosts, England have automatic qualification for the next European Championship in 1996, there is even time for this work to be done. But it is equally probable that the issues will be fudged, that English football will turn in on itself, until another failure sets the whole debate in motion once again. Then, no doubt, there will be recollections of the victory thirty years before and the question will be asked: whatever happened to the spirit of 1966? The myth, and its capacity to disguise reality, will have endured.

References

Critcher, C. (1991), 'Putting on the style: Aspects of recent English football' in J. Williams and S. Wagg (eds.) *British Football and Social Change: Getting into Europe*, Leicester: Leicester University Press, pp. 67–84.

Harris, N. (1971), *The Charlton Brothers*, London: Stanley Paul.

Hopcraft, A. (1971), *The Football Man*, Harmondsworth: Penguin.

Leatherdale, C. (1984), *England's Quest For The World Cup*, London: Methuen.

Pawson, T. (1973), *The Football Managers*, London: Eyre Methuen.

Walvin, J. (1973), *The People's Game*, London: Allen and Unwin.

6 Germany and the World Cup: Solid, reliable, often undramatic — but successful

Udo Merkel

Today, there are not many activities which have a more central place in the national culture of Germany than soccer. Played by hundreds of thousands, watched by millions, it enriches our daily conversation as a fascinating topic, offering vivid descriptions and expressing enthusiastic involvement. Soccer features prominently on the title pages of the print media and the broadcasting programmes of the mass media. It is also a significant part of the leisure and entertainment industries. Professional soccer provides jobs for only a small number of players, but for many people it offers the opportunity to escape for 90 minutes per week from the reality of everyday existence and to join the accompanying culture beyond the confines of the match.

Several recurrent issues dominated the public discussion of German soccer in the 1992-3 season: one was Bremen's championship title after Munich was top of the table over the whole season up to the final day; a second was the return of many outstanding German players from the Italian First Division, the financial paradise for professional soccer players, to the Bundesliga, Germany's elite division. Another was Dortmund's participation in the European Cup Final which they lost to Turin, and a fourth was the progress of an amateur team into the German Cup Final.

Each of these themes in different ways symbolises the most important characteristic of soccer and at the same time offers an explanation for its popularity: the unpredictability of the game. Sepp Herberger, the manager of Germany's international team from 1936-63, expressed this differently: "The ball is round" was his succinct response to a journalist's request to explain a surprising German victory. However, particularly in the second half of this century Germany's achievements on the international soccer scene have been less of a surprise but rather very predictable. Their soccer has been solid and effective, if hardly ever spectactular or magnificent.

Modern soccer originated in England in the last century and quickly spread to Germany where it was initially met with a fair amount of hostility. Some Germans even tried to halt the spread of soccer calling it the 'English Disease'.

However, very soon the first international football match between England and Germany took place in Tottenham. In 1901 Germany was convincingly beaten 12-0. In 1990 during the World Championships in Italy these two teams met in the semi-finals. Germany won after extra time and penalties and three days later became World Champions. In between these two dates lies not only the dramatic Wembley Final in 1966 when England triumphed 4-2 but also the surprising victories by Germany over the 1954 favourites Hungary and the 1974 favourites The Netherlands.

This chapter aims to familiarise the Anglo-American reader with the past and present of soccer in Germany, a topic hardly recognised in the Anglo-American literature; and to provide the ground for comparisons of the historical development of and contemporary issues in this sport with those in America and England.

The focus will therefore be on selected aspects of the development and meaning of soccer as a cultural formation in German society, with emphasis upon the wider context of Germany's international success at soccer which will explain the 'whys' and 'hows' of three World Cup titles and twice as many appearances in the World Cup finals since 1934. The short and long-term effects of the country's most successful tournaments in World and European Championships will also be considered, and particular attention given to the championship of 1974, when Germany was both host and champion.

Origins and early developments

There are three reasons which explain the initial indifference, very often even resistance, of the German middle class, the Bürgertum, to English sports. Firstly, since the early nineteenth century the Bürgertum had been developing its own form of exercise. Gymnastics (Turnen) partly absorbed the energies which in England were employed for the development of modern sports. Additionally, the Turnbewegung provided an organisational framework for the opponents of the idea of sport (Loose, 1904: 684). Secondly, the German intelligentsia asserted that mind and muscular strength were incompatible. Sport was apparently a reflection of western "Zivilisation" but it did not belong to German "Kultur" (Pflaum, 1967: 288). And thirdly,

> while modern sports contributed to the English middle class's attempts at class formation, they could hardly serve this function for the German Bürgertum. With regard to the latter's identity, sports played at most an ambivalent, but mainly a disintegrating role (Eisenberg, 1990: 266).

However, the final quarter of the nineteenth century witnessed a number of changes, particularly a revolution in popular habits. Orthodox Turnen did not seem to satisfy the physical and mental demands of the people any longer. "The new generation wanted fresh air and play" (Dixon, 1986: 135). According to Dixon this was a "natural reaction to new conditions of life" (1986: 134) which were caused by the dramatically fast process of urbanisation, the consolidation of industrial production and the growing fragmentation of everyday life. These modern quests for diversion and motion could be met by sport.

The first to take up and play soccer on a fairly regular basis as a part of the recreational afternoon in their schools were the sons of the German middle class. As in England, the traditional German grammar school, the Gymnasium, played a vital role in the process of the adoption of football. Despite differences between Prussian society and Victorian England in the 19th century their education systems and in particular their schools shared the belief in the doctrine of 'muscular christianity', the apparently positive moral influence of physical exercise and sport.

Historical records mention football in Germany for the first time in 1874 when it became part of the leisure activities of the Martino-Katharineum Gymnasium in Braunschweig whose headmaster was Konrad Koch, generally considered to be the founding father of football in Germany (Hopf, 1979: 54). "After a stay in England, Konrad Koch introduced football into recreational afternoons at his Gymnasium in Braunschweig in 1874" (Mason, 1986: 70).

In 1895, 20 years after Koch introduced football to his students, the first club for male adults was founded in Braunschweig. When in 1900 the German Football Association (DFB) was founded there were so few soccer clubs that rugby clubs, German-Bohemian and other Austrian clubs were accepted. Even in 1904 "only 194 — now merely soccer clubs — with 9,317 members were represented in the DFB" (Hopf, 1979: 74).

The rise of working class football in the early 20th century

In the last quarter of the nineteenth century and in the years up to the outbreak of war in 1914, playing soccer was primarily "a middle class affair" (Lindner and Breuer, 1982: 11), initially played by students and later also by a relatively small number of male middle class adults who founded the first clubs which also attracted many members of the working class. This happened in towns like Braunschweig, "Hamburg, Berlin, Leipzeig, Karlsruhe, Nürnberg, etc." (Lindner and Breuer, 1982: 9). However, "football's breakthrough in Germany was, by and large, less a result of private middle class initiative" (Eisenberg, 1990: 265) than of the emergence of workers' sports clubs and associations. From the 1920s onwards it became the sport of the German industrial working class, particularly in the Ruhr area, a heavily industrialized area in North Rhine (Westphalia) which is still a dominant geographical stronghold of the game.

Up to 1918 the workers' sports movement suffered from severe suppression by the state. Their sports clubs were defined as political parties which meant that the police were allowed to survey them and if necessary to ban their public meetings. It also meant that women, students and apprentices were not allowed to become members of these organisations (Fesser, 1983: 108). Consequently, working class football enthusiasts had the choice of either joining the existing bourgeois institutions or not being able to pursue this sport in an organised way. Due to this legislation it is no surprise that middle class clubs dominated and that most working class clubs were founded in the 1920s, following agitation which achieved the 8-hour working day.

Working class clubs in particular put a lot of effort into generating a distinctive identity. This can be seen in the name of the club, in the choice of a distinctive colour combination, the banner and a particular song. A very common type of name from the beginning onwards contained the aim, the place and the year of foundation of the club. Clubs intending to express their close link to a certain area usually added names such as "Westfalia" (Westphalia), "Germania" (old fashioned form of Germany), "Preussen" or "Borussia" (both Prussia). Particularly popular were names which included a specific attitude in the realm of sport such as "Wacker" (brave), "Phoenix" (phoenix), "Adler" (eagle) or "Vorwaerts" (forwards) or a term which stressed the principle of comradeship and cohesion of the group such as "Sportfreunde" (sport friends) or "Eintracht" (harmony).

The colours of a club not only distinguished teams from each other but also served as important symbols for the cohesion of club members and for affiliation. Very often the colours became synonyms for the official club name like 'the Royal Blue' for SV Schalke 04. Another opportunity for self-expression was usually provided by a song made explicitly for one club. The chosen melody originated from a popular folk song and was supposedly easy to sing; the texts usually focused upon sentimental friendship, loyalty towards the club, linked with the assurance that it will never go under. Flags and pennants also played an important role, very likely to have a shape characterising the club's name. All these props were supposed to symbolise the developing cultural tradition of a club, achieved too by a variety of common activities in play, excursions and celebration of triumphs.

The key issue in an attempt to explain the enthusiasm for football clubs in working class areas and the degree of involvement going beyond the sporting activity is the potential to revive communal relationships in the increasingly differentiated society which Germany was about to become at the beginning of the 20th century. Looking at the history of the Ruhr area it becomes apparent that its inhabitants had to face two dilemmas, the rapidity of social change and the lack of a common cultural tradition. At the turn of this century due to the emergence and expansion of industrial production in the Ruhr area there was an enormous demand for additional workers who came from all over central Europe, particularly from areas which had once been Prussia. "While in 1861 there were altogether 16(!) Polish living in the counties of Rheinland and Westfalen, this number increased to more than 30,000" in 1910. "In 1907, in many mines the proportion of workers from the old German eastern areas and from Poland was higher than 50%" (Lindner and Breuer, 1982: 35-7).

So, a high proportion of people living in the Ruhr area at the beginning of this century were immigrants, predominantly from countries east of Germany. Indeed, it is hardly a surprise that these people lacked a common cultural tradition and therefore found through sporting activity a framework to perform cultural practices which were borrowed from their traditional life in the rural communities which they had left. Putting it in Toennies' terms one could conclude that due to the emergence of "Gesellschaft", an increasingly complex and differentiated German society, those people affected kept up "Gemeinschaft"-like patterns of life in certain enclaves which enabled them to self-locate and identify their place in society (Tomlinson, 1993). So, football and the active participation in the club became for those people an experience of particular depth and intensity.

Post-war developments

> Like their cars, German football is solid, well built, often un-spectacular and seems to go on running. Three World Cup victories and appearances in five of the last seven finals is a phenomenal record that not even Brazil can match (Oliver: 1992, p.289).

After the German Football Association resumed activity in 1946, matches were soon being played on a regular basis. Equally soon it became clear that the traditional working class clubs were going to continue their domination of the German football scene and, indeed, this happened over a period of ten years. During this time football was still very much an amateur game.

Only eight years later, in 1954, the Germans won the World Cup for the first time. Was it merely coincidence that the "Wirtschaftswunder" (the economic miracle) was mirrored by the "Wunder von Berne" (the miracle of Berne) on the soccer pitch?

In 1974 the draw for the qualifying rounds of the World Cup presented the Germans with another memorable achievement when the West Germans had to play the East Germans in the preliminary round. In the past for political reasons both teams had avoided meeting the other. Although the West German team lost 0-1 to the East German side they won the tournament with a victory over Holland, the top favourites.

In 1990, a very confident and optimistic German team went to the 14th World Cup in Italy and won it for the third time thus equalling the records of Brazil and Italy.

Although German teams have always had outstanding players, such as Franz Beckenbauer, their success was usually down to team work. The fact that the Germans have been so successful for such a long time can partly be explained by the amount of soccer players Germany has. In 1993, there were about 5.5 million registered players. Seven hundred of these were professionals from whom the national squad had to be chosen.

Modernisation and preservation of the traditional game

Professionalism in terms of the pursuit of an activity for financial gains was not on the agenda until the 1950s, when the more affluent clubs undermined the system of maximum wages and illegally paid money to players to make them leave their club.

Although there is evidence that some players also received illegal payments on top of the maximum wages (Lindner and Breuer, 1982) the emergence of full-time professionals did not occur before the 1960s. This started with the abolition of maximum wages in 1963, the introduction of one national First Division for professional football, the "Bundesliga", and the abolition of maximum transfer fees in 1968. Consequences were the making of monopolies and oligarchy. The former refers to the process whereby each big town or city brought forth one outstanding club in a monopoly-like position, while the emergence of an oligarchy means the exclusive position of the top clubs in the First and Second Division.

The German Football Association, the DFB, had always been very hostile towards professionalism, but it had to relinquish its resistance since German football was going to lose out to other countries. This had two effects. Firstly, many excellent players left to play abroad: "between 1960 and 1963 there were nine players of the international squad sold to foreign clubs, primarily to Italy" (Lindner, 1983: 61), such as Helmut Haller one of the outstanding players of the 1962 World Cup in Chile who moved to Italy to play for Bologna in the same year. Secondly and more importantly was the introduction of the European Champions Cup in 1956. Apart from organisational problems in determining which German club should compete it was the lack of success which forced the German Football

Association to change its attitudes towards professionalism. In the first ten years of this competition only one German team reached the final, while Italian, Spanish and Portuguese teams dominated it.

The establishment of European Cup Competitions (1956) also contributed to the internationalisation of club football and to the televisualisation of the sport. European matches were predominantly media events and as such they were planned by their inventor, the *L'equipe* journalist Gabriel Hanot.

> Obviously, the organisation of football in the Federal Republic in the 1950s ... was hopelessly out-of-date because the internationalisation presumed the making of oligarchy in one's own country as a prior condition (Lindner, 1983: 62).

This concentration process was carried out expeditiously. Within a few years all big towns produced one major representative club whereas the majority of the traditional small clubs of suburbs or settlements either perished, or were degraded to be farm teams for the provision of talent for senior clubs. Consequently, the local clubs, which dominated German soccer in the first half of this century, have ceased to be symbolic extensions of the local community. For many years the Bundesliga had eighteen clubs — in 1993 there were twenty competing in the First Division, with the aim for this to be reduced to sixteen.

It is not only the monopoly-like position of the big clubs which displays the new shape of football, it is also the new stadia (which are often part of a much larger sports complex located outside residential areas and close to motorways) which show the wide ranging consequences arising from professionalisation. Germany's favourite international venue is the "Olympiastadion" in Munich which was inaugurated in May 1972. "Since then the Olympiastadion has staged, most famously, the World Cup Final in 1974 and the European Championship Final in 1988" (Inglis, 1990: 258).

Professionalisation followed by the processes of internationalisation, televisualisation and commercialisation together led to the making of monopolies and oligarchy and contributed to the emergence of the entertainment-like character of football. These processes were also the means through which football as an element of proletarian culture adjusted to middle class culture. This involved a disintegration of the social and cultural roots of the game, while leaving its fascination as a sport since all these changes did not affect the game itself. Of course, soccer has become more athletic, faster and a more tactical game but the specific fascination remains the same: the relative unpredictability of the result, the necessity to cooperate within a team and to coordinate single activities of players. What has changed are the players (most of them are now considered to be stars), the supporters (nowadays they are referred to as fans), the venues and the clubs (Lindner, 1983: 63).

When Germany hosted the World Cup in 1974 it was very clear that 'Big Business' had become an essential part of the sporting spectacle. Never before had the players been paid so generously. All twenty two members of the German squad received 60,000 Deutschmark (about 40,000 US$) from the German Football Association and 10,000 Deutschmark (about 6,500 US$) for wearing particular boots. The profits of the organisers, too, had never been so large before. The DFB made about 100 Million Deutschmark (about 65 Million US$).

The enormous and almost complete marketing of this World Cup displayed clearly how far the commercialisation process had gone. Sporting values were confined to the events on the pitch. Off the pitch sport and business overlapped to an extent that it was almost impossible to identify differences. For the first time the advertising industry and other commercial interests contributed to the finances of this three week tournament, helping the organisers to make enormous profits.

Football fans both in the ground and at home in front of the television sets got used to many of the commercial elements which were permanently going to accompany the game in the future. Thus, this World Cup contributed significantly to the emergence of a new perception of professional sport, in general, and of a new understanding of professional soccer, in particular.

However, it would be wrong to talk about German football as a part of the entertainment industry in a legal or economic sense since soccer clubs are non-economic organisations and not, like for example their British equivalents, run like private industrial enterprises aiming to maximise profits. From an economic point of view it would also be incorrect to put football on a par with showbusiness because football matches are not staged to generate profits. Any kind of income is supposed to be reinvested into the club, its maintenance, and the promotion of sport for all. Many of the First Division clubs are even financially subsidised by the city or county council because they are seen as regional representatives. As well as big business, there is still substantial local authority backing for clubs in Germany; most of the stadia are still owned by councils and grants are easily available. Therefore it is more appropriate to consider these institutions to be a part of a range of publicly subsidised cultural activities including theatres and museums.

However, the changes football was undergoing in the 1960s must be seen to be linked with the general development of the consumption, leisure and entertaiment industry at the end of the 1950s (Opaschowski, 1980: 7). Reduction in working hours and increased affluence during the period of reconstruction after the Second World War led leisure time to become time for consumption. Particularly, the Germany of the 1960s and 1970s experienced the emergence of a new consumer culture. Consequently, the leisure industry with all its different branches boomed.

Although professional football is economically and legally not a branch of the entertainment industry this sport is competing with traditional forms of entertainment for new customers:

> [This] process involved a transformation of the stereotype of the football supporter. Where once the stereotypical supporter was a working-class man, living for Saturday and inextricably involved — in his own perception — with the fortunes of the club, now he was of undefined class membership (Taylor, 1971: 363).

This point about the English game is equally applicable to the German context.

Williams (1961) showed that there are three possible cultural relationships between an individual and a social group or institution. Applying this system to the realm of football it is possible to differentiate between consumers, customers and members. According to Critcher, a member:

> however illusorily, thinks of himself as a member, and may recognise an informal set of reciprocal duties and obligations between himself and the institution. The customer, more detached, is seeking satisfaction for specific wants, if they are not met over a certain period of time, he may, somewhat reluctantly, take his patronage elsewhere. But the consumer has no loyalty or habit. He

is informed of the choices open to him, and when he wants something will make a rational decision about where he will get the best bargain (Critcher, 1982: 227).

While the majority of traditional supporters certainly belonged to the group of 'members' the successful efforts of football clubs to win new target groups meant that "numerically, the fans gradually step back behind the consumers" (Hopf, 1979: 143).

Parallel to these quantitative shifts, qualitative changes were occurring. The gradual loss of economic and social closeness to the proletarian world meant a complete change in the relationship between club, player and supporter. While the early players and supporters knew each other, lived in the same area and had the same social background, nowadays anonymity and distant admiration determine the relationship between star and fan. Thus, the obligation to the club has also changed fundamentally. While in the past the bond was very emotional and personal and club life an integral part of comradeship and solidarity it is now synthetic symbols, such as flags, kits, badges or scarves which are employed to display the feeling of closeness. This form of fan-team relationship was also conducive to a soccer culture expressing national affiliation and identity. Germany's post-war success in the World Cup can be understood as a modern variant of this emerging dynamic.

Germany's World Cup success story

Germany's first appearance at a World Cup was in 1934 in Italy. Since 32 teams were participating a qualifying round had to be played. The 9-1 victory of the German team over Luxembourg meant that Germany was among the 16 teams which met in Italy under the patronage of the "Duce", Italy's fascist president Benito Mussolini. Due to the problematic situation of the Italian economy he used the World Cup for his political propaganda and although he repeatedly demanded that the state's financial deficits should be reduced, millions of Italian Lira were spent on the World Cup.

Austria and Italy were the favourites for this tournament since the winners of the 1930 World Cup, Uruguay, did not participate. After three weeks of exciting soccer action Italy beat Czechoslovakia in the final while Germany came third beating Austria. The German media were celebrating this victory as if their team had won the World Cup. Their perception was that Germany had proved to be the best amateur team even able to keep up with the best professional teams, such as Austria, Czechoslovakia and Italy.

Four years later in France, only a few months after the annexation of Austria, the German team failed completely although it was composed of the best German and Austrian players. Although the national coach knew of the incompatibility of the two different styles of play with the Austrians playing intuitively and individually and the Germans as drilled workers he, nevertheless, under the instruction of the Nazi regime composed a team with a German defence and an Austrian attack. Theoretically, this could have been a winning formula (even without those players who refused to play for the Nazi regime). However, the rhythms of military marches and Viennese Waltzes did not match at all so that the German team played only two matches before they had to return home. In these matches they met Switzerland with whom in the first match they drew one all so that a replay became necessary which the Swiss team won convincingly 4-2. One and a half years later the Second World War had started, with devastating effects in Europe.

The next World Cup therefore did not take place until 1950 in Brazil where soccer had always been the sport of the white ruling class. Once professionalism was introduced many young players tried to escape their social deprivation through joining the newly founded clubs. Within a few years black players were dominating Brazilian soccer which had become almost a religion, particularly for the black population. The development of soccer in Brazil had an enormous impact on the general progress of the game since the Brazilians were very innovative. They preferred much lighter shoes than the traditional heavy boots, modified the soccer kit and the shorts, introduced floodlit games and most importantly developed new tactics. Due to Brazil's outstanding position in the international soccer scene it was a big surprise to see them losing in the 1950 final to Uruguay.

The 5th World Cup in Switzerland ended with an even bigger surprise than the one four years earlier. Again, the runaway favourite lost in the final while an underdog became World Champion: Germany's team which had not even been seeded among the top 16. However, this under-estimation was very fortunate for Germany, as although they beat Austria

6-1 in the semi-final nobody really thought that they had any chance in the final against Hungary — one of the outstanding teams of this tournament showing everything that good soccer is about: technical skills, perfect cooperation, physical toughness, speed and endurance, imagination and determination.

This Hungarian team, which has often been compared to the Uruguyan squad of the 1920s and to Austria's magical team of the 1930s, made history in 1953 beating England at Wembley 6-3. It was the first time that a continental-European team had beaten the English in England, the Republic of Ireland (having defeated England 2-0 in Liverpool in 1949) being the first non-British side to defeat the English on the latter's home soil.

Sepp Herberger, Germany's team manager, had been to London to see these two sides playing. The term 'Fußball total' has often been attributed to Herberger whose systematic approach to preparation and training was ahead of his time. He rejected one particular hotel as a training camp for his team because of the regular noise created by the nearby church bells and he also sent 'spies' to the training sessions of other teams to collect data and information.

When Germany and Hungary met in the 1954 final in Berne most of the German supporters must have thought of the humilating 8-3 defeat a fortnight before, particularly when Hungary were leading 2-0 after a few minutes. But the Germans managed to equalize in the 18th minute of the match and scored the decisive goal six minutes before the final whistle. It was their excellent mental and physical preparation and their ability to play a very tactical game which had been decisive for their unpredictable success — and of course, a lot of luck.

In this particular historical context of the aftermath of the Second World War Germany's first victory in the 1954 World Cup had an enormous social and national significance. After having been thrown out of FIFA in 1946 and being readmitted in 1950 the German success contributed significantly to the promotion of a national identity and helped the country to be recognised internationally after they had lost the war. By pulling off the biggest shock football has ever seen the Germans improved their image and gained prestige worldwide.

But the new World Champions were not going to be on a lucky streak for very long. After their victory most of the players suffered from a mysterious jaundice and they never played again in the same formation. The German team even lost seven of the following ten matches so that rumours started to spread that they must have been doped in 1954.

In Sweden in 1958 the soccer was magnificent. It was the World Cup of the Brazilian team and their new rising star Edson Arantes do Nascimento, better known as Pelé. Brazil beat Sweden in the final 5-2 while Germany took fourth place after losing 6-3 to France. For some reason the German team left Sweden immediately after the final whistle and did not attend the banquet; this was considered such an insult to the hosts that it was more than five years before Sweden played again against Germany.

In 1962, in Chile, the German team had to pack their bags in the early stages of the tournament after they lost 1-0 to Yugoslavia in the quarter finals.

The 1966 World Cup in England was a sensation in itself since the motherland of soccer had remained in isolation until 1950 when England took part in this championship for the first time. The final in Wembley with its magical atmosphere on big-match days will be one of those memorable moments of soccer's history which only this sport can produce. England was playing Germany and after 90 minutes the score was two all so that the teams went into extra-time. In the 101st minute of the match, Geoff Hurst, the English striker hit the ball under the bar of the German goal from where it bounced back onto the pitch. But the decisive question of whether the ball touched the ground in front of, on or behind the goal line has never been answered. However, the Russian linesman whose death in 1993 was reported by both English and German newspapers approved of the goal. Finally, England scored a fourth goal after the pitch had already been invaded by celebrating supporters. Due to two irregular goals the headline of a German tabloid paper "We lost 2-2" (*Bild*, 31.7.1966) was a fair summary of the events.

Four years later, in Mexico, Germany was third again and Brazil won the World Cup for the third time.

The course of events at the World Cup of 1974 in Germany was less surprising than twenty years previously when the German team had become World Champions for the first time. The Netherlands and the hosts reached the final — very much predicted by experts and knowledgeable fans. However, it was a surprise that South America had sent such weak teams with only Brazil reaching a place among the final four teams.

Most enjoyable to watch were certainly Argentina's efforts to play fast, skilful and creative soccer. Brazil sought however to incorporate traditional European elements into their game, such as toughness, discipline and tactical order — but with little success. As a result the Brazilians fought well but lacked the magical brilliance of the past which almost all supporters had admired so much in Mexico.

What became very obvious at these 1974 World Championships was that a successful football player had to be an all-round athlete showing characteristics such as an athletic physique, skilful technique, physical and mental endurance, strength, fast thinking, and a feeling for tactical arrangements. There were only a very few players of this kind who were both individualist and able to cooperate within a team. Holland and Germany were fortunate since Johan Cruyff ("The King") and Franz Beckenbauer ("The Emperor") were their outstanding personalities in teams, with qualities far above average. There was no doubt that the Dutch had the most gifted team of the tournament, but when it came to the final the Germans had an additional man in their team: their supporters in the Munich Olympiastadion encouraging their team forward after the Dutch had already scored in the first minute of the match before any German player had even touched the ball. As usual, the team of the host nation seemed to be stimulated by the crowd, although the Dutch side was not without noisy support of a few thousand 'Oranje' fans. Equally crucial for the German 2-1 victory was the duel between the artistic Johan Cruyff and the 'terrier' Berti Voigts which was won by the latter.

Despite the early lead of the Dutch the Germans kept cool, played their game down the wings and were rewarded with two goals before half time. The second half was then a match onto one goal. The Dutch constantly attacked the German goal. But a mixture composed of hard work, luck (for the Germans), the nervousness of Johan Cruyff and some excellent defence by the German goal keeper prevented the Dutch from scoring another goal in the second half.

There is hardly any doubt that the result would have been different if the match had been played on neutral ground. Perhaps, these two teams would meet again — in America in 1994 — and it could be again the duel between the Dutch 'artist' and the German 'terrier'. This time it would take place off the pitch since Cruyff and Voigts were managers of their teams — the Dutchman planning to stick to his announcement at the beginning of

1992 that he would coach Holland in 1994, once the side had qualified; and the German staying with his national squad despite his dissatisfaction and constant media attacks on his abilities.

This 1974 World Cup victory could not have happened at a better time. The economy was growing at a fast rate, the left-wing government, committed to creating consensus amongst its people, had just been re-elected and the political climate between East and West Germany had started to improve.

Sixteen years later, in 1990, a very confident and optimistic German team went to the 14th World Cup in Italy. Twenty four teams participated with 530 players of whom 414 in fact played. But never before were so few goals scored: 115 goals in 52 matches (an average of 2.21 per game). However, financially this tournament was a big success. Two and a half million tickets were sold which meant that the organisers made a profit in the region of 170 billion Lira (about 160 million US$).

For the Germans sixteen frustrating years came to an end when their team won the World Cup for the third time within four decades. In 1978, in Argentina, the Germans were eliminated in the second round of the World Cup final tournament. In 1982, in Spain, they reached the final, despite at best modest performances, but lost to Italy 3-1. In 1986, in Mexico, they were again runners-up in the final when they lost to Argentina whose coach Carlos Bilardo had most successfully managed the very difficult task to integrate a number of players working abroad and to form a coherent team — a task Franz Beckenbauer had to accomplish for the 1990 World Cup in Italy since five of his major players were based in Italy.

Despite a lack of formal vocational qualifications Franz Beckenbauer was appointed to be the new manager of the German squad in 1984. According to the "Emperor" — the Germans gave him this nickname because of his outstanding skills and his almost arrogant demeanour both on and off the pitch — it would take at least 10 years before there would be again a first class German team. In Germany, nobody was disappointed with him that this prediction proved an over cautious one, since it took him only six years to bring home the ultimate triumph of another World Cup title through a 1-0 victory over Argentina in Rome.

The international press agreed that it was a very weak final but a just victory for the best team of the tournament which had almost been eliminated by the English side in the semi-finals which had to be decided by a penalty shoot out. Argentina, Germany's opponents in the final, hardly entered the German half and were very unpopular among the spectators because they had knocked out Italy, the hosts (and for many the favourites) of the tournament, in the other semi-final.

For each of the German players this victory meant a premium of 125,000 Deutschmark (about 80,000 US$) — twice as much as their predecessors received in 1974. For the German people at home it meant a night of Italian-style celebrations on the streets on this warm July night. They had more than one good reason for this since Germany had now equalled Italy and Brazil, both three time winners of the trophy.

Germany lost in the 1992 European Championships final to the underdog Denmark, but the Germans were still among the favourites in the United States (Denmark failed to qualify). Qualifying as holders, they had time and opportunity to integrate the excellent players from the former East Germany. Whatever the outcome of the 1994 tournament, there was no doubt that Germany would demonstrate solid soccer qualities displaying traditional and typical German virtues: skills, team spirit, determination and physical strength.

The politics of soccer in Germany

The politics of soccer are as complex as its cultural forms and meanings to individuals and social groups. Soccer has developed under a certain set of circumstances and social relations and fulfils many important political functions in German society.

Like many other sports, soccer provides a variety of politically usable resources. Sport "is, for example, very often seen as a character building agent of socialisation. This perception was part of its very origins in modern times" (Allison, 1986: 12). Although the spirit of competition was counter to the concept and inherent values of Gymnastics, some German educationalists saw the potential educational values of this English game and introduced a 'Games Afternoon' once per week in extra curricular time for those pupils and students who wished to play for example soccer. Initially, these teachers considered soccer to be an ideal means to distract from the idleness of mind and from decadent behaviour, such as pipe-smoking, beer drinking, or attending pubs. Some years later good health was the justification for the incorporation of English games.

When in the late 1920s the first World Cup finals were planned it was commonly assumed that it would take place in Europe since the organising committee consisted of an Austrian, a German and a Frenchman. The German Football Association, however, rejected the suggestion to host the tournament and did not even send a team to Uruguay because it had been agreed that professionals were to be allowed to take part. Although it was common knowledge that some of the top German 'amateur' players were receiving material and/or financial rewards it was the dogmatism and the stubbornness of the DFB which meant that only four European teams, Belgium, France, Yugoslavia and Romania, went to Uruguay.

In 1934, in Italy Germany took part in the 'Campionato Mondiale di Calcio', the World Cup finals, and surprisingly took third behind Italy and Czechoslovakia. Italy's president, the 'Duce' of Italian fascism, understood very well how to use this occasion for his desperately needed propaganda. Although the Italian economy was in a deep crisis sports and in particular football were promoted by the state in a number of ways. "The most skilful players of the most popular sports received considerable state and commercial backing." (Mason, 1988: 98). Only a few days after Italy's victory in June, Mussolini met Adolf Hitler, the German Nazi leader, in Venice. Hitler's regime was able to make even more effective use of sport as a propaganda weapon.

Although Germany came only third in the 1934 World Cup finals the press at home celebrated the team's achievement as if they were the winners of the tournament. The media's point was that the German squad had shown that they were the best amateur team in the world, strong enough to compete on a par with the professionals from Austria, Czechoslovakia and Italy. Under Hitler athleticism was a very important issue on the political agenda. Athletes and teams had very clear orders from the Nazi regime: taking part in international events and being successful were the top priorities. Consequently, top level athletes were promoted by the German state to show the world the nation's superiority and to prove Hitler's racial ideologies. "Hitler had no interest in sport other than this: to express national superiority and internal unity." (Cashmore, 1990: 160) The German soccer team of 1938, however, did not fulfil these politically driven expectations failing completely at the World Cup finals in France.

Another important political resource provided by sport derives from the association with success:

> President Kennedy began the practice of American presidents tele-
> phoning to congratulate winning Superbowl teams. Prime Minister
> Wilson of England, General Videla of Argentina and President
> Pertini of Italy, among others, have all been keen to associate
> themselves with their country's success in soccer's World Cup
> (Allison, 1986: 13).

So are the Germans. In 1974 when Germany won the World Cup for the second time it was the German president Walter Scheel who congratulated the team first. At the same tournament when Holland played Brazil — a match promising to be most exciting since both teams had played exceptionally — 25(!) ministers and ambassadors from all over the world gathered in Dortmund to see this decisive game. Among these were two very prominent football supporters: the foreign ministers of the U.S.A. and West Germany, Henry Kissinger and Hans-Dietrich Genscher.

In 1982, in Madrid King Juan Carlos of Spain, Italy's old President Sandro Pertini and the German Chancellor Helmut Schmidt were numbered among the guests in the Bernabeu Stadium watching the World Cup final between Italy and Germany. In 1990, in Rome the current German Chancellor Helmut Kohl attended the final between Argentina and Germany. The press reported afterwards that he joined the German team celebrating in their changing rooms where one player even poured champagne over him (WAZ, 10 July 1990). But he was not the only top German politician using a popular cultural event to score some points on the popularity scale of politicians. The Home Office minister, who is also responsible for the promotion of top level sports in Germany, also enjoyed the Italian sun and the press coverage of the World Cup final in Rome.

At home, in Germany these two Conservative politicians were not seen very often in football grounds. Since soccer matches have become a popular forum for political demands and public critique of the Conservative government in Germany they had good reason to stay away from football grounds. There have been a number of occasions in recent years when banners with political slogans have been displayed dealing with the indifference of the government towards unemployment, the closure of mines and steel companies, the Unions' demand to introduce the 35 hour working week, higher wages and even enviromental issues, if locally and/or regionally relevant.

However, almost a must for the German chancellor and the president is to attend the annual Cup Final in Berlin, though the symbolic import of this has been lessened since Berlin was no longer in the middle of East Germany, and was scheduled to become the new capital of the 'reunited' Germany. Some German politicians are very keen to be associated with this popular sport even on a club level. A few have joined the board of directors of clubs, such as the Minster for Culture and Education Mayer-Vorfelder in Stuttgart, the Conservative Bernhard Worms in Cologne, and the recently resigned Federal Minister for Economic Policies Jürgen Möllemann. At least one thing is for sure, they cannot do this for personal enrichment since the legal structure of clubs would not allow this. The key issue here seems to be about status and prestige.

Politically, one of the most significant and prestigious matches of the 1974 World Cup finals was certainly the meeting of the two German teams in the preliminary round in Hamburg. The politics of the Cold War period became obvious in the build up to this match. Both sides had always avoided playing each other. The East Germans never had a strong national team so that playing the successful West German side very likely meant to risk their reputation as an outstanding sporting nation. In turn, West Germany was reluctant to play the East German side because it would have meant a further acknowledgement of the German Democratic Republic (GDR) as an independent sovereign state which the West German government had refused to make. Secondly, playing 'the brothers and sisters from behind the wall' would have undermined the ideology of West and East Germans being one big family divided by the expansionist politics of the Soviet Union. However, the West German side lost 1-0 in a disappointing match causing ambiguous feeling among their supporters. On the one hand it was a highly prestigious victory for the GDR, on the other hand it meant that West Germany was playing the 'easier' teams in the next round. However, generally, the World Cup has been less affected by Cold War politics than for example the Olympics due to the fact that the USA and the Soviet Union have never had the strongest national soccer teams.

Equally important in 1974 was for the Germans to re-establish their international reputation as a nation of law and order, after the Palestinian attack on Israel's team during the 1972 Olympics in Munich and the subsequent disastrous attempt of the German police to free the hostages. Consequently, the organisers were deeply concerned about the security of players and spectators and provided an army of security personnel from the forces and the police to protect the participants of the tournament. Some observers labelled the 1974 event 'the World Cup of the Uniforms'. However, there was no doubt that sporting events of this magnitude needed high standards of protection.

Since the Cold War ended, the Iron Curtain has been lifted, and the divided German state 'reunited'. The world's attention has shifted. In Central Europe some of the focus is certainly on the upsurge of a 'new' far right in Germany and their 1930s style violence against marginal and vulnerable social groups. This development is caused by economic turmoil, the steady influx of refugees and asylum seekers and the miscalculation of the Conservative party under their chancellor Helmut Kohl in misjudging the challenge facing the German economy after 'reunification'. However, very soon a counter movement against racism and xenophobia emerged organising demonstrations, public rallies, advertising campaigns, and rock concerts. These activities against the right wing extremism are covering almost all areas of life including soccer. In December 1992, the players of all eighteen clubs in the football premier league took a public stand against neo-Nazism by wearing jerseys during the game bearing the motto: "My friend is a foreigner". In Frankfurt, fans carried banners declaring that "Germany without foreigners is like a piano without black keys" obviously referring to one of the few black players in the German Bundesliga, Frankfurt's top scorer the Ghanian striker Anthony Yeboah. In Munich, at half-time children carrying the flags of the world's countries joined hands to march round the perimeter of the pitch. The venues for these activities were well chosen: firstly, there is evidence that a growing number of football supporter clubs have links to fascist organisations and secondly, it is well known that young fascists attend football matches looking for the opportunity of a fight.

There is no doubt that the players' initiatives and activities are sincere since all German top teams rely on foreign players to fill their ranks, particularly with some players of the World Cup winning team of 1990 (for instance) playing in the Italian league. Many have feared that the exodus of German players to Italy — financially a paradise for outstanding performers — would mean that the standards in Germany are deteriorating. However, in the meantime it has become obvious that the influx of foreign players in the German league has certainly enriched the quality of German soccer, since these players have brought new ideas, fresh impulses and a global dimension to soccer **made in Germany**.

References and further reading

Allison, L. (ed.) (1986), *The Politics Of Sport*, Manchester: Manchester University Press.

Autorenkollektiv (1976), *Fußball in Vergangenheit und Gegenwart*, Berlin (GDR).

Becker, P. (1982), 'Haut'se, Haut'se in'ne Schnauze — Das Fußballstadium als Ort der Reproduktion sozialer Strukturen' in G.A. Pilz, (ed.), *Sport und Körperliche Gewalt*, Reinbek: Rowohlt Verlag: pp. 72 -84.

Cashmore, E. (1990), *Making Sense of Sport,* London: Routledge and Kegan Paul.

Childs, D. (1981), 'The German Democratic Republic' in J. Riordan (ed.), *Sport under Communism,* London: C. Hurst and Company, pp. 6-102.

Clarke, J., Critcher, C. and Johnson, R. (eds.) (1979), *Working-class Culture: Studies in History and Theory*, London: Hutchinson.

Critcher, C. (1982), 'Football since the War' in B. Waites, T. Bennett and G. Martin (eds.), *Popular Culture: Past and Present*, London: Croom Helm, pp. 194-218.

Dixon, J.G. (1986), 'Prussia, Politics and Physical Education' in P. C. McIntosh, J. G. Dixon, A. D. Munrow and R. F. Willetts (eds.), *Landmarks in the History of Physical Education*, London: Routledge and Kegan Paul: pp. 112-155.

Deutscher Fußball Bund (1925), 25 Jahre DFB, Frankfurt.

Dunning, E. (1979), *Soccer: The Social Origins of the Sport and its Development as a Spectacle and Profession*, London: Sports Council/ SSRC.

Dunning, E., Murphy, P. and Williams, J. (1988), *The Roots of Football Hooliganism*, London: Routledge and Kegan Paul.

Dunning, E. and Sheard, K. (1979), *Barbarians, Gentlemen and Players*, London: Martin Robertson.

Eisenberg, C. (1990), 'The Middle Class and Competition: Some Considerations of the beginnings of Modern Sport in England and Germany", in *The International Journal of the History of Sport,* Volume 7: pp. 265-282.

Elias, N. (1978), *Über den Prozeß der Zivilisation*, Frankfurt: Suhrkamp.

Elias, N.and Dunning, E. (1986), *Quest for Excitement: Sport and Leisure in the Civilising Process*, London: Blackwell.

Fesser, G. (1983), 'Von der 'Zuchthausvorlage' zum Reichsvereinsgesetz. Staatsorgane, bürgerliche Parteien und Vereinsgesetzgebung im Deutschen Reich 1899-1906", in *Jahrbuch für Geschichte,* Volume 28: pp. 107-132.

Fürstenberg, F. (1972), *Die Sozialstruktur der Bundesrepublik Deutschland — ein soziologischer Überblick*, Opladen: Westdeutscher Verlag.

Gehrmann, S. (1988), *Fußball-Vereine-Politik. Zur Sportgeschichte des Reviers,* Essen: Reimar Hobbing Verlag.

Hahn, E., Pilz, G. A., Stollenwerk, H. J. and Weis, K. (1988), *Fanverhalten, Massenmedien und Gewalt im Sport,* Schorndorf: Verlag Karl Hoffmann.

Hargreaves, J. (1987), *Sport, Power and Culture,* Cambridge: Polity Press.

Heitmeyer, W. and Peter, J. I. (1988), *Jugendliche Fußballfans,* Munich: Juventa Verlag.

Holt, R. (1990), *Sport and the British: a Modern History,* Oxford: Oxford University Press.

Hopcraft, A. (1971), *The Football Man,* Harmondsworth: Penguin.

Hopf, W. (ed.) (1979), Fussball — Soziologie und Sozialgeschichte einer populären Sportart, Bensheim: Päd Extra.

Horne, J., Jary, D. and Tomlinson A. (eds.) (1987), *Sport, Leisure and Social Relations,* London: Routledge and Kegan Paul.

Huck, G. (1980), *Sozialgeschichte der Freizeit*, Wuppertal: Peter Hammer Verlag.

Inglis, S. (1990), *The Football Grounds of Europe*, London: Willow Books.

Kicker Sportmagazin, 48, 17.6.1991.

Koch, K. (1900), *Die Erziehung zum Mute*, Berlin.

Krüger, A. (ed.) (1984), *Forum für Sportgeschichte. Die Entwicklung der Turn- und Sportvereine*, Berlin.

Lindner, R. (ed.) (1980), *Der Fußballfan — Ansichten vom Zuschauer*, Frankfurt: Syndicat.

———(ed.) (1983), *Der Satz 'Der Ball ist rund" hat eine gewisse philosophische Tiefe*, Berlin: Transit.

Lindner, R. and Breuer, H. T. (1982), *Sind doch nicht alles Beckenbauers*, Frankfurt: Syndicat.

Loose, F. (1904), *Die geschichtliche Entwicklung der Leibesübungen in Deutschland. Der Kampf zwischen Turnen und Sport*, PhD thesis, Erlangen.

Mason, T. (1980), *Association Football and English Society 1863 -1915*, Brighton: Harvester Press.

———(1988), *Sport in Britain*, London: Faber & Faber, London.

———(1986), 'Some Englishmen and Scotsmen abroad: The spread of world football', in A. Tomlinson and G. Whannel (eds.), *Off the Ball*, London: Pluto Press, pp. 67-82.

Mason, T. (ed.) (1989), *Sport in Britain — A Social History*, Cambridge: Cambridge University Press.

Oliver, G. (1992), *The Guinness Record of World Soccer — The History of the Game in over 150 Countries*, Enfield: Guinness Publishing.

Opaschowski, H.W. (1980), *Probleme im Umgang mit der Freizeit*, Hamburg: BAT-Schriftenreihe.

Pflaum, M. (1967), 'Die Kultur-Zivilisations-Antithese im Deutschen' in J. Knobloch (ed.), *Europäische Schlüsselworter. Wortvergleiche und wortgeschichtliche Studien*, Munich, pp. 288-427.

Pilz, G. A. (ed.) (1982), *Sport und körperliche Gewalt*, Reinbek: Rowohlt Verlag.

Pilz, G. A. et al. (1982), *Sport und Gewalt. Bericht der Projektgruppe 'Sport und Gewalt' des Bundesinstituts für Sportwissenschaft*, Schorndorf: Verlag Karl Hofmann.

Planck, K. (1898), *Fußlümmelei. Uber Stauchballspiel und englische Krankheit*, Stuttgart.

Pramann, U. (1983), *Fußballfans — Betrachtungen einer Subkultur*, Hamburg: Stern-Bücher.

Redhead, S. (1991), 'An Era of the End, or the End of an Era: Football and Youth Culture in Britain' in J. Williams and S. Wagg (eds.), *British Football and Social Change*, Leicester: Leicester University Press: pp. 160-186.

Ritter, G.A. (1979), *Arbeiterkultur*, Königstein/Ts.: UTB.

Schulz, H.J. (1986), *Aggressive Handlungen von Fußballfans*, Hamburg: Hoffman.

Stollenwerk, H.J. (1980), 'Soziales Ereignis 'Bundesligaspiel'' in R. Lindner (ed.),*Der Fußballfan*, Frankfurt: Syndicat: pp. 44-51.

Taylor, I. (1971), 'Soccer Consciousness and Soccer Hooliganism' in S. Cohen (ed.) *Images of Deviance* , Harmondsworth: Penguin, pp. 134-164.

———(1973), *The New Criminology: For a Social Theory of Deviance*, London: RKP.

———(1987), 'Putting the Boot into a Working Class Sport: British Soccer after Bradford and Brussels' in *Sociology of Sport Journal*, Volume 4, Number 2, June 1987, pp. 171-191.

Toennies, F. (1887), *Community and Association*, Michigan: Michigan State University Press.

Tokarski, W. and Schmitz-Scherzer, R. (1985), *Freizeit*, Stuttgart: B.G. Teubner.

Tomlinson, A. (1993), 'Culture of Commitment in Leisure: notes towards the understanding of a serious legacy', *World Leisure and Recreation Association Journal* , Volume 35, Number 1, Spring, pp. 6-9.

Tomlinson, A. and Whannel, G. (eds.) (1986), *Off the Ball*, London: Pluto Press.

Waites, B., Bennett, T. and Martin, G. (eds.), (1982), *Popular Culture: Past and Present,* Croom Helm Ltd., London.

Walvin, J. (1975), *The People's Game*, London: Penguin.

———(1986), *Football and the Decline of Britain*, London: Macmillan.

Whannel, G. (1983), *Blowing the Whistle — the Politics of Sport*, London: Pluto Press.

Whannel, G. (1986), 'The Unholy Alliance: Notes on Television and the Remaking of British Sport 1965-85' in *Leisure Studies*, Volume 5, Number 2, May, pp. 129-145.

Williams, R. (1961), *The Long Revolution*, Harmondsworth: Pelican.

———(1983), *Towards 2000*, London: Hogarth Press.

Williams, J. and Wagg, S. (eds.) (1991), *British Football and Social Change,* Leicester: Leicester University Press.

7 Ireland and the World Cup: 'Two teams in Ireland, there's only two teams in Ireland ...'

John Sugden and Alan Bairner

On Wednesday, 17 November, 1993, fate and FIFA conspired to take the Republic of Ireland to Belfast for a vital World Cup qualifying game. In the days leading up to the match, more than two dozen people had been killed in terrorist incidents involving the Provisional IRA and loyalist paramilitary factions. As diplomats in Belfast, London and Dublin struggled to rein the province back from the brink of civil war, tensions between the Catholic and Protestant communities remained as high as they had ever been in the 25 years of the Troubles. In such circumstances, the last thing that the authorities wanted was an event which would force people to openly choose sides between the north and the south. What followed was more than a statement of football partisanship: it was a public declaration of national identity.

It is said that you could have heard a pin drop in Dublin when Jimmy Quinn's volley dipped over Packie Bonner and hit the back of the Republic of Ireland's net to put Northern Ireland 1-0 up. In the four minutes it took for the Republic to find an equaliser, the deep social and political cleavages which keep Ulster on the verge of turmoil were never more clearly expressed. Northern Ireland's national stadium, Windsor Park, was a sea of red, white and blue as the overwhelmingly Protestant support roared on their team. "One team in Ireland, there's only one team in Ireland!" chanted the crowd, reminding Jack Charlton and his team of the taunting which the Northern Ireland side had received while suffering a humiliating 3-0 defeat during the reverse fixture in the qualifying series in Dublin the previous March.

119

Meanwhile, as the Protestant community in Northern Ireland celebrated the opening goal, nationalists, from the safety of their homes or in Catholic bars and clubs, cursed the Reading centre forward's strike which, given that Quinn is a Belfast Catholic, was viewed by many as nothing short of treachery, particularly since his untimely intervention threatened to keep the Irish Republic out of USA '94. At almost the same time as Alan McLoughlin, the Republic of Ireland substitute, hammered home the equaliser, Spain scored the only goal of their game against Denmark in Seville, ensuring that when the final whistle was blown in Belfast, the Republic of Ireland would qualify for the USA by the narrowest of margins. Now it was the turn of Irish Catholics to celebrate. Never in the history of Irish sport had a single game revealed so much about the complex relationship between sport, politics and nationalism on the island of Ireland.

While the Republic of Ireland are currently recognised as a world soccer power, this is a relatively recent achievement. They qualified for the final stages of the European Championships in 1988 and two years later reached the World Cup Finals for the first time after 12 unsuccessful attempts between 1934 and 1986. In fact before Italia '90 the Republic had only previously qualified for the 1924 Olympic Finals in Paris where, after beating Bulgaria 1-0, they were knocked out by Holland, going down 1-2 in the quarter finals.

This lack of success at an international level was the result of several factors, one of which is of crucial importance. In a country with a population of only 3.5 million, association football faces stiff competition from two other codes of football — rugby union and Gaelic. Oliver (1992) estimated that in 1993 there were 2,367 registered adult soccer clubs in the Irish Republic and approximately 80,500 players. At the highest level, senior soccer in Ireland is only played on a semi-professional basis. Domestic competitions are poorly attended by comparison with the other codes which regularly attract bigger audiences than soccer for important matches. At first glance, therefore, the likelihood of attaining regular success on the international stage would appear to be bleak. However, these raw statistics tend to conceal the fact that throughout the twentieth century players born both in the Irish Republic and in Northern Ireland have played football professionally in England and beyond. In addition, and, as we shall discover, of growing importance in recent seasons, there are large numbers of players with Irish ancestry living not only in England, but also in other parts of the United Kingdom who, according to FIFA regulations, are eligible to play for the Republic of Ireland.

Ball games have been played in Ireland for centuries. The oldest of these, the game of Cad, which was popular amongst all Celtic peoples, is thought to have originated at least 1,000 years ago. It involved carrying and kicking a ball across open country and resembled closely the form of football which was banned in England in 1365. But although a sporting ban was introduced in Ireland in the same year by the Proclamation of the Statutes of Kilkenny, the sport to which the authorities had taken exception was hurling rather than football or Cad. This was because of the relative unpopularity of the latter in Ireland and the fact that it was simply not regarded as posing a threat to public order or the status quo. Indeed, football must have been regarded as relatively harmless even as late as 1527 when it was excluded from a ban on all games which were believed to divert people from archery practice. On this occasion, the proscribed sports included hurling and handball, but not "the great foot ball" (Van Esbeck, 1986: 7-11). What is worthy of note here is that although football was still not regarded as harmful it was now accorded the status of an increasingly popular pastime amongst the Irish. Indeed records exist of important seventeenth century football matches held in the Slain area of County Meath and at Fingal near Dublin (ibid: 7). Carrying the ball, however, remained an essential feature of these games.

By the eighteenth century football had become even more popular and, although frowned upon by members of the aristocracy, was played regularly at College Park in Dublin by students of Trinity College. The form of football played was still the carrying game but during the nineteenth century this was replaced in numerous English public schools by a kicking game. This latter form was brought back to Ireland by Irish pupils at these schools either during vacations or on the completion of their studies. The rules of association football were formulated in England in 1867 by the Football Association and football was first played according to these rules in Ireland in 1885. The last recorded game of Cad took place in 1888 between the parishes of Cordal and Scartaglen. Henceforward, although handling was to be a major characteristic of both the Gaelic and rugby codes of football, the kicking game was established as one of Ireland's main sports.

That association football became a major Irish sport, however, is not to suggest that it was received with equal enthusiasm throughout the country and by all its people. Football in some form or another was established as an integral part of Irish sporting tradition. But the emergence of the specific association code owed more to non-native influences. In the southern part of Ireland these were felt most strongly in Dublin and its environs where the Anglo-Irish tradition was most firmly established. This had the effect of making association football, to begin with at least, the preserve of a relatively small, middle-class section of southern Irish society. In the north east of Ireland, on the other hand, the sport was taken up almost immediately by a much larger section of the population. There are three main reasons for this. First, the north east was predominantly Protestant, a majority of its population the ancestors of the original Protestant settlers. Their receptiveness to non-Irish influences was thus greater even than that of the Anglo-Irish community in Dublin. Second, Northern Ireland's close links with Scotland meant that the rapid advances made there in the growth of football had an immediate and direct influence on the introduction of the game in the province. Thirdly, the Belfast area was the most industrialised region in Ireland at the end of the nineteenth century at a time when it was becoming apparent that the real strength of association football was to lie not in its popularity in the great public schools, but in its growth in the industrial regions of Britain. So Ulster's largely Protestant industrial communities provided the ideal conditions for the rapid development of the sport in Ireland and to this day the province's leading clubs are still important focal points of working class culture.

The Irish Football Association (IFA) was formed in Belfast in 1880, five years before association football was played officially in Dublin. The Irish Cup competition was instituted by the IFA and first competed for in 1881. To underline the importance of British influence in disseminating the sport in Ireland, early finalists in the competition included soldiers of the Black Watch regiment and the Gordon Highlanders. In addition, leading Scottish and English teams made guest appearances in Belfast and surrounding areas as gradually the standard of play in domestic circles improved.

To begin with the IFA assumed responsibility for administering association football throughout Ireland and sides from outside the Belfast area competed for the Irish Cup. However, it was not until 1906 that a

Dublin side, Shelbourne, actually won the trophy and Shelbourne (in 1906, 1911 and 1920) and another Dublin club, Bohemians (1908) are the only teams to have taken the Irish Cup out of Ulster.

A similar picture emerges when one turns to the Irish League championship organised by the Belfast-based Irish League authorities and first contested in season 1890-91. No club from outside Ulster has ever won the competition, the history of which has been dominated by Belfast teams. In fact, it was as recently as 1952 that the championship was taken out of the city for the first time, the victors being Glenavon from Lurgan in County Armagh. Again to emphasise the British links early competitors included the North Staffordshire Regiment, the Scottish Borderers and the Royal Scots who withdrew after only seven matches in season 1899-1900 on account of the outbreak of the Boer War and an entirely different challenge in South Africa.

Despite the relative lack of success on the part of Dublin clubs, the game of association football continued to grow in popularity in that city and elsewhere in Ireland. Athlone Town F.C. was formed in 1892, earlier even than Shelbourne (1895) and Shamrock Rovers (1899) and the Sligo Rovers Club was established in 1908. Regardless of the game's growing appeal, however, it remained closely linked with the Anglo-Irish community in Ireland as well as members of the army garrisons and the British administration. As such it was portrayed with some success by nationalists as a foreign game, incompatible with the pursuit of native Gaelic pastimes. This in itself was unlikely to prevent the further growth of the sport even in the most distant parts of the country. At that point, however, politics intervened overtly for the first time in the development of association football in Ireland and the game's various responses themselves took on a political character.

As the issue of Irish independence began to gather momentum, it became increasingly difficult to preserve the unity of football in Ireland. Shelbourne refused to play an Irish Cup semi-final replay at Windsor Park in Belfast in 1919 and further disputes resulted in Dublin clubs withdrawing from the Irish League. As Malcolm Brodie observes:

> unanimity no longer existed in Irish football. Hardline attitudes had developed between Belfast and Dublin. The split, admittedly minimal now, was soon to widen to a chasm (Brodie, 1980: 15).

Finally, the creation of an Irish Free State, from which six counties of Ulster were excluded, prompted the Leinster Football Association to break from its parent body, the IFA . Immediately, as Malcolm Brodie reports:

> Eire newspaper advertisements described matches in Dublin as being under the 'Football League of Ireland' while games in Belfast were merely 'Belfast and District' (ibid).

Henceforward association football was to be organised separately in the different states of Ireland with the Irish League and the Irish Football Association continuing to preside over the games affairs on the northern side of the border and the League of Ireland and the Football Association of Ireland(FAI) assuming control in the south.

The impact of political and cultural division was now more overt than had been the case before partition. These political implications can be discerned in two distinct but related areas: first, the nature of football relations between Northern Ireland and the Irish Republic; and second, the football relations between the vying communities within Northern Ireland.

The FAI was formed in 1921 and became affiliated to FIFA in 1923. The League of Ireland championship was first contested in 1921-22, being won by St James' Gate of Dublin who also won the national cup competition in its inaugural year, 1922. By far the most successful side in the domestic development of Irish football has been Shamrock Rovers although other sides including Dundalk, Shelbourne and Bohemians have enjoyed sporadic periods of preeminence.

An international side representing the Irish Free State (as it was then designated) played for the first time on 28 May, 1924 in the Paris Olympics. Two other matches were played that year including the team's first ever victory, 3-1 over Estonia, also in Paris. The following year the United States were beaten 3-1 in Dublin. Perhaps indicative of the cool relations between the Ireland and Great Britain, the Free State did not play any of the United Kingdom's teams until 1946 when England came to Dublin and won 1-0. Three years later, the Irish team exacted its revenge by beating England 2-0 on English soil at Goodison Park, home of Everton F.C. Thus, Ireland became the first "foreign" team to beat England in England, more than four years before Hungary's much better known triumph at Wembley in 1953.

During this period the Belfast-based IFA continued to select representative sides from players born throughout the island, fielding them under the name of Ireland and, thereby, making relations difficult between the two associations .

On the international front, the politics of football operate at two levels: on the one hand, the attitudes of football administrators in Ireland and, on the other, the perceptions and behaviour of football supporters. Of the former it can be said that relations between administrators on different sides of the border have typically been far more amicable than those which have existed between their political counterparts. Nevertheless, the existence of two separate administrations on the same island, the political identity of which is contested, has created unavoidable difficulties. In 1954, these reached a peak when at the annual congress of FIFA, the FAI proposed that only teams playing under its control should be described as Ireland. At that time, and indeed into the 1960s, the IFA continued to describe its representative sides as Ireland, the title of Northern Ireland becoming common only in the 1970s. This was resented by Dublin-based officials. Yet it should be remembered that long after partition, the IFA continued to select its international sides on an all-Ireland basis and this situation did not change until 1950, the last all-Ireland selection being made in that year for the game against Wales at Wrexham. Furthermore, despite the tacit admission by the IFA that it now lacked any authority over Irish football outside Northern Ireland, there was no likelihood that it would forfeit the right to be seen as representing Ireland. With the support of the other home unions, therefore, the IFA sought to resist the FAI's challenge and the 1954 proposal was defeated. Thus, we have the strange situation of two Irelands competing in major international football competitions: a source of some terminological confusion to radio and television commentators.

The fact that the two sets of administrators are now able to peacefully co-exist is the result of a realistic appraisal of the context in which they find themselves. First, given the political impasse which now exists, it is likely that the two separate political entities in Ireland will remain as they are for the foreseeable future. Separate governing bodies for the game of football are a straightforward acknowledgement of that fact. Second, given the relatively small size of Ireland's population the situation which prevails allows for a larger number of football administrators per head of

the population than would normally be the case. Thus, the sports administrators may have a vested interest in a pragmatic acceptance of the
existing state of affairs.

These factors should be borne in mind when one considers the
widespread resistance to the idea of an all-Ireland football team or the
concept of an all-Ireland League competition. The other decisive factor
however is the response of football supporters, particularly in Northern
Ireland, to proposals of this nature.

Since the late 1970s, Northern Ireland and the Irish Republic have
clashed in six full international matches (in 1978, 1989 and 1993 in Dublin
and in 1979, 1988 and 1993 in Belfast). Thanks in part to major security
operations and restrictions on away supporters, these games have passed
off with a minimum of crowd disturbance. That is not to deny, however,
the intense rivalry generated by these occasions. For many supporters the
confrontations were invested with a significance well in excess of that
which is usually attached to international football games, even those
between such long-standing rivals as Germany and France or Scotland and
England. Here, for many, were the latest instalments in the unfolding story
of tribal conflict between two warring communities. It is ironic in these
circumstances that the composition of the two sides on view has tended to
be at odds with the picture conjured up by such graphic imagery.

With the appointment of Jack Charlton, a former English international
player and World Cup medal winner, in the 1980s the FAI began to turn to
players whose links with Ireland are through grandparents rather than
parentage or place of birth. This has led to the selection by an English
manager of international sides in which less than half of the players were
born in Ireland and, thus, recognisable as natural members of the Irish
nationalist community. The IFA has also selected players designated as
Northern Irish despite having been born outside the Province but, in
general, this policy has been less strenuously followed than it has been by
the FAI, hence northern scorn at some of the latter's selections and the
popular joke that the letters FAI stand for "Find Another Irishman!"
Nevertheless, Northern Ireland's team selections are themselves far less
pristine than those who regard competition between the two Irelands as a
re-enactment of old battles might wish to believe.

In truth, it is doubtful if the Republic could have achieved so much had
it not been for Jack Charlton's creative use of FIFA's rules governing

players' qualification for international duty. By pursuing players who qualify to play for the Republic through their eligibility for an Irish passport, which includes people who have at least one Irish grandparent, Charlton has effected a massive increase in his recruitment base, enabling him to construct a team which owes as much to Ireland's diaspora in Britain as it does to Irish-born players.

Indeed the Irish manager's somewhat promiscuous selection policy has provided Northern Protestants with a particular source of grievance. Until earlier this year, the rules governing the selection of players for Northern Ireland were dictated by an agreement made between the four UK 'home' associations which laid down restrictions based on players' or players' parents places of birth. This rule was introduced to avoid confusion when the English, Welsh, Scottish and Northern Irish football associations were selecting players for the 'home' internationals which were discontinued in the early 1980s.

Along with the other UK associations, the IFA has now adopted FIFA's rule which extends eligibility to the place of birth of grandparents. However, this came too late to claim Alan Kernaghan, who, although born in England, was raised in the North and played schoolboy international soccer for Northern Ireland. Although he was disqualified from playing for Northern Ireland until the IFA's recent rule change, that did not prevent him opting for the Republic on the basis of his grandparents having been born in Belfast before partition.

In addition, the pursuit by both the FAI and the IFA of players on the basis of which passport they are entitled to hold is certain to lead to conflict, since players from Northern Ireland can claim both British and Irish citizenship. There are already signs at youth level that, as the Republic's achievements eclipse those of Northern Ireland, increasing numbers of talented young players, particularly those from the nationalist community, are looking south to develop their international careers.

The IFA has always selected Catholic players, not only whilst it reserved the right to select all-Ireland teams but even since its acceptance of a narrower field of influence. Some of these Catholics, most notably Pat Jennings, Northern Ireland's most capped international player, attained legendary status in the eyes of Northern Ireland's supporters. Paradoxically, however, many of those who encouraged Jennings so vociferously were also likely to sing songs which directed abuse at the Catholic religion and to wave the colours red, white and blue to attest to their loyalty to the union. For many years this complex relationship was accepted as both unavoidable and, ultimately, harmless and it did little to deter Catholics from supporting the national team, which after all included members of their own community. Indeed, they could derive considerable amusement from hearing Protestant supporters break off from a chorus of "The Sash My Father Wore" to sing the praises of big Pat from Newry or former Gaelic footballers, such as Gerry Armstrong and Martin O'Neill. This is a perfect illustration of the sanguine attitude towards sectarian abuse which most Northern Irish people have tended to adopt even during the lowest points in the current Troubles.

But the real tensions lie just below the surface and, by the mid 1980s, they had begun to make a serious impact on supporters' attitudes towards the Northern Irish team. Then, for the first time, substantial abuse was directed from the terraces towards Catholic players in the side, most notably Anton Rogan. In response, the IFA took the unprecedented step of warning that the Spion Kop at Windsor Park on which the most overt manifestations of loyalism had always been displayed would be closed for future international matches if the practice continued. But why had it begun in the first place and what are its implications for support for the national team?

The reason why Rogan was specifically singled out for abuse is that not only is he a Catholic from West Belfast, perceived in loyalist eyes as being almost entirely inhabited by republicans and fellow travellers, but he was chosen to represent Northern Ireland as a Glasgow Celtic player. The lingering influence of the Scottish game is highlighted by the widespread support in Northern Ireland for the major Glasgow teams which follows the same sectarian pattern as in Scotland itself. Given the enthusiasm of Northern Ireland Protestant football supporters for Celtic's traditional rivals, Glasgow Rangers, the presence of a Celtic player in the national squad naturally drew a less than enthusiastic response which was soon trans-formed into outright hostility when Rogan made mistakes on the field of play. Indeed, another player similarly abused by supporters was Allan McKnight, himself a Protestant but also a Celtic player when first selected to play for Northern Ireland. However, by itself the Celtic connection fails to provide a full explanation for the increased hostility shown towards Catholic players in the 1980s, since in previous years Celtic players had been accepted by Northern Ireland supporters. Indeed, former

Celtic players Bertie Peacock and Charlie Tully are remembered as two of the greatest and best loved players to have represented Northern Ireland in the post-war era.

A further explanation for the hostility shown towards Rogan is that it is the product of frustration on the part of the Northern Ireland followers. During the early 1980s the national side had enjoyed a period of unprecedented success, qualifying for the final stages of the World Cup in both 1982 and 1986 and scoring notable victories against Spain in Seville (1-0, 25 June 1982) and West Germany in Belfast (1-0, 17 November 1982) and Hamburg (1-0, 16 November 1983). As experienced players retired and no immediate replacements were found it became clear that the later years of the 1980s would be dedicated to team-building and little success could be anticipated. Exacerbating the problem, in the eyes of supporters, was the fact that the Republic of Ireland was enjoying international success. For the first time it seemed as if the balance of football power in Ireland was shifting south. This realisation was underlined when the Republic defeated Northern Ireland convincingly in Dublin on October 11, 1989 in the qualifying round of the European Championships.

Against this backdrop, criticism of Rogan and others can be seen as a response to what was regarded, in sectarian terms, as an enemy within. However illogical, particularly in the light of success enjoyed with Jennings as the last line of defence, Northern Ireland's relative decline *vis-à-vis* the Irish Republic was attributed by some, many of whom would have found the concept difficult to articulate, to the presence of players in the team whose ultimate loyalty to Northern Ireland in general was questionable. This in turn raises broader political questions about the status accorded to the national football team in loyalist popular culture.

The third, and most serious, reason for the insults hurled at Anton Rogan is that the nature of support for Northern Ireland has undergone a gradual transformation during the course of the Troubles. Central to unionist ideology is a sense of being under siege, heightened by the signing of the Anglo-Irish agreement which seemed to prove to many Protestants that their fears of being abandoned by Britain were well justified. As early as the late 1970s in fact the Ulster Defence Association (UDA) together with some Unionist politicians had come to accept that it might be necessary at some point for Northern Ireland to become independent in order to avoid the danger of incorporation into the Irish Republic. So many symbols of

Protestant popular culture, however, are essentially British that the idea of independence demands for its acceptance a profound transformation in Protestant attitudes. In turn this requires the existence of organisations and emblems which are exclusive to Northern Ireland and can sustain popular support for the demand for independence.

Few symbols were better equipped to serve this purpose than the Northern Ireland football team. It was living proof that Northern Ireland was and is a separate political entity whatever politicians in Dublin and London might claim and nationalists in the Province might aspire to. During the 1980s, union jacks were replaced on the terraces by Northern Ireland flags and Windsor Park, the national stadium but also home of Northern Ireland's most loyalist club side, Linfield, became an increasingly unfriendly place for Catholics — symbolised by the message 'Taigs Keep Out' ('Taig' being a term of abuse for Catholic) daubed on a wall near one of the approach routes to the ground.

The expression of cross-community tension through football was given added prominence at the beginning of 1992 when a local newspaper, the *Sunday Life* (5.1.92), drew attention to comments made by Linfield manager, Eric Bowyer, in a Linfield fanzine. Bowyer made it clear that in the prevailing circumstances he could not envisage signing a Catholic player. Despite the policy reiterated by club secretary, Derek Brooks, not to "exclude from its staff anyone by reason of colour, race or religion" (2.2.92), Linfield came under attack from Father McManus, spokesman for the Irish National Caucus in the United States, who demanded that the IFA sever its ties with Windsor Park and threatened to disrupt Northern Ireland's participation should they qualify for the 1994 World Cup finals in the United States. The secretary of the IFA, David Bowen, defended Linfield from the charge of sectarianism and pointed out that the IFA's relationship with Linfield is underpinned by a £3 million programme of ground improvements largely funded by the Government. Although Mr Bowen acknowledged that a boycott campaign would be embarrassing, he was confident that his organisation would receive full backing from F.I.F.A (26.1.92).

In March, however, after relentless lobbying by the Irish National Caucus, Coca-Cola threatened to withdraw sponsorship from the IFA. In addition, Thorne-E.M.I. ended their sponsorship of Linfield. While the company stated that this step was taken because of a down-turn in the economy, many believed that this was as a result of the bad publicity which the club had received over the Bowyer affair. In the face of such pressures Linfield took the unprecedented step of holding a press conference at which they declared themselves to be a non-sectarian organisation, stating further that:

> People of all classes and creeds are welcomed at Windsor Park, both for Linfield games and for internationals, and the Management Committee strongly refute the scurrilous and unfounded allegations made by Father McManus and his associates and their campaign to have commercial sponsorship withdrawn from soccer in Northern Ireland (*Irish News*, 19.3.92).

Club officials went on to detail the 70 Catholics who had played for the club since its inception in 1886. Close examination reveals that although many of these individuals played for the club in the post-war era, most did so in the period before the Troubles began in earnest in the late 1960s. Very few Catholics had played for Linfield since that time and they had all been recruited from outside of Northern Ireland. However, after considerable efforts, in the summer of 1992 they managed to sign one relatively unknown local Catholic. This was followed by the signing of two Catholic players from the Irish Republic and, subsequently, at the beginning of the 1993-94 season, a high profile player from the North's Catholic community. It remains difficult, however, for Linfield to sign a Catholic player from any of Northern Ireland's more staunchly nationalist areas, not least because of the range of problems which would confront such a player in his local community. In the prevailing circumstances, therefore, it is unlikely that Linfield's reputation as a Protestant symbol will be seriously challenged by token gestures.

This does not present a problem for the majority of those who at present constitute Linfield's and indeed Northern Ireland's support. It is precisely because the Northern Ireland football team remains as one of the strongest reminders of the Province's separate political identity that Protestant supporters have remained loyal and regard Catholic shifts in allegiance as the latest example of the perfidy of the enemy within.

None of this is to suggest that a majority, or even a substantial minority, of Northern Ireland's supporters would favour independence as a solution to the present political crisis. What it highlights however, is that under siege, people turn for solace to that which they can claim to be exclusively their own. The success of the Northern Ireland team was a source of comfort as well as of joy. When success receded into history, the enemy within would inevitably be the first to be singled out and blamed.

A survey carried out in 1990 has demonstrated that affiliation to and support for national football teams by Northern Irish football supporters tends to reflect the complexity of the issue of religious/national identity in the Province. 100 Catholic and 100 Protestant football supporters from the greater Belfast area were invited to rank in order England, Northern Ireland, Wales, the Republic of Ireland and Scotland according to how they would prefer to see them finish in an imaginary international soccer tournament. Of the Catholics an overwhelming 91% wanted the Republic of Ireland to come first. Only 8% wished to see Northern Ireland win the competition, but 62% hoped that they would come second behind the Republic. 64% of the Catholic sample placed England in last place behind third placed Scotland and fourth placed Wales. On the other hand, 88% of Protestants surveyed wished to see Northern Ireland victorious, followed by either Scotland(41%) or England(39%). 60% placed the Republic of Ireland fourth or last. Significantly, however, more than 40% of the Protestant sample placed England lower than third place with 24% wishing to see them last behind Wales. In addition, in the event of the Northern Ireland national team being disbanded, respondents were asked to declare whether they favoured Northern Irish players representing an All-Ireland or an all-U.K. team. 85% of Catholics favoured participation in an all-Ireland team. Protestant opinion was evenly divided with 43% preferring participation in an all-UK team and 42% opting for an all-Ireland side.

These results confirm that Protestants clearly identify with Northern Ireland and have little regard for the team of the Republic, except perhaps when they are playing against England as happened in the 1988 European Championships and the 1990 World Cup. The fact that many Northern Irish Protestants choose to support the Republic of Ireland over England cannot be taken as exemplifying a more general leaning towards Dublin. On the contrary, it illustrates the depth of mistrust generated within Northern Ireland's Protestant community by the many and varied attempts by successive English-dominated British governments to settle the 'Irish question' in Northern Ireland by admitting Dublin into the apparatus of political negotiation.

On the other hand, the majority of Catholics who follow football feel themselves to be best represented by the team of the Republic and, furthermore, they would prefer the Northern Irish team to be subsumed by an all-Ireland organisation. According to the author of the survey, these preferences are indicative of deeper seated political sentiments:

> The rejection of the Northern Ireland team and Windsor Park, which to Catholics symbolises Unionism in the form of the Union Jack flag, the British national anthem and the chanting of sectarian abuses probably conveys most Catholics' rejection of the Northern Ireland state. A state which they feel has nothing to offer them in terms of a history, a culture or an identity (McGivern, 1991: 87).

At international level, therefore, many Catholics in Northern Ireland have turned their attention to the Irish Republic's team, partly no doubt because of the latter's recent achievements but at least as importantly because they feel that they are unwelcome intruders at Northern Ireland games. Yet, Catholics continue to play for the national side and, despite the rival attraction of Gaelic sport, they play an active role at all levels of the game within Northern Ireland.

It is only when full account is taken of the above that the politicisation of the 17 November, 1993 match at Windsor Park can be understood. A month earlier, Jack Charlton was hoping that this game would be meaningless other than as a celebration of his team's qualification for USA '94. A month can be a long time in football and in politics. Three Spanish goals in Dublin, a Provisional IRA bomb in a fish shop in the Shankill Road in Belfast and a spate of loyalist paramilitary revenge killings combined to ensure that the contest was anything but meaningless.

Even before the episodic upsurge in sectarian violence it is doubtful if many northern Protestants would have welcomed the prospect of a summer-long celebration of the Republic's achievements in the USA, particularly since Northern Ireland had failed to qualify from the same group. Contrast this with the situation when Northern Ireland qualified for the World Cup finals in 1982. Apart from the most hard-line nationalist circles, both communities celebrated the success of Billy Bingham's team in reaching the quarter-finals in Spain. As we have seen, this was helped by the fact that half of Bingham's team, including Northern Ireland's most capped player, Pat Jennings, team captain Martin O'Neill and top goal scorer Gerry Armstrong were Catholics. At least as important in terms of attracting Catholic support was the timing of the team's success, during a period when soccer in the Republic was in the doldrums.

How things have changed, both on and off the field since then. Once the Republic's soccer team became successful it was inevitable that most northern nationalists would shift their allegiance from a team symbolising union with Britain to one which showed off Irish nationhood to the world.

This Catholic exodus has been accompanied by a gradual drift away by more liberal-minded Protestants who have been turned off both by Northern Ireland's poor performances and by the sectarianism of sections of its supporters. While they remain followers of the northern team, albeit passive ones, this group of fans has quietly applauded the Republic's qualification and a few may even travel to the USA to support them. This will prove once again that it is much easier for northern Protestants to be Irish and proud of it when they are away from the island. Indeed, had the boot been on the other foot, with Northern Ireland instead of the Republic going to the USA, it is likely that the team and their supporters would have been viewed simply as 'the Irish' by most of their American hosts.

Indeed, the relationship between sport and Irish identity is very complex. Although the Irish national team sports remain hurling and Gaelic football, it has taken a 'foreign' game to demonstrate that Ireland has come of age in the sporting arena. An all-Ireland final at Croke Park is a parochial affair compared with a major soccer international. Indeed, while association football has long been considered by Gaelic purists as a foreign(i.e. British) threat to Irish national culture, it is only in recent years that soccer has seriously challenged Gaelic games for the mantle of 'the' national game of Ireland.

The success of the Irish national soccer team has given a massive boost to the profile of a sport which was already on an upward curve. While the claims made by the founder members of the GAA at the turn of the last century, that association football was essentially an English game, had a degree of plausibility, as we approach the turn of the next, soccer is beyond question a universal game with global popular appeal. Despite concerted advertising campaigns on television and in the newspapers, when senior politicians openly rejoice at the nation's success in soccer, it is difficult for the GAA to convince today's generation of Irish games players that choosing association football over Gaelic games is a betrayal of their national heritage. On the contrary, the GAA runs the risk of being portrayed as anachronistic and introspective. As Bowman remarks:

> In the middle term they (the GAA) must be concerned at the appeal of televised world-class soccer. Ireland is one of the few countries where three codes of football prosper. But it would be naive to presume that all three can prosper indefinitely. Many astute observers reckon that the threat must be to Gaelic football (*Sunday Times*, 23.4.89).

This view is supported by *The Irish Times* columnist, Michael Finlan, who recognises the growing cultural power of soccer throughout Ireland, believing that it is well on the way to usurping the authority of the GAA and becoming the national sport:

> We do seem to have reached the stage where soccer, a once-reviled symbol of foreign yokes and repression, is threatening to become the national game of Ireland. And — oh the shame of it! — it's all largely the work of an Englishman who has cast a wonder-working spell on an Irish team which has some members who'd have trouble identifying a shamrock and might punch you out for using swear words if you tried the cupla focail (native language) on them (*Irish Times*, 8.6.90).

As Finlan suggests, it must be particularly worrying for the GAA that this is happening at a time when, with an English management team and a large proportion of current international players having been born on the mainland, the influence of the British on the development of the game in Ireland is stronger now than at any time since the last century. Undoubtedly, the main reasons why many gifted young Irish sportsmen such as Roy Keane, Niall Quinn, Kevin Moran and Mal Donaghy ultimately opted to play soccer rather than Gaelic games is that soccer afforded them the opportunity to display and test their abilities in an international arena and earn a good living. Furthermore, the country's participation in international soccer tournaments provides the whole nation with an opportunity to join in the promotion of Ireland on the world stage. While an all-Ireland Gaelic final at Croke Park may have the status of a national institution, it cannot rival an appearance by the Republic of Ireland in the quarter finals of the soccer world cup as an occasion for mass celebration.

Despite the challenge of soccer to the GAA it is likely that Gaelic games and association football will continue to flourish since each provides in differing ways an element in the development of Irish national identity. It is possible that rugby union will be the game which is increasingly under pressure. A few schools remain the backbone of the sport and attempts to broaden the game's base have been largely unsuccessful. Indeed even the game's traditional strongholds are less reliable than in the past, not least because the involvement of teachers from religious orders, happy to spend countless, unpaid hours in the propagation of the sports, can no longer be guaranteed (*Irish Times*, 26.10.93).

Nevertheless, none of this is to ignore the relatively fragile hold which soccer has over the Irish sporting public. Despite the handsome sum of money which has accrued from international matches played, ironically at the Irish Rugby Football Union(IRFU), headquarters, Lansdowne Road, and more significantly from qualification for major international competitions and the attendant sponsorship deals, especially with Opel, association football remains something of a poor relation in the context of Irish sport. Facilities are poor, even those provided by some members of the League of Ireland's Premier Division. As Emmet Malone puts it:

> part of the problem lies in the history of the game here with many clubs springing up on pitches owned by public or private landlords, who had no desire to see them properly developed for use as a soccer club and who, therefore, tended to hamper the natural progress which might have been expected as the game flourished (*Irish Times*, 13.10.93).

Thus despite the game's growing popularity, soccer teams cannot make the same sort of profits as those enjoyed by rugby and Gaelic clubs whose facilities are massive by comparison and used for a whole range of social activities. At the tip of this iceberg is the fact that the FAI has no national stadium, unlike rugby's Lansdowne Road and the GAA's Croke Park. The FAI has renewed its contract with the IRFU until 2006 and, thus, put an end to speculation that it was about to support the development of a national stadium in south-west Dublin. Unless the FAI carefully husband the grass roots of soccer within Ireland it is unlikely in the long term that the Republic of Ireland will be able to sustain its challenge to the perennial top nations on the international stage.

Given the huge Irish diaspora in the United States, it is undeniable that the qualification of the Republic's team for the 1994 Finals was demanded by Irish supporters and the competition's American organisers with almost equal degrees of intensity. These are the Finals that the Republic had to be in, even if they never qualify again. As far as the future of soccer in the Irish Republic is concerned, however, the qualification tournaments in the years ahead will be of crucial importance. The present squad contains a number of players, such as Bonner, McGrath, Whelan, Houghton, Aldridge, who are unlikely to play in many international matches after 1994. Jack Charlton too, may be thinking in terms of new challenges, either in football or more realistically beside his beloved salmon runs. Perhaps the experience of the Republic's northern neighbours is about to be repeated — a period of success followed by a relatively fallow time.

The final irony of course is that whilst British football in general examines its own collective navel and asks — what went wrong? why didn't we qualify for USA '94? the British game will be represented by an Irish team consisting of players born in various corners of the British Isles, who have learned their trade in English league football and who are managed by an Englishman who has used tactics which owe far more to Charles Hughes (the Director of Coaching for the English FA) and his position of maximum opportunity than to traditional Celtic values. It will annoy Irish supporters considerably to hear their team being appropriated by English commentators, but given the way the gap between the domestic soccer scene in Ireland and an international team ranked sixth in the world by FIFA has been bridged, perhaps the appropriation will not be entirely unwarranted.

Will there ever be "one team in Ireland, only one team in Ireland"? Certainly, each time the pendulum of fortune swings in favour of one or other of the Irish teams, conversation turns to the idea of a united side, capable of qualifying regularly for major international tournaments and of attaining even better results than have so far been achieved by either Northern Ireland or the Republic when going it alone.

However, as we have argued elsewhere, few things in Ireland, including sport, can be divorced from the politics of division (Sugden and

Bairner, 1993) and it is impossible to consider the unification of the Irish in association football without also thinking about political arrangements for the government of Ireland, north and south. In the wake of the last meeting between the two separate Irelands in Belfast, Michael Finlan was moved to write:

> The fact that two parts of the small island of Ireland should be battling each other in a soccer game at all perfectly demonstrates the artificial and absurd separateness of the two places. Just as the two soccer teams should be combined into one mighty squad of players, perhaps under the joint management of a Protestant and a Catholic, to take on the world, so should the parts of the island finally come together in an atmosphere that would scrupulously respect and protect the traditions and ethos of both warring factions (*Irish Times*, 19.11.93).

Such an idea could only have been floated at the end of 1993 when according to some analyses there was a greater possibility of peace breaking out in Ireland than at any time in the past 25 years, and when the Irish and British premiers could issue a joint statement urging a peace settlement. However, while Finlan is correct to link the possibility of an all-Ireland football team with the prospects for a united Ireland, as anybody who was at Windsor Park the night of 17 November 1993 will realise, there appears to be little support for either proposal within the Protestant community. If the current attitudes of many northern Protestants towards the existing Republic of Ireland soccer team are in any way indicative of how the public at large might respond to closer cultural and political union with the south, it has to be said that it is likely that a divided Ireland and two teams in Ireland will be the status quo for the foreseeable future.

References

Brodie, M. (1980), *One Hundred Years of Irish Football*, Belfast: Blackstaff.

Irish News, Belfast, various dates.

Irish Times, Dublin, various dates.

McGivern, N. P. (1991), 'Examinations of patterns of association football support as a way of determining national identity in Northern Ireland'. *Unpublished B.A. dissertation*, University of Ulster.

Oliver, G. (1992), *The Guinness Record of World Soccer. 'The History of the Game in over 150 countries'*, Enfield: Guinness Publishing.

Sugden, J. and Bairner, A. (1993), *Sport, Sectarianism and Society in a Divided Ireland*, Leicester: Leicester University Press.

Sunday Life, Belfast, various dates.

Sunday Times, London, various dates.

Van Esbeck, E. (1986), *The Story of Irish Rugby*, London: Stanley Paul.

8 Italy and the World Cup: The impact of football in Italy and the example of Italia '90

Pierre Lanfranchi

What did Italy produce in the last decades? Cars, Fellini, Ferrari, wine — and the biggest football league in Europe. Football passion in Italy is connected to good results and to a great organisation. The World Cup 1990 in Italy was the occasion to note how football was an essential phenomenon in the Italian society.

Furthermore, the World Cup provided the occasion for a new definition of the sport. As one commentator put it:

> The sporting scene was a constant vortex of images, of narration, of references that were present in all kinds of media and activities — from recreation to advertising, from the politics of enterprises to politics tout court. This was a phenomenon so blinding that it was precisely difficult to see.[1]

Given the strong passions so strongly anchored in the habits and customs of the Italian public, soccer in Italy (contrary to British or German soccer traditions) has never been attached to social class identity (i.e. defined as the sport for the working class). Rather, it has operated as a vehicle for social integration, social mobility, and local identity. Soccer clubs in Italy play the role of centres or 'nodes' around which social communities are formed. There have been numerous examples in the past where the fortunes of the local soccer club have generated a sense of communal identity and pride and a means for overcoming objective, socio-economic and political difficulties. Pundits have labelled soccer in Italy as the 'lay religion'. Attendance at Sunday afternoon games has substituted for the regular attendance of Sunday morning mass. In fact, Sunday morning is important now as the pre-game, preparation phase of the competition rather than as a moment set aside for religious reflection and practice.[2]

Soccer in Italy benefits from an interest that is not equalled in any other country on the European continent. Part of the interest in the game is generated by the national pool or lottery, *Totocalcio,* that is played in the country and abroad by millions of people and generates significant profits for the lucky winners. *Totocalcio* in Italy represents the most popular weekly 'lottery' that at one time or another everyone has tried to win and use as a means of getting rich in a quick and legal manner. Thus, soccer in Italy represents a complex combination of social ritual, economic enterprise, community identity, and national pastime that confronts sociologists, historians, and political scientists with the need to make a series of difficult distinctions between the presence of symbolism versus substance in the playing of the game and in the industry that has blossomed on the fringes of the sport. It is not a coincidence that a French specialist on Italian history has focused on the evolution of the game over time as a way of studying the manifestations and changes in the national character.[3]

In Italy, where soccer is a broadly based and intensely felt social phenomenon, it is difficult to achieve the detachment from the game necessary for serious analysis. Soccer is ephemeral, yet it has a powerful impact on its environment. We could say that it has the capacity of creating its own world; it generates its own heroes and rules that defy the logic of the outside world.[4] This is a world where the sports star and sports journalist rule supreme. Sports journalists, as a group, have been subject to significant criticism for their lack of intellectual legitimacy and order, but the sale of sports newspapers and magazines and the number of viewers tuning in to television programmes focused on sports commentary demonstrate that their power of attraction has been on the increase for over half a century.[5] One could argue that soccer has replaced politics as the national pastime in Italy.

The following table (Table 1) illustrates the extent of this media constituency.

Table 1:
Audience of Italian sporting programmes on Public TV (RAI)

CHAN-NEL	TITLE	TIME	DAY	Total	Children [4-15]	Men [15+]	Women [15+]`	SHARE %
				INDIVIDUALS (in 1000s)				
Raiuno	90 minuto	18.10–18.50	SUN	6828	799	3129	2900	53.82
Raiuno	La domenica sportivo	21.45–22.35	SUN	4193	564	2229	1631	30.82
		23.00–24.00		1346	131	753	462	23.00
Raiuno	Lunedi sport	15.15–16.30	MON	460	65	213	182	8.53
Raiuno	Mercoledi sport	20.10–20.45	WED	1994	1600	5985	4389	45.68
		22.35–24		1123	100	619	403	16.82
Raiuno	Sabato sport	14.10–16.00	SAT	329	86	432	312	12.92
Raidue	Campionato di calcio al serie A	18.40–20.05	SAT/ SUN	2303	320	1350	933	19.00
Raidue	Tg2 Domenica Sprint	20.00–20.10	SUN	4564	587	2306	1792	24.68
Raidue	Tg2 Sportsera	18.00–18.50	MON–FRI	1574	121	753	699	17.15
		17.00–17.50	SAT	362	61	368	233	10.80
Raidue	Tg2 Sport	20.10–20.25	MON–SAT	3426	392	1508	1526	16.29
		14.00–17.00	SUN	2338	223	1298	817	26.51
		17.45–18.00	SUN	1822	201	946	675	13.84
Raidue	45 minuto	15.20–17.45	SUN	1063	118	494	451	10.60
Raidue	Tuttocampionato [al interno dei Tg]	13.15–13.30	SAT	5522	470	2459	2593	35.15
Raidue	Tg2 Dubbing	18.45–19.00	SAT	2058	250	1017	791	15.57
Raidue	Tg2 Sportselte	23.00–24.00	SAT	622	58	330	234	8.27
Raitre	Domenica goal	18.35–18.50	SUN	1112	123	588	401	9.17
Raitre	Il processo del lunedi	22.20–22.40	MON	2369	191	1285	893	19.61
Raitre	Campionato di calcio serie 8	(several)	SAT SUN THUR	459	40	257	162	3.11
Raitre	Tg3 Derby	12.00–19.00	MON SAT	895	90	471	334	8.20
Raitre	Sport-regione	19.40–19.50	SUN	1566	184	732	650	7.67
	Sport-regione del lunedi	19.40–19.50	MON	1539	148	700	690	7.11

Source: Minerva, L. (1989) *Di pallone bella rete*, Rome: ERI: 143.

One of the other peculiarities of the Italian soccer phenomenon, is, without any doubt, the constant success of football matches. The more important clubs: Milan, Inter, Juventus, Napoli, AS Roma attract attendances of more than 40,000 per match. AC Milan and Naples had more than 60,000 season-ticket holders in the season 1990. A recent work on AC Milan supporters attending the matches showed on one hand the 'social normality' of the supporters (see Table 2); on the other hand the large potential market they are offering to the media and press industry.[6]

Table 2: Occupation of AC Milan supporters 1990

Occupation:	N	%
Workers	144	28.8
Craftsmen	38	7.6
Services	130	26.0
Commercial Branch	47	9.4
Liberal Professions	35	7.0
Business Managers	11	2.2
Teachers	5	1.0
Other	10	1.6
Not in work (student, unemployed)	82	16.4
Total	502	100.0

Given these elements, it is possible to begin to appreciate the significance of the Word Cup in a country where soccer assumes a special place in the use of leisure time throughout the year by a large portion of the (particularly male) population.[7] Without doubt students of contemporary events in Italy need to study such events to fathom the national character and understand how Italy is adopting to its post-capitalist economy and social structure. What we want to do in this chapter is to analyse the impact of the World Cup on the country: what were the roles played out by its various stars, how did the public reflect the contradictions inherent in the event, what was the role of the powerful soccer industry and of a powerful national soccer federation, what impact did the stadium renovation projects have on public policy and how well did Government policy maintain control over the public contracts that were generated by the World Cup competition? The answers to these questions are of great interest in revealing the undercurrents of Italian popular culture and society that are not normally studied by political scientists but which are of great importance in the daily lives of the Italians and in revealing the trends characterising the society in the short- and the medium-term. In staging an event of this size, the organisers of the 1990 World Cup attempted to transmit a 'modern' image which, incidentally, did not differ substantially from that proposed by Mussolini in 1934 at the only previous World Cup competition organised by Italy. What we will try to do in the following section is to interpret the contents of this image and in the subsequent section we shall concentrate on analysing soccer's contemporary place in Italian society.

The staging of the World Cup

As Jean Baudrillard wrote about Heysel, the Belgian disaster where 39 people lost their lives in a crowd disorder that took place at the European Cup between Liverpool and Juventus from Turin: "this catastrophe is basically the explosive form that is taken by the absence of any event ... It is the political void, the silence of society and of history".[8] In a similar fashion the World Cup can be conceived of as an extreme expression of an ideological no man's land. On one hand, the staging of the event was supported by the vast majority of Italians who saw the event as an opportunity to highlight the achievements of Italian society and the opportunity to win another World Cup title to add to their most recent 1982 victory in Madrid. The goal that the national and international soccer federations wanted to achieve through the staging of the Italian World Cup was to consecrate the return of a 'drug free' sport and, more importantly, the achievement of a greater level of sportsmanship among the players and fans. After the Heysel and Bradford (England) disasters there was the need to stop the decline in the popularity of the sport and consolidate its traditional image as the sport of the masses which enjoyed the largest and most extensive worldwide audience.

On the other hand, the event was fraught with great uncertainty. There was a tremendous fear among the organisers that the event would be marred by violence generated by unruly fans attracted to the country by the competition. Strict police measures were employed to keep any prospect of pervasive and massive violence under control.

The Italian authorities were also sensitive to the role that the media could play in fanning the flames of violence in the stadiums. They wanted to absolutely avoid what had become commonplace in the UK where reporters were sent out by the media to follow and report on fan violence rather than cover the match. From this approach, the event that made the news was the violence and not the game.[9] The Italian and international soccer authorities did not want the 1990 World Cup to be remembered as a statement on social disorder rather than a sporting event. Special care was taken in sites where England played its matches. In Cagliari, Sardinia the English and Italian authorities worked in tandem to control the potential problems that could be generated by the expected influx of 5,000 English fans. Ian Taylor has written that the root cause of English fan violence was "clearly not a problem to do with football, but politics".[10] A politicised over dramatisation of potential disorder was, in fact, often an excuse on the part of the host organisation to hide its inability to prepare adequately for the event and all of its consequences. The Italian soccer authorities, relayed by the major press, tried continuously, during the month preceding the event, to make a clear distinction between the football world associated with football lovers, the 'true fans' and "a kind of social pollution that has contaminated the youth movement in general".[11]

Once the World Cup competition was over everyone awoke to the fact that the lack of violent incidents was one of the most important events that did not take place. The potential for violence had attracted the attention of most observers at the beginning of the competition, and the lack of violence subsequently allowed the Italian press to sustain the view that the issue of soccer hooliganism was a phenomenon peculiar to English fans and not applicable to the entire international soccer community.

Given the exaggerated emphasis of the need to keep at bay the fear of an 'overwhelming violence', what followed after the World Cup was an uncontrolled optimism and the denial of the problem by pretending that the World Cup had defeated forever the potential for fan violence in the Italian stadiums.[12]

The event

The spectacular image of Italia '90 was above all one of the ability to undertake a great enterprise, provide a concrete example of the potential for growth and creativity, and demonstrate the contribution that Italy could make to the growth of Europe in the future. The COL (Italian World Cup Organising Committee), directed by the young and dynamic manager, Luca Cordero di Montezemolo, formerly manager of the Ferrari Formula 1 racing team and the Italian entry — Azzurra — in the America's Cup had estimated on the eve of the World Cup that the economic potential of the competition was approximately 320 billion lire (245 million dollars).[13] Only half of this sum would come from ticket sales, and the other would be generated by sponsoring institutions.[14] The manager of Italia '90 was the ideal expression of the new-wave hero (a charismatic individual in his private life and with personal ties to show business) of the show which would crown the world's best soccer team and identify the new players that would dominate the game in the 1990s.[15] Soccer was increasingly becoming identified as a business, and as such it needed a recognised and successful business manager to set the tone.

The COL represented the epitome of a modern enterprise that had adopted the Italian model of economic decentralisation and the turning away from the dependence on public subsidies to finance the staging of international sporting events. In addition, it represented in its structure all of the characteristics of the originality of Italian neo-liberalism. The Italian organising committee was, after all, a public undertaking (presided over by the then PSI Minister of Tourism Franco Carraro and later mayor of Rome), and the Italian manifestation of the International Soccer Federation (FIFA). Its liberal philosophy was in line with the tastes of the day in general society as well as in the sports federation where "sponsorship is acceptable to the measure that it results from a contract freely entered into by the contracting parties".[16] Even if the COL did not have the authority to choose the official sponsors of the Mondiale (Coca-Cola, Philips, and Gillette) that poured 13 billion lire into the coffers of the organisation, it did stipulate the contracts with the official suppliers (all Italian) from Olivetti to the State Railways (FS). We should also not forget that the money supplied by RAI (State Communications System), Fiat, and the National Bank of

Labour (BNL) amounted to more than a 60 billion lire contribution to the organisation.[17]

In this sense, the World Cup reflected precisely one of the major developments in Italian football in the 80s, the growing importance of private sponsorship. Italy was the last of the mainland European countries to permit the sponsors to have their name printed on the League Club's football shirts, in 1981. In the last season before shirt sponsorship, sums from sponsorship in the Serie A (Division 1) totalled 5.9 billion lire. Seven or eight years later, in 1989, the sponsoring income for the Serie A team increased more than 3 times to 21.6 billion lire. For the major Italian enterprises football and sport generally are considered as an excellent market supplier. Major firms like Parmalat (milk and food industry), UPIM (big stores from Fiat group) or Benetton (Fashion), who is sponsoring all the team-sports in the city of Treviso and a Formula 1 Racing team, are considering sport as a perfect expression of modern Italy.

There was really no great difference in the establishment of relations with the organising committee by private *vis-a-vis* public firms. The image of the World Cup served only to strengthen the worship by public opinion of competitive enterprise and to reduce the distance between Europe and the United States in the use of a sport as an occasion to mount a national cultural spectacle.

The realisation of significant profit margins in a sports event of this size was certainly one of the biggest successes of Italia '90. When the organising committee for the 1994 World Cup (during the Autumn 1990) contacted Luca di Montezemelo to offer him the position as head of the committee, the request was interpreted by the Italian press as a confirmation (it was said 'by recognised experts in the field' of sports capitalism) of the success of the 'made in Italy' management of the World Cup.

The World Cup also offered the national federation the opportunity to verify whether the American approach to sports had taken over a significant part of the Italian scene. After the acquisition of the Milan team by Silvio Berlusconi in 1985, Italian soccer had assimilated well his stated goal of:

> completely transforming the organisation of soccer into a business-oriented venture, well integrated into the activities of the FININVEST holding company and treated like every other sector of the company's industrial and commercial enterprise.[18]

The commercialisation of soccer occurred, above all, in its affirmation on television. In this domain, the American model is summarised in a single phrase: "television is effectively a professional sport and professional sport is television".[19]

Despite the fact that all of the stadiums were completed in time for the competition, the imperfections in the choice of construction sites was revealed once the rains started. The grass surfaces in the Milan, Rome and Turin stadiums were more appropriately labelled as swamps rather than as soccer playing fields.

'Size' was for decades a characteristic that accompanied World Cup projects, and it was usually operationalised in the construction of huge stadia. In 1930 during the first World Cup competition Uruguay constructed the 'Monumentale' stadium, and the 1950 World Cup in Brazil was held in the 'Maracana' stadium which holds up to 200,000 spectators. For a long time, the efforts of the organisers were primarily concerned with stadium capacity, the benefits coming from ticket sales.

However, twenty years later architects and urban planners responsible for stadium projects became more concerned with other aspects of the competition, and the notion of the size of stadiums was brought into line with the ideals of post-consumerism. Stadiums had to be 'more practical, comfortable, cleaner, and safer'. The adoption of these criteria inevitably had the impact of creating stadia that, for the most part, "reduced the potential for spontaneity and consequently failed in increasing the quality of life".[20] The goal of the Italian organisers was to create stadia with sitting room only accommodation in numbered seats and to have a maximum number of these seats under a roof. In the Milan stadium only the playing field was not covered. The new stadia needed to provide easy and quick cleaning, and they had to be extremely functional. The facilities built or restructured for the World Cup were supplied with ultra-modern facilities (video screens, telephones, VIP sky boxes) and they represented 'jewels' of modern architecture reflecting the genius of Italian design and functionality.

If one considers stadia policy as a good image of auto-definition of a regime, the recent evolution has shown that the stadium building policy has been often connected with 'Tangentopoli', the political and economic institutional crisis. The cost of this modernity may have been over-estimated and part of the money landed on the political parties.

The first World Cup to be held in Italy (in 1934) produced stadia designed by the renowned architect Pier Luigi Nervi in Florence and the Littoriale stadium in Bologna (today called the Dall'Ara stadium).[21] These stadia became part of the country's contemporary architectural patrimony and symbolised the modernist aspirations of Futurism. The 1990 constructions were, in a parallel fashion, supposed to reflect the increased quality of Italian infrastructure, the renewal of Italian creative passion, and the marked individualism that continued to characterise Italian architecture and society. Through this expedient, the construction of the stadia was supposed to reflect, in essence, Italy's post-war democratic ideals.

Stadia have for a long time been taken by the media as a reflection of the country's economic, social and political climate. In 1973 in Chile and in 1978 in Argentina the stadia were taken as symbols of the dictatorship. In 1985 at Bradford and in 1989 at Hillsborough, UK the old, 'English style', stadia were the sites of real human tragedies. The blame for these tragedies went beyond the physical aspects of the stadiums and were, in fact, attributed to the breakdown of social order and consensus in the Thatcher era.[22]

Italy chose, in contrast to the Fascist regime, to respond to the exigency of the World Cup with the objective of using the occasion to emphasise in its stadia the concept of public safety and democracy; the result was what critics labelled the 'demystification' of the World Cup stadia.[23] One could decry the passing of the 'old' 75,000 seat San Siro stadium of Milan which only had one of its four levels of seats covered. But the new stadium was, according to the 'soft ideological' model which has become dominant in politics as well as in architecture, destined to become the place for public entertainment as part of the new European approach to major sporting events. Stadia could no longer be the site for strong passions. Despite the dictates of the plans developed by the promoters of the World Cup, the result was quite different.

On the fields — the other World Cup — Toto, Diego and the Modern North

Changing the name of football to calcio before World War 1, Italian football chroniclers recorded a potential origin of the game in a medieval Florentine court game. But, for decades, they developed an internationally known

Italian style: *the catenaccio* personified by Helenio Herrera and the Inter Milan team of the nineteen sixties. From the thirties on, Italian football was associated with the big club "la decchia signora" (the old lady), the Juventus. The history of the game was connected strongly with the Juventus history and its owner — the Agnelli Family, owners of Fiat, presidents of the club from the mid-twenties. In 1934, when Italy won its first World Cup, two major elements of the club were Luis Monti and Raimundo "Nummo" Orsi. Both were Argentinian internationals coming to Turin for big money and the latest Fiat model. Monti was an extremely strong defender — the Italian press used the word, virile — and Orsi an extremely fine forward, exposing the fascist aspirations 'back to the fatherland' of this sort of Italian. The defensive trio — Combi, Rossetta, Calligaris — won with the club five successive championship medals 1931-35.

During the 1950s Gianpiero Boniperti, local idol, was in the middle of the team to win new medals with John Charles and the Argentinian Omar Sitori. In the seventies and eighties, the club won, as national champions, all three European Cups and had eight world champions in the World Cup winning side — including the goalkeeper Dino Zoff aged 41 (who won in 1986 his 22nd and last championship).

For the Agnelli family and Fiat, the 1990 Italian soccer season was nothing short of a disaster. After the departure of the French star Michel Platini (that coincided with the arrival of Berlusconi as the head of A.C. Milan), the "Juve style" of soccer appeared to have become obsolete in comparison to the Milan Juggernaut and the rising fortunes of the team from Naples and its captain Diego Armando Maradona. The World Cup competition did not seem to hold out very good news for the Juventus players.

Despite these pessimistic forecasts, the World Cup proved to be a boon for the personal fortunes of Juventus and the Agnelli empire. The revelation of the competition was Salvatore Schillaci, the centre-forward of the national team and Juventus. The other major star of the Italian team was Roberto Baggio, a recent Juventus acquisition. Baggio had emerged as an Italian soccer prodigy in the Florence (Fiorentina) team. A few weeks before the initiation of Italia '90, Juventus bought Baggio for a sum in excess of 20 billion lire. Sports commentators observed that the price paid for the player represented 'his weight in gold'. The purchase of Baggio was a significant addition to the Juventus team and constituted a substantial profit for the Pontello family that owned the Fiorentina team. However, the Pontello family had to pay dearly for the sale of Baggio. For days enraged Fiorentina fans besieged the Pontello family residence and Fiorentina offices in Florence. The street demonstrations and occasional rioting eventually convinced the Pontello family to sell the team to the Checchi-Gori group.

The spectacular goals by Schillaci and Baggio in the World Cup restored the splendour to the Turin Juventus empire.[24] The emergence of the Sicilian Schillaci in a top Northern club had an important impact on the north-south divide in Italy, reviving the memory of the first economic miracle which in the 1950s and 1960s had fuelled a massive transfer of workers from the rural south into northern urban factories. Schillaci's exploits and the enthusiasm that they generated among the fans served to reconcile a large number of Italians with their past.[25]

Juventus is not the team of the city of Turin — this role is taken by the local rival, Torino — but the team from all Italy. In the 1982 team, Zoff came from Fruil (on the North-East), Gentile from Sicily and Libya, Tardelli from Tuscany, Porio from the South (Lecce), Scirea from Bergamo, Cabrini from Cremona, Causio from Lecce too.

Totó (the diminutive of his name, Salvatore, adopted by all Italians) appeared to possess all the characteristics of the stereotypical, although a bit anachronistic, Sicilian worker transferred to the north. He was born in a poor neighbourhood in Palermo and fit perfectly with the image of the Juventus fans recruited *en masse* from the ranks of the poor, southern Italian working in the northern factories. On the field Toto was surly and clever in finding his opportunities for scoring, but in normal life he was simple and timid. In every goal scored by Schillaci (he finished the World Cup with the highest tally of goals), this hard-working, humble Italy of the 1970s awoke once again and rejoiced. Gone were the thoughts that the simple Italian players had inevitably to give way to the arrogance of the Berlusconi who bought his special breed of modern player abroad.

Prior to the World Cup, Schillaci seemed to be destined for a supporting role in a world of modern soccer embodied by teams like A.C. Milan. He was an ordinary man in a sport destined for exotic heroes.[26] While the players who had dominated the previous Italian championship had come from middle-class backgrounds and always played in national clubs, Schillaci did not play in the top league until twelve months before the World Cup. He had emerged as a promising player at the late age of 26 (an age at which the destiny of most players is already consolidated) during his stint with the Sicilian team of Messina, a team playing in the second Italian league (B league). The public image projected by Schillaci reassured his native region and all southerners that he had not turned his back on his origins and that he had worked his way to prominence through hard work and sacrifice.[27]

The affirmation of Schillaci could be considered as a symbol of conservatism in Italian football, of a traditional 'good old Italian style' with working class players — but Schillaci was not just a machine, a normal player. Diego Maradona was another case of a player who could not be compared with a machine. The fantastic Argentine player upset the established social order and hierarchy of Italian soccer. Before the beginning of the World Cup, he had attracted a lot of negative press due to his frequent remarks in the media that served to exacerbate the north-south split. Certainly his minor escapades with the Naples criminal element, extra-marital affairs, and unwillingness to follow orders were annoying, but he made up for it by helping Naples win the Italian championship (the 'Scudetto') to the chagrin of the supporters of A.C. Milan and northerners in general. Maradona had responded to the Neapolitans' cry ('allow us to dream') at the moment of his triumphant arrival in the southern city by winning the Italian championship twice and reversing the traditional roles between northern and southern teams in the Italian league with a sense of determination and revenge[28]. 'Naples champion, screw the nation' was a commonly heard Neapolitan slogan.[29] As a consequence, the national Italian press and, especially, northern public opinion never forgave him for his unruly behaviour.

From the opening match in Milan in which Argentina found itself playing Cameroon (the quintessential dark horse of the World Cup), the public tone was defiant. Given that Maradona had asked Neapolitans to root for Argentina rather than the Italian national team, the Italian crowds turned vehemently against Maradona and Argentina. When the Argentine national anthem was played in the opening ceremonies, the partisan northern crown whistled from the beginning to the end, and every time the

Argentinian captain touched the ball a loud boo rumbled throughout the stadium.

The furore generated by Maradona led the Italian press to begin to question the national loyalty of the Neapolitan public. Polls were taken to find out whether Neapolitans would follow the advice of Maradona or root for the Italian team. Antonio Matarrese, DC deputy and president of the Italian soccer federation, felt obliged to issue on television a call to Neapolitans to demonstrate their support for the national team, that is, the 'azzurri'.

Maradona replied to Matarrese by addressing his Neapolitan fans with the following observation:

> For 364 days out of the year you are considered to be foreigners in your own country; today you must do what they want by supporting the Italian team. Instead, I am a Neapolitan for 365 days out of the year.

The Maradona squabble turned what could have been considered a minor press skirmish into an important national issue.[30] During the municipal elections at the beginning of May, the Lombard League certainly benefited from a rather favourable anti-southern sentiment generated the week before by the Neapolitan victory in the soccer championship; the victory by Naples was seen as a slap against northern Italy, a defeat for the hardworking honest, and rich part of the country by the poor, subsidised, and lazy south.

The elimination of Italy in the semi-final match against Argentina in a match played in Naples (in front of a crowd that applauded the Argentine anthem but rooted for Italy) only reinforced the national press' hostility against Maradona. The absence of Italy from the final game was lived as a national trauma[31]. As a consequence, the Italian public took sides and rooted vehemently for Germany in the final match.

The tears shed by Maradona at the end of the game and the German victory seemed to exemplify the epitome of a northern revenge against the up-start south. In the end, the superior strength of the north had vanquished the fantasy and passion of the south: the social order had been re-established.

These remarks are a comment on the strong relationship existing in Italy between sport, and especially football, and social life. But football is particularly significant because it made it possible in less than half a century to make a strong cultural patrimony of a large part of the population.

All the excess expressed during the World Cup was simply a perfect reflection of the importance of the very idea of a game between equals in a society in which the concept of equality is not taken seriously.

Notes and references

1   G. Vigarello, O. Mongin, 'Le nouvel âge du sport', *Esprit*, 125, 1987, April-June, p.1.

2   I borrow this term of 'lay religion' from Eric Hobsbawm. Marc Auge, for his part, classified the infatuation for soccer as a form of ritual practice, 'Football, de l'histoire sociale á l'anthropologie religieuse', *Le Débat*, February 1982, pp.59-67. Italian sociologists have been interested in the phenomenon of soccer through the studies of violence in the stadiums. The works of Antonio Roversi, *Calcio and Violenza in Europa*, Bologna, *IL Mulino*, 1990, approach the phenomenon from different positions. Soccer has also been studied from the point of view of social history. See the debate in the review *Italia Contemporanea*, 176, September 1989. As I noted elsewhere, it would be particularly revealing to construct a diagram taking into account, on one hand, the daily sport publications and their circulation in different European countries and, on the other, the historical and sociological publications treating the sport phenomenon. The second graph curve would be, without doubt, inversely proportional to the first. See P. Lan-franchi, 'Nei meandri della Storia dello Sport', *Italia Contemporanea*, 176, cit.

3   Pierre Milza, 'Le football italien. Une histoire a l'échelle du siecle', *Vingtieme siêcle*, 26, April-June 1990, pp. 49-58.

4   It is worth taking note of the ardour generated by the television programme on RAI3 conducted by Aldo Biscardi entitled 'Processo del Lunedi' (or the Monday trial). This programme is without doubt the television programme most highly criticised by the Italian intellectuals. It perfectly illustrates the absurdity and intensity of the interest displayed by Italian soccer fans, commentators, and the game's general public. The lofty tones and the flowery language of the discussion serve to accentuate the grotesque and fascinating aspects of the sport. The programme dissects the events and personalities of the previous day in such a detailed and captivating way that the private channels run by Silvio Berlusconi offer 'L'appello del martedi' (the Tuesday appeal) as a way of building on the

appeal generated by the Biscardi programme. Soccer has become, therefore, one of the central instruments in the war for viewers and sponsors fought out by public and private television channels.

5   See on this subject the books published by two of the most famous Italian sports journalists: Gianni Brera, *Storia Critica del Calcio*, Milan, 1978, and Olivero Beha, *Anni di Cuoio, l'Italia di Oggi allo Specchio del Calcio, Il Suo Sport Piu Amato, La Sua 'Malattia' Piu Contagiosa, in cui Si Riflettono Vizi e Vitu di un Popolo Tifoso Fino al Midollo*, Rome, Newton Compton, 1987. On the importance of soccer in the daily publications, see the film on the fans of Naples proposed by the Swiss Romanda television: 'Passion et rituels du foot', made in collaboration with a group of French ethnologists. One must remember that Italy is the only European country that has four daily sport publications distributed nationally. One of these the *Gazetta dello Sport*, boasts a place among the three daily publications with the highest circulation.

6   A. Dal Lago, R. Moscati, *Regalateci un sogno. Miti e realta del tifo calcistico in Italia*, Milano, Bomprani, 1992: 33-55.

7   The proportion of female supporters is similar in the two bigger surveys conducted on Italian supporters — 16% in Bologna, and 18% in Milan in the age category 19-25, Dal Lago, Noscati, *op cit*, 37; A. Rovsi, *Calcio Lifo e violenza. Il teppismo calcistico in Italia*, Bologna, e nulino, 1992 p.69.

8   Jean Baudrillard, 'Heysel', *Autrement*, 'L'amour foot', 80, May 1986, pp.159-163.

9   Eric Dunning, 'Soccer as a political football: the game in Britain now and in the future', paper presented at the conference 'Le football et L'Europe'. European University Institute, Florence, May 1990, EUI Colloquium Paper 123/90.

10   Ian Taylor, 'English Soccer in 1990: Possibilities and Problems', European University Institute, Florence, May 1990, EUI Colloquium Paper 123/90.

11   Interview with Pierre Verbrugghe, Prefect of Paris, in the newspaper *Le Monde*, 14 November 1990, about youth vandalism and riots in Paris during the Autumn of 1990.

The fears concerning the Italian fans were unfounded, as observed by Antonio Roversi:

> The young Italian fans — called 'ultras' — have never been particularly stimulated by the undertakings of the national team and the games played by the national team have never represented a motive for pitched battles between the Italian 'ultras' and analagous groups supporting the opposing team.

See 'La Violenza calcista in Italia 1970-1989', text presented to the conference *Calcio e Violenza in Europe. Cause e Rimedi*, Bologna, May-June 1990. The National team became after the world cup a subject of opposition between Italians, having different kinds of supporters in cities like Palermo and Florence (where the team was criticised).

[12] See on this point the pertinent observations of Allessandro Dal Lago in *Descinzioné di una Battaglia*, pp.147-150 and of Michael Eve, *Dentro Inghilterra. Ragioni e miti di una identita*, Marsilio, Venezia, 1990, pp.224-231.

[13] The exchange rate that can be used to generate the dollar equivalents of the sums cited in this article is 1,300 lire/$ US.

[14] *Il Sole 24 Ore*, June 4, 1990; PierLuigi Marzola, *L'industria del calcio*, Nuova Italia Scientifica, Rome, 1990 p.180.

Official sponsors: Canon, Coca-Cola, Anheuser Beer Busch, Philips, Fuji-Films, Gillette, JVC.

Official Furniture: Alitalia, Fiat, Railroad Ilalians, INA (Insurance), Olivetti, RAI (Italian Television), BNL (Bank), STET (Communication).

[15] Alain Ehrenberg, 'Le show meritocratique', *Esprit*, cited in Vigarello and Mongin, 'Le nouvel âge du sport', cit.:266-283.

[16] This form of liberalism attributed to sports federations is evident in the proposal made by Mariano Ravazzolo, director of the office of the president of the Italian Olympic Organising Committee (CONI), *Panorama*, 15 April 1990 et id. 'Le sponsorisme dans le sport italien', *Esport, Revue Juridique et Economique du Sport*, 13,. 1990, 2 pp.85-88.

[17] *Il Sole 24 Ore*, 10 December 1988.

[18] Gian Paolo Caselli, 'Which way for the Italian football industry?' presentation at the colloquium 'Le football et L'Europe', European University Institute., Colloquium Paper 122/90.

[19] George H. Sage, *Sports and American Society*, Addison Reading, 1974 (2), p.6. In Italy the income from television rights has more than doubled between 1985 and 1989, Gian Paolo Caselli, 'Il calcio da sport a impresa capitalistica' in R. Grozio (ed.), *Catenaccio e Contropiede. Materiali e Immaginari del Football Italiono*, Pellicani, Roma, 1990, p.27-38. One witnesses the same pheno-menon in France as in Spain, cf. Wladimir Andreff, Jean-Francois Nys, *Le sport el la télévision. Relations economiques: Plurité d'intérets et sources d'ambiguités*, Dalloz, Partis, 1987. In France the scheduled volume of broadcasts of soccer games has increased from 55 hours in 1984 to 275 hours in 1989, and the percentage represented by the television rights in the budget of professional clubs has increased from 1% in 1980 to 40 per cent in 1988. See Jean-Francois Nys, 'L'economie du football en France in *Le football et l'Europe*, EUI, Colloquium Paper, 103/90.

20 Jean Francois Bourg, *Football Business*, Oliver Orban, Paris, 1986, pp.180-181.

21 The Littoriale was constructed in 1927, see Vera Ottani, 'Lo stadio di Bologna. Quando un campo e monumento da tutelare', in *Azzurri 1990 Storia bibliografica emerografica iconografica della Nazionale Italiana di Calcio e del Calcio a Bologna*, La Meridiana, Rome 1990, pp.129-132.

   See too: John Bale, 'Football and Topophilia: the Public and the Stadium' in P. Lanfranchi (ed.), *Il calcio c il suo pubblico*, Napoli, ESI, 1992 p.221-240.

   Miguel de Moragas, 'Football, télévision et identité européenne', in *Le football at L'Europe*, European University Institute/Colloquium Paper, 128/90.

22 See the moving testimony of Ian Taylor 'Hillsborough: 15 April 1989. Some personal contemplations', *New Left Review*, 77, Oct.-Nov. 1989 p.89-100.

23 On the political use of the stadium during the Fascist regime, P. Lanfranchi, 'Bologna, the team that shook the world', *The International Journal of the History of Sport* 8, 1991,3 pp.336-346. The stadia were named after Fascist heroes like Berta in Florence, or Mussolini himself in Turin and were never conceived, like the British stadium, just for football. The pluri-sportive use was a central element. A recent history of Italian football came to the same conclusions. A. Papa, G. Panico, *Storia sociale del calcio in Italia*, Bologna, le Mulino, 1993.

24 For a discussion of the 'Juve style', see Christian Bromberger, Alain Hayot and Jean-Marc Mariottini, 'Allez l'OM! La Passion pour le football a Marseille et a Tourin', *Terrain*, 8. 1987, pp.8-41; Ch. Bromberger, 'L'Olympique de Marseille, la Juve et le Torino. Variations ethnologiques sur l'engouement popularie pour les clubs et les matchs de football' *L'esprit*, 'Le Nouvel age du sport', cit., p.174-195. The Juve style is symbolised by three 'Ss': simplicity, seriousness, and sobriety'.

25 Pierre Milza, cit. see footnote 3 above.

26 We subscribe to the point of the image of the sport as the supreme eulogy of the ordinary man, A. Ehrenberg, 'L'etoffe du heros', *Cahiers internationaux de sociologie*, 20 September 1988. Id. *le culte de la performance*, Paris Calmenn-levy, 1991.

27 The press gave a lot of prominence to his affirmation that: "Yes, I am a southerner".

28 Such is the title of a conclusive chapter in his excellent book Robert Ciuni, *Il pollane di Napoli*, Shakespeare and Company, Milano, 1985 pp.75-91.

29 Christien Bromberger, 'Ciuccio e fuochi artificio. L'immaginario di Napoli attraverso il suo football', *Micromega*, 4, 1990, pp.171-181.

30 In a poll directed by Roberto Moscati and Alessandro Dal Lago among the A.C. Milan fans, one of the questions asked was: Which soccer player do you hate the most? The almost unanimous answer was Diego Armando Maradona. In response to the follow-up question of 'why', those inter-viewed gave sixty different answers. Maradona and the Naples team had generated a tremendous amount of animosity in the Lombard capital. op.cit.: 52.

31 Nine of the twenty-two Argentinian or German players were members of Italian teams. If one adds the fact that Italian teams won five out of the six international championships at stake during the last two years, it seemed reasonable to think (at least for the Italian press) that Italy was on the point of attaining in soccer the hegemonic power that was comparable to that of the United States in sports such as basketball and baseball.

9 Japan and the World Cup: Asia's first World Cup Final hosts?

John Horne and David Jary

Introduction

On Thursday 28th October 1993 the final matches of the Second Qualifying Round for the World Cup Finals of the Asian Football Confederation were being played in Doha, Qatar. With 30 seconds remaining Japan were leading Iraq 2 goals to 1 and seemed to have secured a place at the 1994 Finals of the World Cup. Then, from a corner kick, the captain of the Iraqi team headed an equalising goal, which sent Saudi Arabia and Japan's closest, rivals South Korea, through to the US Finals instead.

For the Japanese team, and over 1,000 of their supporters who had accompanied them to the Gulf, there was a sense of disbelief. For those millions of Japanese watching at home — in what, remarkably, amounted to the fifth largest television sport audience ever in Japan — the feeling of anti-climax was profound. Despite failing to qualify, however, the role of hosting the finals in the Asian continent for the first time may well be the compensation that Japan eventually receives.

In this chapter we attempt to look at Asian soccer, and the prospects for soccer in Japan in particular, in as objective light as possible. What is the reality behind the sudden interest in soccer in Japan? Will Japan become the dominant footballing nation in Asia, and then the world?

It has been very easy to be dismissive about Asian football, and Japanese ambitions for soccer in particular. One, characteristically British, soccer journalist told us that the Asian Cup (which Japan won in 1992) has about as much significance as the minor-league Freight Rover Trophy in England. The J-League — Japan's first full-time professional soccer league

launched in May 1993 — will in all probability be given the same treatment. Alternatively it might be dismissed as another opportunistic
commercial ploy to create more Yen out of the burgeoning leisure industry,
either directly or indirectly through television deals, franchises, and
associated merchandised spin-offs which the Japanese, with too much
money in their pockets, are gullible enough to buy. Some may even see it as
a more sinister attempt to control the hearts and minds of the young
generations of Japanese whose prospects for life-time job security and ever-
increasing affluence may just be about to collapse as Japan's "bubble
economy" bursts. Worst of all, for football purists, the quality of Japanese
soccer is thought likely to be too drilled and imitative, without much flair
or real hope of success on the global football stage.

Certainly the number one sport in Japan, baseball, has always been on
the receiving end of negative comparisons by US commentators. So
perhaps it is only to be expected that the reaction in England, the birthplace
of soccer, would be equally dismissive.

In writing about Asia, the Orient, and perhaps especially Asian sport,
there are two interrelated distortions to guard against: 'eurocentricism' and
'orientalism'. Most histories and accounts of sport are riven with Western
and, especially in the case of soccer, eurocentric bias. In American accounts
of baseball in Japan, for example, there is an arrogance, often masked as
cultural relativism, about the supremacy of the *real* game (Maitland, 1991;
Whiting, 1977). In the case of soccer, a predictable number of assumptions
have filtered into recent accounts of the development of the game in Japan.
BBC sports reporter Ray Stubbs introduced a profile of the former England
soccer striker Gary Lineker on his new life in Japan, broadcast before the
1993 FA Cup Final, with the line, 'From the serene to the ridiculous' (BBC1
TV, 15 May 1993, 1.10pm).

Japan's recent investment in soccer has been interpreted by some as an
imitation of the USA in the wake of the latter's success in securing the
World Cup Finals in 1994. Just as in the US case in the 1970s, Japan is seen
as relying upon the importation of ageing stars from South America and
Europe to generate interest in the game. In time, it is suggested, enthusiasm
will fade out in the same way as interest in the USA has in the past. Even
after the staging of the World Cup Finals in 1994, few people think that the
professional game will take off in the United States. Reasons offered for

soccer's likely demise in the US range from the absence of a solid working class base outside the hispanic population centres, to the nature of the game in a culture which wants an outright winner at the end of 90 minutes. But should the Japanese experience be judged by the US approach to soccer? Such assumptions reflect an ethnocentric western bias, embracing the notion that Japan is still somehow under American occupation, with its sports forms held securely within an American sphere of influence.

Our consideration of the planning involved in the launch of the first full professional soccer league in Japan in May 1993 — the J-League — will reveal a different picture, and suggest that soccer in Japan may be just about to take off in a way that will confound the footballing pundits as much as the post-war success of the Japanese economy at first puzzled some financial analysts.

Any consideration of sport in Japan, and the East in general, also has to overcome the bias of 'orientalism' (Said, 1978). Here the attempt to understand cultural activities in Asian societies is framed by sets of entirely speculative assumptions about their 'uniqueness' — especially the distinctiveness of the 'Oriental mind' as opposed to the 'Occidental mind'. This is something which some Japanese writers have also perpetuated themselves. In the rest of this chapter we will attempt to avoid such a bias as we consider soccer in Asia, modern sport in Japan, and the prospects for soccer in Japan. Among the questions which will be addressed are the relative permeability of national cultural boundaries, including the extent of 'Americanisation' and the openness to processes of 'globalisation' evident in Japanese sports forms.

Soccer in Asia

African and Asian membership of FIFA in its own right has grown in the post-1945 period. In the 1950s FIFA created the zones for football confederations which have helped less well-developed footballing nations establish their international profile. Additionally João Havelange's succession as FIFA President in 1974 was partly enabled through the support he received from Asian and African representatives who felt his election would improve their position on the game's international body. A significant part of the attraction is that the football World Cup is on a par with the Olympic Games as a major global sports festival. The estimated worldwide audience for the final in recent years has reached hundreds of millions. Yet the World Cup Finals have most often been played *without* representatives from the two continents that contain the majority of the world's population — Africa and Asia.

It is worth considering then the numerous constraints on the successful development of Asian football in world cup soccer and soccer in general. Three chief obstacles stand out — the vast distances and organizational problems involved in arranging sport across Asia; the relative economic underdevelopment in many cases and also the political instability of the area; and the existence of other, indigenous and imported, sports traditions.

Asia is an enormous continent and as a result the Asian Football Confederation (AFC) is huge. It comprises not only the South-East Asian countries — China, Taiwan, North and South Korea, Singapore, Hong Kong, and Japan — but also the Gulf States (Saudi Arabia, Iran, Iraq), and smaller countries such as Malaysia, Indonesia, and the Phillipines. As Guy Oliver (1992: 817-818) states, "Riyadh and Seoul are as far apart as Madrid and Rio de Janeiro". Apart from the logistical problems this presents, the AFC has also been the most overtly political, or at least most affected by political forces, of the regional football confederations. Israel was originally included in the AFC, until it was expelled because of the rift with the Arab nations which joined the AFC in the 1970s. Israel has subsequently found a home in Europe (just as in the Eurovision Song Contest!). Relationships between the People's Republic of China and Taiwan have created another major crisis for the confederation. Taiwan were expelled, but have been allowed to return. The AFC has also had to juggle relations between the "two Koreas", the communist North — heroic conquerors of Italy in the 1966 World Cup held in England — and the rapidly industrializing South — venue of the 1988 Olympic Games.

Membership of FIFA fluctuates, but of the 168 or so members in 1993, 92 were in the African, Oceania and Asian zones (*World Soccer*, July 1993: 56-7). These 92 members only have at most six places in the final tournament. Thus a major impediment to Asian involvement in the World Cup has been the large number of elimination games required in order to qualify. With relatively few places for the large number of countries involved, the barriers to entry to the World Cup Finals are much higher for nations outside Europe or the Americas. Winners of the Asian zone have often had to play off against a team from Oceania, or in the case of Israel in 1958, Wales. On that occasion the Welsh won and were able to join the other British Football associations at the World Cup Finals for the first and only time.

One obvious way of circumventing the problem of qualification would be for an African or Asian country to host the final championship tournament. Guy Oliver suggests that it is a question of when, rather than whether, the World Cup will be staged in an African or Asian country. It is unquestionably the case now that the race is on between Japan and the two Koreas to stage the first Asian World Cup Finals, possibly in 2002. South Korea successfully bid to host the 1988 Olympic Games in Seoul against a rival bid from Nagoya, Japan's fourth largest city. Rivalry between Japan and Korea is an additional source of tension in the region. Before 1994 both Koreas had made one World Cup finals appearance each. 1966 was the year that North Korea took the honours in England — losing to Portugal 5-3 in one of the most memorable world cup quarter-final matches, whilst South Korea's only finals appearance was even earlier (1954 in Switzerland). The South Koreans finished bottom in their group which included the eventual champions (West Germany) and the runners-up (Hungary).

Another factor inhibiting the development of a strong footballing tradition in Asia is "the lack of a well-founded club structure in the majority of countries" (Oliver, 1992: 817-818). In part this is because of the existence of other, indigenous and imported, sports traditions which have often been inhospitable to soccer — most notably the popularity of baseball where the US influence has been greatest, and in former British colonies where 'elite colonisers' have influenced the spread of the 'elite' team games of cricket, hockey, and rugby football. With other sports occupying the market niches that might have become occupied by soccer — until recently — the game has not been organised into fully professional leagues. Hong Kong, with its strong links with Great Britain, retains the longest lasting professional soccer league. In recent years the club sides dominant in the Asian Champion Teams' Cup have been from Japan or Saudi Arabia, where facilities and experienced coaching staff could be afforded. South Korea launched a professional 'superleague' in 1983, attaching teams to some of the country's biggest industrial companies. This is the route that Japan has taken with the launch of the J-League in May 1993.

Understanding sport in Japan

Although men are expected to control their emotions and hide sadness, it is occasionally all right for a man to cry .... If you see a Japanese in floods of tears, it does not necessarily mean that he or she is sad. It can be a sign of great happiness, as when one's home team has won at baseball. This form of tears is called *ureshinaki* ('happy crying'). (*Living Japanese Style,* Japan Travel Bureau 1992: 170).

> Although the Japanese work hard, they play hard too... For most people...the problem with leisure activities is finding both the time and the space to make them possible. (*Japanese: Language and People,* BBC Books, 1991 192).

The ideology of 'orientalism' casts a long shadow over our understanding of Japan and Japanese culture. There is a danger that everything will appear strange, exotic, and inscrutable. The two quotations above remind us that the Japanese, in their day-to-day lives, are faced with dilemmas and behave in ways, that are actually quite familiar to us in the West. That Japanese society strikes some visitors as heavily underpinned by hier-archical relationships, for example, can actually be related to the positive encouragement given to reforming Meiji statesmen in the 1880s by the English sociologist, Herbert Spencer (Benedict, 1992: 80-81).

On the other hand it would be unwise to go completely to the other extreme and say that everything is the same as in the West, now that Japan has become 'westernized' in terms of the lifestyles and aspirations of its people. The truth is that Japan, like other countries, has its own very specific pattern of development, or 'modernization'. This in turn is reflected in its culture and sport. As Brian Moeran (1991: 200) notes, "a modern, non-native sport is not necessarily practised in Japan in the same way as in its country of origin".

Japan has often been remarked upon by western observers for its "exceptional" status — as a hybrid society — combining elements of pre-modern and advanced industrial society. Yet it experienced a period of planned social isolation for over 260 years during the Tokugawa period (1603–1867). The Meiji Reforms begun in 1867 saw a dramatic modernization programme, including the introduction and subsequent growth of modern sports and leisure activities. Contemporary Japanese leisure is marked by a combination of traditional and modern or 'native' and 'non-native' activities. Since 1945 skiing, golf and American football have been imported from the West; mahjong was borrowed from China centuries ago; whilst sumo and judo are native to Japan.

Skiing has come to be very popular in the winter months — Japan has already hosted the Winter Olympic Games once and Nagano in the Japanese 'Alps' is host of the 1998 event. Golf retains its tremendous popularity despite a chronic lack of space and the enormous costs of club membership . Golf swings can be seen being practised in two-tier driving ranges as well as with rolled-up newspapers on station platforms!

As in most advanced industrial countries sporting events are heavily sponsored by large corporations: motor companies finance car racing teams; securities firms contribute to tennis tournaments; airline companies donate to marathon races. Still, sumo wrestling and baseball remain the two most popular spectator sports in Japan. Sumo tournaments occur every six weeks or so. They are reported extensively in newspapers and magazines and are broadcast on television and radio. The baseball season opens in the Spring and there are games almost every day until the end of the season in winter.

Baseball, which was first introduced to Japan in the late nineteenth century, has been organised into professional leagues since 1936. Since the late 1950s there have been two professional leagues, the Central League and the Pacific League, each with six teams in them. Most of the teams are named after the main Japanese companies which sponsor them, usually with the addition of a nickname, often an English-derived name of an animal. Hence the Swallows, Dragons, Tigers, Whales and Carp play in the Central League, whilst the Lions, Hawks, Buffaloes and Orix, play in the Pacific League. In 1991 the average gate for each game ranged from 52,000 for the Yomiuri Giants (Tokyo) to 16,000 for Lotte (sponsored by the Korean based confectionary company of the same name).

Japanese baseball, as with soccer and other modern sports, now has a vocabulary that has been described as "Japlish" — many of the words and phrases used to describe the tactics, rules, and basic organization of the game are Japanese renderings of English words. During the 1930s many of the English words were replaced by Japanese equivalents, but since 1945 they have returned. Compared with US baseball there are noticeable differences: the size of grounds, which are much smaller; the quality and style of play, which even sympathetic observers consider to be on a par with the Minor Leagues (Maitland, 1991: 8); and, perhaps most importantly, the psychology of the game.

The mid-summer High School baseball competition is seen as *"the* baseball event in Japan"(Maitland, 1991). It provides a good illustration of the Japanese approach to the "all-American game", and sport in general.

The pursuit of apparently difficult 'accomplishments' is a fundamental aspect of Japanese culture, according to social anthropologists. Learning is based largely on imitation and repetition; perfection is achieved through conforming to expectations. Perseverance and suffering are integral to the process and only after many years could one contemplate introducing any originality. Through this participants can develop *seishin* ('strength of spirit'). The application of devotion, dedication and perseverance to whatever is being undertaken can lift it from the mundane to the realm of art (Hendry, 1987: 157ff). The mass media report the High School baseball games as psychological struggles between the *pitcha* ('pitcher') and the *batta* ('batter'). The focus is upon each player's *shinbo* ('perseverance'), *gaman* ('endurance'), *gattsu* ('guts') and especially *seishin*, qualities which are rated amongst the highest Japanese virtues. In this way baseball comes to epitomise being Japanese. Whilst team games are viewed in individualist ways, the 'true' Japanese athlete submerges individuality into 'selflessness' — a Zen-like state of 'no mind'. Hence participation in individualistic sports (such as sumo, karate and kendo) may reinforce the group-oriented social ideology (Moeran, 1991).

In contemporary Japan the tension between traditional conceptions of 'groupness' and western notions of 'self' may be part of the explanation for the relative lack of success in international sport and soccer in particular. But it would be falling into the trap of 'orientalism' to leave it there. Mental and psychological processes are important, but if we are trying to account for the similarities and differences between nations in their sporting patterns we also have to take account of the international and national circumstances that created the conditions in which individual choices for sports are made (Stokvis, 1989: 23).

The development of soccer in Japan

According to Ruud Stokvis (1989) if we want to explain the varieties and differing amounts of sports participation in any one society we need to consider changes in the world system within which the society exists, as well as changes in the socio-economic and class structure of the society concerned. In addition religious beliefs, age, gender and 'race' relations will affect the development of, and patterns of participation in, sports.

Since the latter half of the nineteenth century, when the diffusion of modern sport began, competition for dominance amongst the industrial core countries has shaped the process. Britain/England was predominant, alongside Germany, in the nineteenth century and early twentieth century. During the 1920s the USA and the USSR emerged as dominant world powers. However, in sport English dominance continued, except in the USA, US colonies and the Pacific region, including Japan. So, although it is known that a form of *kemari*, a game borrowed from China, and in some ways remarkably similar to soccer, was played in Japan from the 2nd to 19th century, it is only in the post-1945 period, and especially since the 1960s, that soccer's popularity has soared.

Whilst in 1991 soccer ranked as 22nd in terms of sports participation by the total population, it was second in popularity to baseball amongst the 15-19 year olds (Asahi Shimbun, 1992: 65 and 66). Soccer has enjoyed greater involvement and more popularity than baseball in high schools for the past five years. Since it is arguably the schools that are the most important institutions for the growth of broad-based participation and interest in sport, these are healthy signs. In what is still considered by many as a strikingly patriarchal society, even Japanese women's soccer has been quite successful recently. There is an organized national women's competition and at the FIFA World Cup for Women Japan qualified for the finals held in China in 1991 with 27 goals for and only 1 against. In the same group as the eventual winners, USA, they failed to win a match at the finals, but again the seeds of interest are apparent. A survey conducted in December 1992 found 31.4% of respondents wanting to attend a J-League game at a stadium, compared with 33.5% for baseball. Soccer was most appealing to children and young adults.

The men's game did not get properly underway until the formation of the first Japanese amateur soccer league in 1965. Composed of company teams, it produced players such as Sugiyama (Ryuichi) of Mitsubishi and Kamamoto (Kunishige) of Yanmah, who helped fuel interest in the sport through their success in Mexico in 1968 when the Japanese Olympic team gained a third place bronze medal. In the 1970s and 1980s, whilst a few solitary individuals played in professional leagues in Europe and elsewhere, the promise of the Olympic Games achievement was not maintained. Soccer in Japan did not take off again until the end of the 1980s when three club sides played in the Finals of the Asian Champion Teams' Cup — two of them emerging as winners (Furukawa in 1986 and Yomiuri in 1987).

In 1992 whilst the national side won the Asian Cup, amateur teams like Mitsubishi Motor, Furukawa Electric and Toyota Jidosha were lucky to attract 2,000 spectators. But in 1993 full-time professional soccer in the shape of the J-League was launched with a massive injection of capital (possibly totalling £20 billion) and a large marketing campaign. Reborn as Urawa Red Diamonds, JEF United and Grampus Eight, each with a mascot, team song and colours, these three teams, along with seven others, were expected to attract between 15,000 and 30,000 fans twice a week. This they did in the first half of the 1993 competition, yet each club was still expecting to lose one billion Yen (approximately £6 million) each year for at least the first five years. The bid to host the 2002 World Cup is costing £40 million alone. In addition, different local government authorities are involved in projects to build new soccer stadia by the year 2000 or before, with minimum capacities of 40,000. In Yokohama, the second largest city in Japan, adjacent to Tokyo, the Marinos and AS Flugels will share the largest one, to be completed by 1997 at a cost of £375 million. Cynics may still say that even if the bid is not successful a lot of money may be made by television stations, sports outfitters, advertising agencies, magazine companies, stadium builders and concrete suppliers (Popham, 1993: 28). At the outset McDonalds was offering J-League gifts, and telephone cards with soccer emblems are all the rage. Soccer "boutiques" sprang up in many of the large department stores with a wide range of J-League endorsed products. One estimate by a subsidiary of the giant Nippon Life insurance company has predicted that soccer may spawn business worth 110 billion Yen (£650 million) in its first year. Marketing specialists in Japan, a true 'consumer culture', are hoping that Japanese youth will start to favour soccer shirts as fashion items ahead of the traditional baseball uniforms.

Soccer in contemporary Japan

On its launch, most of the J-League teams were located in the large population centres stretching out from Chiba Prefecture in the east to Hiroshima
in the west. Table 1 shows how the J-League lined up in May 1993.

Table 1:   The J-League line-up 1993

Club	Main Sponsors	City	Population
Verdy	Yomiuri, Hihon (press, TV)	Kawasaki	1,153,000
Marinos	Nissan (motors)	Yokohama	3,211,000
Antlers	Sumimoto Metal, Kashima	Kashima	45,000
JEF United	JR East (rail) Furukawa Electric	Ichihara, Chiba	not available
Red Diamonds	Mitsubishi	Urawa	417,000
Sanfrecce	Mazda (motors) Hiroshima	Hiroshima	1,062,000
Gamba	Matsushita Electric ("Panasonic")	Osaka	2,512,000
AS Flugels	All Nippon Airways (ANA)	Yokohama	3,211,00
	Sato Kogyo	Kyushu Island (West Japan)	not available
Shimizu S-Pulse	Shizuoka (TV)	Shimizu	240,000
Grampus Eight	Toyota, Tokai Bank	Nagoya	2,098,000

Sources: *World Soccer*, May 1993, pp. 4-5;
           Asahi Shimbun, (1992) *Japan Almanac 1993*, Asahi Shimbun, Tokyo, p. 36.

The ten teams in the J-League in 1993 were formed out of teams which
competed in the old Japan Soccer League (JSL). The JSL is now the JFL
(Japan Football League) which has two divisions (J1 and J2), each consisting of 10 teams each (see Table 2 overleaf). These lower divisions involve
some semi-professional company teams that applied to join the J-League,
such as Yamaha, Hitachi and Fujita, whose technical skill is not much
different from that of the J-League teams. Alongside motor cycle, musical
instrument, electrical goods and construction concerns, the teams in J1
and J2 include computer companies (Fujitsu), pharmaceuticals (Otsuka;
Tanabe), metal (Toho Titanium; NKK; Seitetsu), telecommunications (NTT)

171

and oil and petrochemicals (Cosmo). It was planned to expand the J-League to 16 or 18 teams over the next ten years and to eventually allow relegation and promotion between the J-League and J1.

Table 2: Professional and semi-professional soccer in Japan

| J-League Clubs: | Japan Football League (JFL): | |
	J1	J2
Verdy	Kyoto Shikou	Osaka Gas
Marinos	Chyuo Bohan	NTT Kanto
Antlers	Yanma	Toho Titanium
JEF United	Fujita	NKK
JRed Diamonds	Tokyo Gas	Tanabe Seiyaku
SanFrecce	Yahama Hatsudoki	Kohu
Gamba	Fujitsu	Honda
AS Flugels	Hitachi	Cosmo Sekiyu
Shimizu S-Pulze	Otsuka Seiyaku	Seino Unyu
Grampus Eight	Toshiba	Kawasaki
Seitetsu		
Plus: Regional League; Prefecture Lecture		

Source: Adapted from *J-League Magazine*, Tokyo (1993): 125.

So is the dream of sending the national team to the World Cup Finals, let alone hosting them in Japan, purely an aspiration to accomplish the impossible in the midst of great adversity — an 'accomplishment' on a grand scale? Rather than impossible, it might be more accurate to consider Japan's challenge as highly likely to succeed. Japan first entered the World Cup in 1950 but has never reached further than the third round of the qualifying tournament (in 1986). In 1992 the national team won the Dynasty (East Asia) Trophy and the All-Asia Cup. They entered the second round of the Asian Football Confederation elimination group for the 1994 World Cup Finals as winners of their first round qualifying group with a 28-2 goal aggregate. Expectations were high, and the 2-2 draw which pushed them into third place, a non-qualifying position, could understandably be seen as devastating. It is still likely, however that the Japanese will rebound from this setback and redouble their efforts to secure the first Asian based World Cup Finals.

172

Given the description above of the Japanese approach to baseball, their football might be expected to be well drilled, yet without flair. Maybe this was so in the past, but according to David Miller, reporting in *The Times*, (17 May 1993), the first day 2-1 defeat of Yomiuri Verdy by Yokahama Marinos "spectacularly demonstrated the potential of the best of Japanese football. Strange to say, the Japanese, so programmed in business, on the football field have the fluidity of Brazil".

The first match, in which the English star Garry Lineker's team Grampus Eight were beaten 5-0 by Kashima Antlers, was a reminder that soccer is a team game not merely dependent upon foreign imports.

Kashima were the potential underdogs of the J-League. Kashima is a small town (by Japanese standards) of 45,000 people located on the coast 60 miles north-east of Tokyo. Ibaraki Prefecture, the local authority in which the town resides, alongside the biggest local employer, Sumimoto Metal, spent more than $70 million to bring back the Brazilian, Zico, world footballer of the year in 1983, from retirement and were also building a new stadium. Despite only one appearance by Zico, Kashima's reward was to become the champions at the halfway stage of the J. League season.

The politics of popular culture as expressed in soccer

The tension between exploitation and cultural expression lies at the heart of popular culture. Is soccer in Japan (and elsewhere) being used as a form of social control? It can be seen in this light (Vinnai, 1973). Writing in *The Times*, David Miller (13 May 1993) also identified this possibility in the formation of the J. League in Japan:

> The intention is for club football to do for this country what the likes of Aston Villa, Preston North End, Blackburn Rovers and West Bromwich Albion did for England at the end of the 19th century: create regional identities that will focus local people's energy and affections, radically alter the traditional Japanese dominance of professional sport by the corporate business world, and decrease population migration towards Tokyo.

Such a vision of deliberate social planning through the establishment of soccer in Japan is partly supported by the absence of a team based in the capital Tokyo. In Kashima local government officials justify the £71 million investment in the Antlers with the argument that "Young people are leaving, so we are building this stadium as a way to revive the area" (cited in *The Japan Times*, 7 April, 1993).

True, the J-League was a deliberate plan to secure a basis for soccer in Japan and in the medium term to secure the World Cup in 2002. But, we might ask, why not? Might it also be seen as a potential space for the creation of local 'belongingness' and class and group solidarity (Mason, 1980; Tomlinson, 1986)? The support is there. Baseball is still most popular, but soccer could become popular too. American influence is tolerated, but not so welcome anymore. Requiring the teams to be independent companies (and not just company teams) and requiring them to limit the number of foreign players in a club to five (and on the field of play to three, at any one time), seems to support the seed-bed idea behind the League. Without the opportunity to play in such a competitive atmosphere, the home-grown talent could not hope to develop further. Most of the matches were televised live by local TV networks. 18 out of the first 90 matches were also screened live on nationwide television. Unlike the coverage of baseball where transmissions of *naitas* (night games) which exceed a specified time are often cut short, soccer fits well into television schedules. There is also the example of corporate and local authority partnerships in producing the stadia and the teams: the Antlers are fully supported by the local city (Kashima). Would not such partnerships be welcomed in Britain?

The political uses of soccer in relation to the World Cup

Why does Japan want the World Cup in 2002? Four factors are important: finace; regional pride; intra-regional competition; and internal consumtion strategies.

First, in terms of television audiences, after the Olympics, World Cup football is the second biggest global sports event. It is the largest team game festival without a doubt and attracts a massive worldwide audience. If baseball has the World Series, the football World Cup is undoubtedly the world *soap opera*; '*Dallas* with balls' as O'Connor and Boyle (1993) suggested recently. The investment promised for the game may be difficult to sustain without a project like the hosting of the World Cup Finals to sustain ambitions.

Second, FIFA has been interested in locating the finals in Asia or Africa for some time. The South (Africa) is too unstable and relatively impoverished, even if the quality of football has up to now been perceived as more developed than that in the AFC. The 1988 Seoul Olympics demonstrated what could be accomplished in the South-east Asian area. Japanese soccer may have come good at exactly the right time — in terms of national success and local interest.

Third, the Koreans (the South in conjunction with the North) may also be putting in a bid to host the 2002 World Cup Finals, especially in the wake of the South's success in qualifying for the 1994 Finals. This would be consistent with the longstanding love/hate relationship between Korea and Japan. With many deep-seated conflicts — the Japanese occupation of Korea from 1910-1945 being just one of them — still within living memory to fuel competition for such events as well as economic success, Asian countries as major players in soccer could be seen as merely another chapter in the continuing story of the 'de-centering' of the West.

Fourth, underlying all of this, and linking economics with culture, there is also the fact that at the end of its long boom the Japanese economy is deeply troubled, needing to find new ways of sustaining property and land values and the general impetus of the economy (McCormack, 1991), while at the same time also finding new bases of social integration. With the relative decline of the work ethic and the need to create new forms of consumption also associated with the above tendencies, the promotion of new patterns of sport and leisure involvement is an obvious step. Recent national and corporate planning in Japan has explicitly targetted sport and leisure as a remedy for both economic and cultural ills. Given its world stature, soccer is obviously a vital ingredient in this strategy. The goal of hosting the World Cup is a part of this process.

Globalization, national identity and sport

A number of recent scholars (Maguire,1990; Wagner, 1990; Klein, and McKay & Miller, 1991; Kidd, 1991 and Guttmann, 1991; and also see Houlihan, 1994) have considered the transformations of sport and society that are linked to the *globalization* of world social relations. What is happening to sport in the context of globalization? What can we learn about globalization from this case study of soccer in Asia and Japan in particular?

"Globalization" according to Anthony Giddens (1989: 727) is best understood as:

The development of social and economic relationships stretching world-wide. In current times, many aspects of people's lives are influenced by organizations and social networks located thousands of miles away from the societies in which they live. A key aspect of the study of globalization is the emergence of a *world system* — that is to say, for some purposes we have to regard the world as forming a single social order.

Globalization is the key concept in attempts to move beyond a debate between 'modernisation theory' and 'dependency theory' in explanations of global development. It mainly developed in response to the growth of major trends and phenomena which transcend national borders — economic, political, social and environmental. The 'new nations' are no longer new, the term 'Third World' is no longer accurate, and the 'cold war' is over.

Japan has often been presented as a "special case", as presenting some puzzlingly different patterns of development and culture from the 'Western' model.[1] In the case of soccer, and perhaps modern sport, globalization is best understood not as a new phenomenon. Rather it is because the scope and pace of global integration has quickened dramatically since the 1970s that globalization appears a more useful way of understanding the contemporary social world. There are three current arguments about the impact of globalization on cultural and national identity (Hall, 1992: 300): first, that national identities are being *eroded* as a result of the growth of cultural homogenization and the 'global post-modern'; second, that national and other 'local' or particularistic identities are being *strengthened* by the resistance to globalization; and finally that national identities are declining but *new* identities of hybridity are taking their place.

Talk about the erosion of national identities links to older arguments about cultural imperialism and "Americanization". Yet, undoubtedly, cultural homogenisation is too simplistic and exaggerated a picture of developments. Hall (ibid: 306) notes three qualifications to this view. First, globalization can go hand in hand with a strengthening of local identities, though this is still within the logic of time-space compression. Second, globalization is an uneven process and has its own 'power-geometry', that is, different social groups and individuals enjoy very distinct relationships to the effects of time-space compression. Third, globalization retains some aspects of Western global domination, but cultural identities everywhere are being relativized by the impact of time-space compression.

In Japan, in the late 1980s, attempts to strengthen local and national identities could be seen in the pronouncements of leading Japanese politicians that veered toward biological explanations for Japanese economic success. The 1980s also saw a growth in the number of calls to rearm the Japanese army and a reawakening of interest in traditional Japanese cultural activities including those associated with *bushido* ('the way of the samurai'). A sometimes manifest, and often latent, ethnic absolutism in Japan could be seen as an attempt to sustain "an identity that coheres, is unified and filters out threats in social experience" (Sennett, 1971: 15).

On the other hand, one result of globalization, in terms of identity formation in North America and Britain, as well as in Japan, has arguably been a "proliferation of new identity-positions together with a degree of polarization amongst and between them" (Hall, 1992: 306). Hence the second and third possible consequences of globalization are that there might be a strengthening of local identities as well as the production of new identities. There is evidence of this third possible consequence of globalization — the creation of new identities. In Japan in the 1980s the word *shinjinrui* was coined to describe a 'new generation' of young people involved in novel cultural and artistic activities. The word may no longer be in vogue in Japan, but the existence there of large numbers of youth who are "as familiar with hamburgers as *onigiri* (rice balls), Guns n' Roses as *ikebana* (flower arranging), and folding a paper packet of cocaine or heroin as folding an *origami* crane" (*The Face*, April, 1993: 63) cannot be denied. Just as in British society where it has been argued that both Afro-Caribbean and Asian communities are often "treated as 'the same' (i.e. non-white, 'other') by the dominant culture" (Hall, 1992: 308), the 'new people' in Japan are considered as "outsiders". Whilst some of these will undoubtedly become in time part of the establishment, others will remain outside the mainstream.

Conclusions — will soccer 'take-off' in Japan and will Japan host the 2002 World Cup?

Whether by an accommodation with traditional Japanese culture or by an association with the creation of new personal and national identities, will the recent promotion of Japanese soccer be successful? It is obviously impossible to give a definitive answer. However, we believe that there are several strong influences at work which may help professional soccer to succeed in Japan:

First, the relative decline of Japan's previous manufacturing base and the necessity to create a new economic impetus in the service economy including new leisure industries, not least those activities which can be large users of land and for construction, helping to sustain speculative land and property values as well as promote regional development (McCormack, 1991);

Second, an associated questioning of the 'work ethic' in Japan and the search for new stimuli in a leisure oriented consumer culture;

Third, a history of state intervention in the promotion of national adjustment to new economic conditions;

Fourth, the fact, as Robertson (1987) suggests, that Japan has been such a 'systematic selector of ideas for import' and has the capacity to assimilate, and at the same time 'Japanize', foreign sports, for example, golf and baseball — the syncretic factor;

Fifth, a suggested cultural preference for team games within Japan, which are seen as character-building as well as socially integrative (Moeran, 1991);

Sixth, high rates of participation in sports of many kinds in Japan, and a rapid growth in rates of participation in soccer in particular in recent years, for women as well as men (Saeki, 1989);

Seventh, a history of previous successful utilisation of sports and major sporting events in the promotion of cultural and national integration, for example, the introduction of Judo in 1880, the Tokyo Olympics, of 1964, and the forthcoming Winter Olympics in 1998.

If the staging of the World Cup in the United States proves effective in relaunching the professional game there this too is likely to add impetus to professional football in Japan, which has, at least since 1945, closely followed US patterns of sports development. Given that Japanese sport has hitherto operated very much within the American sphere of influence, and given also that US soccer has failed to establish itself as a major spectator sport, it will serve to underline the suggestions we are making about the prospects for Japanese soccer if, in conclusion, we draw a series of general comparisons between Japan and the United States. As summarised in Table 3, while soccer has established itself as a mass participation sport in the US and the same is true of Japan, consideration of a number of further key differences between the two countries, however, suggests that attempts to establish Japanese soccer start with a number of clear advantages compared with the US (cf. Sugden in this volume).

Table 3: Prospects for 'take-off' of soccer in Japan as a mass spectator sport — A comparison of the USA and Japan

	USA	JAPAN
1. Soccer a mass participation sport	Yes	Yes
2. Degree of entrenchment of existing spectator team sports	High - deterrent to entry of 'new' sports	Moderate - opportunity for entry of new sports
3. Extension of geographical territory	Long distances between main centres, creating difficulties for the establishment of a national league	Smaller territory and geographical concentration of main centres
4. Role of sport in defining national identity	Identity defined primarily in terms of distinctively 'American' sports	Identity defined in part through distinctive sports, but 'syncretic' cultural tradition, including adoption of foreign sports with potential for enhanced Japanese sports identity in world terms
5. Planned use of sport in 'social engineering'	Low	High - history of planned utilisation of sport for national integration
6. Economic factors currently favouring promotion of soccer in Japan	Hosting 1994 World Cup Finals comparatively inexpensive; and accessible nature of soccer as a cultural activity	Economic downturn and declining emphasis on 'work ethic' and both economic and social demand for expanded leisure. The goal of obtaining the 2002 World Cup part of wider strategy for leisure

Maybe US professional soccer will again fail to take-off, despite the stimulus of hosting the World Cup. Maybe professional soccer in Japan will not succeed either, despite the factors suggested as potentially in its favour. But Asia *is* a preferred site for a future World Cup tournament, and Japan is attractive as a host on the basis of its economic capacity and relative political stability. Even if soccer in the US does not move forward from the World Cup, though, our guess would be that the Japanese initative may well succeed; that Japanese professional soccer has more than a 'sporting chance' of prospering, and that Japan *will* host the World Cup in 2002.

Acknowledgements

Many thanks to Hisao Nojima, Masayoshi Seino, Takayuki Yamashita and Shin Kawaguchi for help with obtaining and translating the material upon which much of this is based.

Note

[1] The exceptional nature of Japanese development — combining aspects of ultra-modernity with apparently pre-modern social relations and cultural traditions — once puzzled sociologists expecting to find 'convergence' with other industrial societies or simple 'modernization' along western lines. Fortunately good sociological practice is now increasingly defined as combining the "sociological imagination" with historical and comparative analysis.

As highlighted recently by Robertson (1987) the long recognised Japanese capacity for a 'syncretic' response to foreign belief systems and cultural forms is a particularly significant example of the retention of complexity and diversity within the globalization process. Robertson suggests that there are central "features of Japanese life which have historically, and are currently, facilitating a carefully calibrated rhythm with respect to external involvement" (p. 37).

It is in such terms that the new sociological interest in place, space and localities helps make better sense of the Orient as well as the Occident. The new spatially aware sociologist insists on studying the specificities of particular places *and* the broader forces which shape and *are shaped* by particular local circumstances and histories. Hence capitalism is shaped by, and thus varies between, different social structures in different places. The existence of different capital*isms* and moder*nities* has effectively been recognised.

References

Asahi Shimbun (1992), *Japan Almanac, 1993*, Tokyo: Asahi Shimbun Publishing Company.

Benedict, R. (1992),*The Chrysanthemum and the Sword* [1946], Tokyo: Charles E. Tuttle Company.

The Face, (1993), 'Japan's New Generation', No. 55, April 1993.

Giddens, A. (1989), *Sociology*, Cambridge: Polity Press.

Guttmann, A. (1991), 'Sports Diffusion: A Response to Maguire and the Americanization Commentaries', in *Sociology of Sport Journal* , Volume 8, Number 2: pp. 185-190.

Hall, S. (1992), 'The Question of Cultural Identity', in S. Hall et al. (eds.) *Modernity and its Futures*, Cambridge: Polity Press.

Hendry, J. (1987), *Understanding Japanese Society*, London: Croom Helm.

Houlihan, B. (1994), *Sport and International Politics*, Basing-stoke: Harvester Wheatsheaf.

The Japan Times (1993).

Japan Travel Bureau (1992), *Living Japanese Style*, Japan: JTB.

Japanese: Language and People, (1991), A BBC Course in Japanese, BBC Books.

Kidd, B. (1991), 'How do we find our own voices in the "new world order"? A Commentary on Americanization', in *Sociology of Sport Journal*, Volume 8, Number 2: pp. 178-184.

Klein, A. (1991), 'Sport and Culture as Contested Terrain: Americanization in the Caribbean', in *Sociology of Sport Journal*, Vol. 8, Number 1: pp. 79-85.

McCormack, G. (1991), 'The Price of Affluence: The Political Economy of Japanese Leisure', *New Left Review*, Number 188: pp. 121-134.

Mckay, J. and Miller, T. (1991), 'From Old Boys to Men and Women of the Corporation: The Americanization and Commodification of Australian Sport', in *Sociology of Sport Journal*, Vol. 8, No. 1: pp. 86-94.

Maguire, J. (1990), 'More Than a Sporting Touchdown: The Making of American Football in England 1982-1990', in *Sociology of Sport Journal*, Volume 7, Number 3: pp. 213-237.

Maitland, B. (1991), *Japanese Baseball: A Fan's Guide*, Tokyo: C. E. Tuttle Co.

Mason, A. (1980), *Association Football and English Society 1863-1915*, Brighton: Harvester.

Miller, D. (1993a), column in *The Times*, 13th May.

———(1993b), column in *The Times*, 17th May.

Moeran, B. (1991), contributions to *Japanese: Language and People*, op cit.

O'Connor B. and Boyle, R. (1993), 'Dallas with balls: televised sport, soap opera and male and female pleasures', in *Leisure Studies*, Volume 12, Number 2: pp. 107-119.

Oliver, G. (1992), *The Guinness Record of World Soccer*, Enfield: Guinness Publishing.

Popham, P. (1993), 'A star in the East', *The Independent Magazine*, 17th April.

Robertson, R. (1987), 'Globalization and Societal Modernization: a Note on Japan and Japanese Religion', in *Sociological Analysis*, Volume 47, 5: pp. 35-42.

Saeki, T. (1989), 'Sport in Japan', in E. Wagner (ed.), *Sport in Asia and Africa*, USA, Westwood Press.

Said, E. (1978), *Orientalism*, London: Routledge & Kegan Paul.

Sennett, R. (1971), *The Uses of Disorder*, Harmondsworth: Penguin.

Stokvis, R. (1989), 'The International and National Expansion of Sports', in E. A.Wagner (ed.), *Sport in Asia and Africa*, Connecticutt, USA: Greenwood Press.

Tomlinson, A. (1986), contribution to 'Ideas on Sport — Play, Power, Performance', broadcast by Canadian Broadcasting Corporation, 2nd October 1986.

Vinnai, G. (1973), *Football Mania*, London: Ocean Books.

Wagner, E. (1990), 'Sport in Asia and Africa: Americanization or Mundialization?', in *Sociology of Sport Journal*, Vol. 7, No. 4: pp. 399-402.

Whiting, R. (1977), *The Chrysanthemum and the Bat*, New York, USA: Avon Books.

World Soccer, various issues, London: IPC Magazines.

10 Norway and the World Cup: Cultural diffusion, sportification and sport as a vehicle for nationalism

Matti Goksøyr

Introduction

In his history of World Soccer Guy Oliver (Oliver, 1992) opened his commentary on Norway with an acknowledgement that the Norwegians might create an "odd shock ... at international level", such as defeating Italy in 1991 and so precipitating that giant football nation's exclusion from the finals of the European Championships in the following year. Oliver asserted confidently, though, that "Norway are one of Europe's perennial underdogs and they look set to stay that way". But the results of Norway's endeavours in its qualifying group for the 1994 tournament belied this prophesy. Norway commanded a group in which the other qualifier was Holland/The Netherlands; and from which England emerged towards a painful post-mortem on its failure to win a place in the 1994 Finals in the USA. What, then, were the roots of the game in this Nordic country of 5 million people? Until 1993, Norway's most prominent success was in the 1936 Olympic Games when they lost to the highly 'professionalised' and Mussolini-inspired Italians in extra-time, at the Berlin Games so closely associated with Hitler. On the way to this semi-final Norway defeated Germany, prompting Hitler, as Oliver puts it, "to storm out of the stadium in a rage". This successful Norwegian side also qualified for the 1938 World Cup, losing to Italy (again in extra time) in the first round.

The purpose of this chapter is simply to touch upon a few questions and aspects of football's development concerning diffusion, sportification and national identity. In football's development, two processes are central: first, the globalisation of football, meaning a transition from a local traditional game to a worldwide activity performed in the same way the world over (Smith, 1990) — implying that two contestants can, principally, take part in the same contest, although a few minor cultural differences may exist with regard to style of play or attitudes to the game; second, something which I, even in an English-speaking collection[1], will call sportification — that is to say, the development of football from a pastime with the typical characteristics of a game into a modern sport. This implies that a rational frame of achievement-orientation and competition distinguishes how modern football is performed and perceived. What have these processes meant for sport's function concerning national identity? How can there be national identity in a global sport?

Football has been touched upon from many aspects in sports history literature (Mason, 1988). So has the globalization of the game, but to a much less degree (Tomlinson and Whannel; 1986: Tomlinson, 1986). Still, it is not the global development which is at focus here. It is rather to present one example of a process which started in England in the last century. One of the countries which was affected by this was Norway, a country whose geographical proximity to Britain may have led to an early introduction of football.

The game was introduced in the middle of the 1880s, which was not particularly early compared to neighbouring countries. But what is more interesting here is that the game needed time to develop and become firmly rooted in the national sports culture. Although other ballgames had been common, football when it turned up for the first time was a completely new and unknown sport in Norway. The launching of this imported game along Norwegian shores can be analysed both as a kind of cultural diffusion (even cultural imperialism)[2] and in a frame of sportification. Traditionally the diffusion of English sports to Norway has been attributed to student's and businessmen's personal knowledge of the game after stays in England, supplied by the role played by Britons travelling or stationed abroad (Mason, 1986). Hence, the introduction of football is put into models of general "internationalisation-processess". I would argue that these can give coarse and not very nuanced pictures.

Theories have been formed on the spread of football *out* of England. Harold Perkin has given a historical explanation of the diverse diffusion of British sports: the spread was dependent on the persons who went out to rule the Empire and the ones who went to Europe (Perkin, 1989). To the Empire travelled mostly young men from the upper classes with public school backgrounds to convey the power of the Empire and British culture (Mangan, 1986). Rugby and above all cricket were the outward signs that Britons were ruling the colonies[3]. To Europe on the other hand, travelled engineers, tradesmen and officials — social groups who brought their variant of the British sports culture, namely football. Although this theory underestimates the fact that in many cases foreigners went to Britain and picked up a game they liked, it seems plausible and strengthens a view that the social spread of the game in Britain was a precondition for the game to diffuse to Europe. But the explanation still leaves us with a remaining question of why it took such a long time from the introduction of the game to a real "take-off" in the development of the sport in receiving countries.

Historical problems concerning the spread of new sports should be discussed in an overall perspective taking into account the dynamics both in societies and in sport. The crucial point for the spread of new cultural impulses is that the receiving society has a high degree of receptability. But the tricky question remains: what are the concrete conditions which determine whether a cultural impulse — in this case the game of football — is compatible?

From the studies in Norway I will argue that material conditions such as leisure, housing, income or in other words a surplus of time and money to spend, can be considered as necessary, but not sufficient conditions for an explanation. Cultural conditions varying according to social background must also be considered, as they were influential in terms of interest and "taste" and thereby the way sport was conceived in the various social groups (Bourdieu, 1986). Norbert Elias's point on a growing "functional democratisation" could also be considered here[4]. But in addition one should ask whether there were sport-immanent features which influenced the social reception of a new activity?

Was the physical modelling of a sport decisive for its compatibility? Apparently not. Regarding patterns of physical movement another British game like cricket was much more similar to traditional Scandinavia "stickball" games. Still cricket has had problems to find a proper ground on which to grow and prosper outside the former British Empire, while football eventually experienced a break-through.

Does this mean that some sports or games are more easily transmittable over cultural borders than others? There are great variations in the way different sports are received in different parts of the world (Markowitz, 1990). Some sports are obviously more popular than others on a world-wide scale; they seem to be transmittable at a minor cultural cost. It is, however, difficult to claim the "cultural neutrality" as opposed to "cultural intensity" of some sports, without looking at larger societal and cultural processes[5]. The important thing here is that football — although being considered culturally neutral, perhaps more in retrospect after its triumphs over most of the world — actually did have problems in being assimilated into some nation's sports cultures.

The fact that football was nowhere near a familiar way of practising physical exercise meant that the game got of to a troublesome start in Norway. The taste for football was restricted to special layers of people, according to social background, age and sex.

"Football was vulgar" was a common statement of informants from the upper and upper middle classes of Bergen[6] — apparently having changed their minds since their own playing days. It was, nevertheless, the boys from the upper middle classes who served as entrepreneurs and promotors of the game. In the first decades after its introduction, football survived only as a school sport, as an activity for boys in the secondary and higher schools, somewhere between a compulsory part of the education in physical exercise and a voluntary game after school.[7]

However, around World War 1, football went through a process of thorough social diffusion in the cities, creating for the first time an element of identity connected to the game. Football contributed to build-up of street and neighbourhood identity in workers' districts; apparently, this was a reason for the "old boys" to disregard the game, as always in retrospect.

Sportification is a central concept for understanding these processes. The term cannot be dealt with fully here[8]. I will, however, argue that the inherent perspective of the concept can be rewarding when applied to the development of football.

An urge for bigger and more rational arenas at which to compete, was one side of sportification, along with an emphasis on audience. Spectators became a regular ingredient of sport. Onlookers were literally to be counted. This happened although the new clubs and associations of the new sports (being predominantly amateur) originally were not particularly spectator-oriented. The activity was to a large degree participant- or club-related. However, competitions fascinated more people than the actual competitors. The modern enclosed sports arenas were to imbue the area surrounding the activity with an increasing interest. It should be noted though, that this was a long-term development. The first sports grounds were in the first instance designed for the activities that were to take place. Facilities for spectators were few or non-existent around the turn of the century[9].

However, along with a growing social diffusion of the game, football experienced a break-through as a spectator sport at the end of World War I. This had effects on emergent influential elements like excitement, tension-equilibrium and differentiation, which must be passed over here, except for one element of sportification that led to more exciting matches and more spectators.

When the Norwegian Football Association — as late as 1937 — voted to introduce a national series in addition to the cup, it should be seen as an outcome of a long-term development. The cup had held a central position in Norwegian football, and still today the cup-winners are given the title of "Norwegian champions". This means that the national championship is awarded on a system that is democratic and open, and rewards the ability to take the one chance, more than long-term based evaluations. However, a series system was a much more rational way of measuring achievements than a knock-out competition. The consensus of this in the "football community" has led to a general (also international) agreement that the status of the league winners is superior to the cup winner. In such a perspective sportification can be an analytical tool to bring us somewhat further in an historical analysis than merely to register empirically that the Football Association at their 1937 assembly voted to introduce a national series system. Such a perspective can uncover some short-term economic and political motives for the decisions, as they were presented at the assembly.

Now, did sportification influence the identity perceived in the game of football? The modern sport that emerged in Norway, from the last half of the 19th century, was a mixed product of cultural impulses. Both the originally German "turnen" and the Swedish gymnastics were eventually converted into Norwegian sports (or idrett)[10]. The same thing happened a few decades later to the British sport. From the perspective that culture is a process in continuous change as it interferes with other cultures, it is interesting that the first major survey of sport in Norway, published in 1891, chose not to treat ballgames in general and football in particular, extensively, for the following reason:

> Possibly the future will show, that these amusing English ballgames may prosper also amongst us. For the time being, however, these games are so weakly based, that I dare not call them Norwegian (Urdahl, 1891).

Football (association) rules had been published already in 1886, accompanied with attempts to introduce Norwegian terms. It was L. Urdahl who tried this (Urdahl, 1886). Still, football was definitely conceived as an English sport in 1891. When the Norwegian Football Association was founded in 1902, only three clubs took part. However, the long-term development gradually made football into a natural ingredient of Norwegian sports culture. Shortly after World War 1, the game had reached a level of registered Association members equal to other mass sports like skiing, gymnastics and track and field athletics. During the 1930s it surpassed the others to become, in quantitative terms[11], the number one sport — by the last decade of the century approximately half a million Norwegians were registered as members (including many children under 16), which was around one eighth of the entire Norwegian population.

Another part of this development was that the national team, having played internationals since 1908, from the end of World War 1 experienced a significant rise of interest in their performances. A break-through regarding both public attendance and achievements occurred in 1918 when Norway for the first time won an international, defeating both Sweden and Denmark in the same year. In 1920 the national team for the first time defeated the big nation, England, at the Antwerp Olympics. Since then, a regular peak used to be the (previously) annual matches against the former union brother Sweden — matches that aroused national sentiments long after the union of 1905 had been settled. Another brief high occurred around the national team in the last half of the 1930s. This was particularly roused by the notable victory over Germany in the Berlin Olympics in 1936, with Hitler present on the terraces, symbolising that a small nation could overcome a great power (Bussard, 1989). A growing cultivation of *national* sports *heroes* like the "bronze team" of the Berlin Games, in the last half of the 1930s, also functioned as part of the reconciliation that marked the political history of these years in Norway. In sport, as well as on other fields, the tendency was to move away from class struggle towards national communion (Goksøyr, 1994).

This illustrates one of the functions a national team can have, even through an originally imported sport like football. The game, by its immense international expansion, has been a difficult field in which to assert oneself, or precisely because of that, there has been a latent interest in the national team and its potential, quite startling in its manifest forms. The famous outburst by the radio reporter Bjorge Lillelien after a World Cup qualifier victory over England on 19th September 1981, illustrates this well. I quote just a small bit: "We are the world's best, we are the world's best. We have defeated England — England, land of giants; Lord Nelson ...". Then he went on listing famous Englishmen whom 'we' had all defeated. If we stretch Norwegian football history all the way up to 1993, we will find that this interest has not diminished.

The last point to bring up here is connected to the fact that the celebration of possible successes, more now than before, is so clearly marked with national symbols. At the same time modern life is — according to (among others) Anthony Giddens — characterized by a reduction of traditional identities based on social class and even nationality. Such belongings are losing their decisive importance for a person's social identity (Giddens, 1991). How should we then interpret the increasing use of national symbols in football?

The identity that is revealed and exposed during international football matches is without doubt national. However, its duration and operation is limited to the time around the match itself. This kind of national identity could therefore, with a borrowed Scottish term, be called 90-minute nationalism (Jarvie, 1992). What is worth noticing with this kind of national sentiment, is that it is not binding outside of the match and its surroundings. The 90 minute nationalism has no consequence for other political matters. I will argue that this kind of nationalism matches, not only cultural fascination for football in Scotland, but characteristics of so called modernity.

Eric Hobsbawm's recurrently quoted phrase, building on Benedict Anderson — "the imagined community of millions seems more real as a team of eleven named people" (Hobsbawm, 1990:143) — says something about a football team as a carrier of national expressions. However, to me this is a statement more of *identification* than of *identity*. Hobsbawm's observation could be made of any national team — from England, Scotland, Argentina and Brazil to Norway and the Faroe Islands. It does not say anything about the role and function of the particular sport in the national culture.

Although it has for long been the biggest sport, football has due to its foreign and international origins, not been rooted as deeply in traditional Norwegian culture as the Number 1 "national sport", skiing. Norwegians were not born with bats in their hands or footballs at their feet, but with skis[12]. Today football has become part of the global culture. One question is therefore: How can something which is essentially global in its character, represent local, regional or national identity?

I will argue once more, that what the sport provides is an opportunity for collective identification with the chosen ones. The game itself can, in spite of current success, hardly be claimed to represent any Norwegian identity more than it would for most other nations, and considerably less than for nations like the British and the Latin. It is in the collective identification that football's force as a spectator sport lies.

A final remark: It is, as we have seen, paradoxical that so called modernity calls for a growing marking of identity through national symbols. After all, the 'national' has often in the West been regarded as the other side of 'modern'. But it also characteristic, because other belongings have been weakened, and have left something like a vacuum, making '90-minute nationalism' an answer to contemporary urges for short and un-committing, but also strong and sometimes fortune-bringing, identity. Such a transitory identity is more than before connected to achievements and success, which the stirring of 'national sentiments' around the Norwegian national team during 1993 illustrated. Norway's success in qualifying for its first World Cup Final for fifty-six years is, in part at least, testimony to the power of such national sentiments when stirred, as well as to the aspirations and organisation of a moderate playing squad.

As Erik Thorstedt (goalkeeper of the London club Tottenham Hotspur) has put it, the Norwegian manager, Egil Olsen, adapted "direct" methods, based on a classically "English" combination of strength and determination, and moulded moderate parts into an effective whole. Norway completed the qualifying group matches undefeated, a model of consistency. A country with only 1,810 clubs, almost all amateur based, and 300,100 players (as opposed to England's 42,000 clubs, including 300 professionally-based ones, and 2.25 million players)[13], its achievement warrants the outpouring of national sentiments to which it gave expression. That the "chosen ones" achieved such unambiguous superiority over England, the founders of the game, gave further fizz to the cocktail of Norway's success, and to soccer's function as a vehicle nationalism in the build up to the Finals of 1994.

Notes

[1] On the semantic monstrosity of the concept, see M. Goksøyr, 1988.

[2] If we are to take the circumstances around the first football matches on Norwegian grounds in 1886 literally — officers and cadets from the fleet of the British Empire displayed British sports culture. The naval cruise functioned as a launching of British football. In two of the three largest cities which the fleet visited, the British made their influential input to the introduction of the game. There is, however, little reason to believe that the officers themselves felt and acted as football "missionaries". A conscious ideology for the diffusion of British culture in Europe corresponding to what took place inside the British Empire did not exist (see note 3).

[3] Consider the British saying of Sudan: "A land of Blacks ruled by Blues". (Anthony Kirk-Greene; 'Imperial Administration and the Athletic Imperative', in Baker and Mangan, 1987).

[4] The question to raise here is: would the extension of the network of interdependency chains and an increasing balance of power between social groups, i.e. "functional democratisation", mean that the social spread of sport could be accomplished with more inclination? (See N. Elias, 'Introduction', in: Elias and Dunning, 1986:12-13.)

[5] Ali A.Mazrui, 'Africa's triple heritage of play: Reflections on the gender gap', in Baker and Mangan (1987), claims the culture neutrality theory.

6   E.g. Rolf Sundt (b.1890) in personal interview, June 1984.

7   See M. Goksøyr, 1989 and 1991.

8   Studies like Bernett (1984) and Elias (in Elias and Dunning, 1986) have been influential for my understanding of the term.

9   Henning Eichberg's term for this enclosing process is "parcellisation", meaning that sport went from open and nature-like surroundings to arenas fenced in "behind walls and inside halls" (Eichberg 1979). The last was not so relevant for football, but the process was parallel. The historical "parcellation" process can of course not only be seen in the perspective of sport's inner dynamics. It can also be seen as part of an urbanisation process, driving youngsters away from previously open common grounds.

10 "Idrett" is the Norwegian concept which is not 100% translatable to sport. Historically, it includes some ideological component.

11 In January 1940 the Norwegian Football Association had c.70,000 members, while the ski association had c.51,000, and the associations for gymnastics and athletics included around 25,000 members each. Also in the workers' sports movement football was by far the largest sport. Because of the relatively informal organisation of the workers' sport movement, no figures exist for this. A calculation might point, though, to a figure not far from the 70,000 in the Football Association.

12 The concept "national sport" is problematic. The traditional Norwegian sports identity has been built upon winter sports mainly, and outdoor recreation, in other words "nature sports" with a less degree of "parcellation". But what is in the expression? Who defines it? How is it explained? The literature in many ways lies between two extremes: 1) A sport where "we" have international success, or 2) an activity that is regarded as a carrier of "national virtues" and as such is more central to a nation's cultural heritage than others.

13 These figures are taken from the UK's *Independent on Sunday*, 28th November 1993, full-page feature "After Taylor", p.12. "Taylor" is the English soccer team manager, who had resigned earlier in the week following England's failure to qualify for USA '94.

References

Bussard, J-C (1989), 'Les Jeux de 1936 dans la presse suisse de langue Francaise', in Renson, Lammer, Riordan and Chassiotis (eds.), *The Olympic Games through the Ages, Proceedings of the 13th International HISPA Conference,* Olympia, May.

Baker, W. J. & Mangan, J. A. (eds.) (1987), *Sport in Africa: Essays in Social History* London: Africana Publishing Co.

Bernett, H. (1984), 'Die Versportlichung des Spiels', in *Sportwissenchaft,* Volume 14, Number 2.

Bourdieu, P. (1986), *Distinction: a social critique of the judgement of taste,* London: Routledge.

Eichberg, H. (1979), Der Weg des sports in die industrielle Zivilisation, Baden Baden: Nomos 1973, 2. Auflage 1979.

Elias, N. and Dunning, E. (1986), *Quest for Excitement — Sport and leisure in the civilising process ,* Oxford: Blackwell.

Giddens, A. (1991), *Modernity and Self-Identity — Self and Society in the Late Modern Age,* Cambridge: Polity Press.

Goksøyr, M. (1988), 'The development of modern sport in Norway in the 19th century. A question of sportification', *Paper for the Seoul Olympic Scientific Congress,* Seoul 1988.

———(1989), 'Prestasjonsuialing eller posering? Den engelske sporten i norske omgivelser, in *Norsk Idrettshistorisk Arbok.*

———(1991), Idrettsliv i borgerskapetsby En historisk undersøkelse au idrettens utuikling og organisering i Bergen pa 1800-tallet, Dr. scient-dissertation, Oslo.

———(1994), 'Phases and Functions of Nationalism. The Norwegian experience of international sports impulses', in J.A. Mangan (ed.), *Nationalism and Sport,* London: Frank Cass.

Hobsbawm, E. (1990), *Nations and Nationalism,* Cambridge: Cambridge University Press.

Jarvie, G. (1992), 'Sport, Nationalism and Cultural Identity', in Lincoln Allison (ed.), *The Changing Politics of Sport,* Manchester: Manchester University Press.

Mangan, J.A. (1986), *The Games Ethic and Imperialism: Aspects of the Diffusion of an Ideal*, Harmondsworth: Viking.

Markowitz, A.S. (1990), 'The other American Exceptionalism: Why there is no soccer in the United States', *International Journal of the History of Sport*, Volume 7, Number2.

Mason, T. (1986), 'Some Englishmen and Scotsmen Abroad: The Spread of World Football', in Tomlinson and Whannel (eds.), *Off the Ball: the Football World Cup*, London: Pluto Press pp.67-82.

Mason, T. (1988), 'Football and the Historians', *International Journal of the History of Sport*, Volume 5, Number1.

Oliver, G. (1992), *The Guinness Record of World Soccer — the history of the game in over 150 countries*, Enfield: Guinness Publishing.

Perkin, H. (1989) 'Teaching the Natives how to play: Sport and society in the British Empire and the Commonwealth', *International Journal of the History of Sport*, Volume 6, Number 2.

Smith, A.D. (1990), 'Towards a Global Culture?', in M. Featherstone (ed.), *Theory, Culture and Society*, Volume 7, Numbers 2-3, June, pp. 171-191.

Tomlinson, A. (1986), 'Going Global: the FIFA Story', in Tomlinson and Whannel (eds.) (1986), *Off the Ball: the Football World Cup*, London: Pluto Press: pp. 83-98.

Tomlinson, A. and Whannel, G. (eds.) (1986), *Off the Ball: the Football World Cup*, London: Pluto Press.

Urdahl, L. (1886) 'Lidt om Fodboldspil efter associations' regler, in *Norsk Idraetsblad*, Number22.

————(1891) Norsk Idraet Skildringer og skisser fra norsk sportsliv, Kristiania.

11 Sweden and the World Cup: Soccer and Swedishness

Alan Bairner

It is undeniable that the 1958 World Cup Finals are more commonly associated with Brazil, who won the competition for the first time, than with Sweden, the host nation. In a variety of ways, however, the championship itself, and the game of football more generally, tell us a great deal about Swedish national identity. What follows is a defence of that assertion.

Olle Montanus, a character in August Strindberg's *The Red Room*, asks "can anyone tell me anything Swedish in Sweden other than our pine trees and firs and iron mines?" (Strindberg, 1967:223). At first glance, his concern might seem surprising given Sweden's reputation, in modern times, for having avoided the politics of nationalism (Elklit and Tonsgaard, 1992). However, more than 80 years since Strindberg's death, not only is the question pertinent, but the debate on Swedish national identity has gathered momentum and assumed even greater significance in the face of threats, real and imagined, to the Swedish way of life (Ehn et al., 1993). The new challenges include Sweden's proposed membership of the European Community, a new world order which might make the country's long-standing commitment to neutrality increasingly less relevant and the impact of large-scale immigration affecting the balance of a hitherto relatively homogeneous population. In response to such developments, the question is asked with growing urgency — "what will happen to the Swedes?" (Daun, 1992:179).

It is possible that the Swedes' well deserved reputation for tolerance and compromise will ensure that nothing much happens to them. But more extreme possibilities exist. On the one hand, Swedish identity might become weakened as European identity grows (Daun, 1992). On the other hand, the next few years may witness increased *försvenskning* — the process by which Sweden is becoming more Swedish (Ehn et al., 1993). The purpose of this essay is to explore the issue of Swedish national identity by examining football's role in highlighting and enhancing key elements of Swedishness.

As Grant Jarvie points out, "sport, in all its different forms and contexts, often contributes to quests for identity" (Jarvie, 1993:61). This is at least as true of Sweden as of anywhere else. According to Billy Ehn "sport in twentieth century Sweden has become one of the most emotional areas for expressing nationalism" (Ehn et al., 1993:204). More than that, "in Sweden there is scarcely another field where love of one's native country is expressed so strongly and in unison by so many people" (Ehn et al., 1993:206). This is consistent with the prominence given to sport in Sweden where at least 4 million people (out of a population of 8.6 million) are involved in some form of sporting activity. Foremost amongst a large number of popular sports are skiing, athletics, ice hockey, bandy (indoor and outdoor), orienteering, sailing, table tennis, ten pin bowling and gymnastics. Furthermore, tennis, golf and motor sports, although played by fewer people, have given Sweden a high international profile. However, as Tomas Peterson observes, "football is the biggest single sport in Sweden, both in terms of players and spectators, and it has a strong position within the Swedish Sports Confederation" (Peterson, 1993:19). Sweden has 3,250 football clubs or sports' clubs with football sections, with over one million members and 162,566 licensed players (over the age of fifteen). There are, in addition, some 330,000 youth footballers (Svenska Fotbollförbundet, 1992). Football's popularity with so many Swedes, young and old, male and female, makes it an ideal starting-point for an investigation into what it means to be Swedish.

In the light of the game's popularity, however, it is ironic that Sweden's contribution to what is undeniably the greatest episode in the history of Swedish football has tended to be overshadowed by other factors. In the summer of 1958, Sweden hosted the World Cup Finals and, on 29 June, at the Råsunda Stadium in Stockholm, the national team played Brazil in the final match of the tournament. That game, Sweden's only appearance to date in a World Cup Final, and the competition which had preceded it are now best remembered for two reasons, neither of them directly related to the host nation's performance either on or off the field of play. First, the World Cup Finals received television coverage for the first time, thereby underlining football's status as the world's favourite game. Second, Brazil, who beat Sweden 5-2 in the final, became the first and, so far, the only team to win the World Cup outside of their own continent. Not only that but their victory was the prelude to a golden period in the history of Brazilian football which was to include two further World Cup wins as well as the accession to the title of 'the greatest player in the world' by Pelé who, as a seventeen-year old, made the first of his many appearances in the World Cup Finals in 1958.

Given the importance of each of these aspects of the 1958 Finals, it is not entirely surprising that the role of Sweden both as hosts and as beaten finalists has become little more than a footnote in the history of football. Of the game against Brazil, Orvar Bergmark, a member of the Swedish team, comments that "at that time, it would have probably been better to sit in the stand and enjoy all their skills instead of being exposed to them" (Nilsson, 1979:191). One should avoid creating the impression, however, that the Swedes had little or no right to appear in the Final of the World Cup. In earlier Finals, Sweden had finished fourth (1938) and third (1950) and Sweden's footballers had won Gold Medals at the 1948 Olympic Games as well as Bronze Medals in 1924 and 1952. Indeed, it was testimony to Sweden's position as an important footballing nation (at a time when this was the pre-eminent criterion) that the Swedish Football Association (Svenska Fotbollförbundet — SFF) had been invited to play host to the 1958 tournament.

The 1958 Finals consisted of four qualifying groups. Group One, consisting of West Germany, Czechoslovakia, Northern Ireland and Argentina, was based in Halmstad, Malmö and Helsingborg. Group Two's members, comprising France, Scotland, Paraguay and Yugoslavia, played their matches in Västerås, Norrköping, Örebro and Eskilstuna. The members of Group Three, Sweden, Hungary, Wales and Mexico, played at Råsunda and in Sandviken. Finally, Group Four, with Brazil, England, the Soviet Union and Austria, was contested in Uddevalla, Gothenburg (Göteborg) and Borås. In the quarter finals, Brazil beat Wales 1-0 in Gothenburg, France beat Northern Ireland 4-0 in Norrköping, West Germany beat Yugoslavia 1-0 in Malmö and Sweden won 2-0 against the Soviet Union at Råsunda. The semi-finals were played at Råsunda, where Brazil beat

France 5-2, assisted by a Pelé hat-trick, and at Nya Ullevi in Gothenburg where Sweden, playing away from Stockholm for the only time in the competition, beat West Germany 3-1. The match to decide third and fourth places was played in Gothenburg, with France beating West Germany 6-3 and so came the Final with the hosts matched against the favourites.

Sweden opened the scoring with a fourth-minute goal by Nils Liedholm. Vava equalised for Brazil six minutes later and then put his side into the lead in the thirty second minute. In the second half, a fifty-sixth minute goal by Pelé made it 3-1 and Zagalo made it four for Brazil in the sixty eighth minute. Agne Simonsson got one back for Sweden in the eightieth minute but, in the last minute of the game, Pelé scored his own second and his team's fifth goal and Brazil had finished comfortable as well as deserving victors. Many of the Brazilian team which played that day are still remembered wherever football is discussed — Gilmar, Djalma and Nilton Santos, Didi, Garrincha, Vava, Zagalo and, of course, the inimitable Pelé. Although the Swedish team at the time contained some equally talented players — Kurt Hamrin, Gunnar Gren, 'Nacka' Skoglund, Liedholm and Simonsson — they are remembered now, if at all, only in Sweden or by the most dedicated football enthusiasts elsewhere. Yet it could all have turned out so differently. After all, the Swedish team was only ninety minutes away from winning the World Cup.

Even had Sweden won the Final, it is highly improbable that they would have gone on to make the sort of lasting impact on world football which the Brazilians were to achieve. To have won the World Cup at all, however, albeit as hosts, would place Sweden alongside England in the competition's roll of honour as one of only two World Cup winning nations to have won the trophy only once. In addition, the future trajectory of the Brazilian side might have been radically altered had they lost to Sweden in 1958. Would they have proceeded to win the World Cup in 1962 and again in 1970? How would Pelé's career have developed? These are, of course, hypothetical questions to which there are no empirically based answers. On the basis of the actual evidence, however, we can certainly say that the 1958 World Cup Finals were of great importance to Brazil, but, hopefully, without ignoring their significance for Sweden. In fact, the tournament highlighted certain recurring tendencies in Swedish football which relate to the broader issue of Swedish national identity.

First, the achievements of the Swedish team confirmed the high standard of Swedish football which could stand comparison not only with football in considerably larger countries but also with other realms of activity in which Sweden had enjoyed success, most notably industrial development. Second, hosting the World Cup Finals was indicative of a more general desire on the part of Swedes to involve themselves in the affairs of the international community. Third, the enthusiastic response given by the Råsunda crowd to the victorious Brazilians provided evidence of the degree to which Swedes had managed to replace crude nationalistic sentiments with a genuine capacity to respect and admire the qualities of other people. Arguably this was facilitated by the nature of the opposition since far less generosity of spirit had been exhibited by the Gothenburg crowd for the semi-final tie with West Germany. Overall, however, efficiency, international responsibility and a sense of justice are all characteristics which have commonly been attributed to the Swedes and each was evident during the 1958 World Cup Finals. Like all stereotypes, however, the image thereby created offers only a partial insight. To gain a fuller understanding of Swedish identity, it is necessary to look more closely at the development of football in Sweden and, in particular, to assess the character of the game at a time when the issue of what is involved in being Swedish is coming under ever closer scrutiny. The first part of this study will focus specifically on the Swedish approach to football, the second on the ways in which football reflects and even contributes to contemporary developments in Swedish society.

There is as yet no single, incontrovertible theory as to when and where football was first played in Sweden. In the early 1880s, the game was introduced in Stockholm by members of the British Embassy staff. At roughly the same time, Scottish workers brought it to Gothenburg and to Gävle where a man called Robert Carrick invited Swedish boys to a training camp at which they were taught to play football. In due course, Gefle IF, founded in 1882, became the first football club in Sweden.

Thus it appears that football arrived in Sweden almost simultaneously by way of a number of different routes. Two things, however, are certain. First, the extent of British influence was considerable and was to remain an important feature in the development of Swedish football. Second, the west coast port city of Gothenburg quickly established itself as the early centre of

Swedish football and it has retained a prominent position ever since. The oldest Swedish football club still in existence is Örgryte IS, formed in Gothenburg in 1887, and, in 1895, the game's first governing body (The Swedish Sports and Athletic Association) was also established in Gothenburg. The first Swedish football championship, played on a knock-out basis, was won in 1896 by Örgryte who repeated their success in each of the next three years until Allmänna Idrottsklubben (AIK) took the championship title to Stockholm for the first time. In 1902, an unofficial national governing body was set up in Stockholm and, two years later, a section for football and hockey was established within the Swedish Sports Confederation. The name Svenska Fotbollförbundet (The Swedish Football Association) was officially adopted in 1906 and it was voted into FIFA the following year.

The early years of the Swedish championship which, from 1910 until 1925, was complemented at irregular intervals by an unofficial league, were dominated by clubs from Gothenburg and Stockholm, whose rivalry continues to play an important part in Swedish domestic football today. The 'big city' domination was ended in 1921 by IFK Eskilstuna but, even then, the unofficial league competition that year was won by Örgryte with their Gothenburg rivals Göteborgs Atlet och Idrottssälskap (GAIS) in second place and Stockholm's Hammarby IF third. The forerunner of the present-day Allsvenskan (Premier League) was not contested until 1924-5 with GAIS triumphing over city rivals IFK Göteborg and Örgryte who finished second and third respectively. Indeed, Göthenburg clubs won the first four Allsvenskan titles until a more significant challenge to the Göthenburg-Stockholm axis was mounted by Helsingborgs IF, from Sweden's west coast, who won the title in 1928-9 and 1929-30 and repeated these back-to-back successes in 1932-3 and 1933-4. IFK Norrköping won the championship for the first time in 1942-3 and Malmö FF secured their first title in 1943-4. These two clubs then proceeded to dominate Swedish football until the 1950s, since when the championship title has been shared by a number of leading clubs with only Åtvidabergs FF's victories in 1972 and 1973 doing anything to alter the pattern. Since 1981, various experiments have taken place in an attempt to improve the entertainment value of Allsvenskan with play-offs, knock-out competitions and mini-leagues being used to identify the champions. In 1993, however, it was decided to revert to the system which had been in place from 1924 until 1981.

Including the early competitions, the Swedish Championship roll of honour has Malmö FF and Örgryte sharing first place with 14 victories each and IFK Göteborg second, having won the title 13 times. Other clubs with a history of successes are IFK Norrköping (12 titles), AIK (9), Djurgården IF (from Stockholm) (8), GAIS (6) and Helsingborgs IF (5). The history of the Swedish Cup competition is shorter and considerably less illustrious. It was first contested as recently as 1941 and was not even competed for in 1952, 1954-66 and 1968. Malmö FF have achieved by far the greatest number of Cup victories (14) with IFK Norrköping in second place (5), followed by AIK and IFK Göteborg with 4 wins each.

Turning from domestic competition to international football, Sweden played its first international match on 12 June, 1908, beating Norway 11-3 in Gothenburg. In 1912, the Olympic Games were held in Stockholm and football benefited from the general upsurge in sporting interest which followed the event. There were international victories over Finland as well as Tsarist Russia who lost 1-4 to Sweden in Moscow on 4 May 1913. But there were also heavy defeats at the hands of England and near neighbours Denmark who beat Sweden 8-0 in Copenhagen and 10-0 in Stockholm during 1913. It was not until 1916 that victory against the Danes was finally achieved.

During the 1920s and 1930s, Sweden began to enjoy success in international competitions. The Bronze Medal for football was won by the Swedish team at the 1924 Olympic Games held in Paris and, in 1934, Sweden competed in the World Cup Finals for the first time, losing 1-2 to Germany in a quarter-final match played in Milan. Four years later, the Swedish team reached the World Cup semi-finals at which stage they lost 1-5 to Hungary. They were subsequently beaten 2-4 by Brazil and finished the competition in fourth place. But even greater achievements were to follow in the period after the Second World War.

At the 1948 Olympics in London, the Swedish team won the Gold Medal by beating Yugoslavia 3-1 in the Final. Two years later, a Swedish side, denied the presence of foreign-based professional players by SFF's commitment to amateurism, went to the World Cup Finals in Brazil and was good enough to gain third place in the mini-league which replaced the final knock-out competition that year. A second Olympic Bronze Medal was won at the 1952 Games in Helsinki when Sweden beat West Germany 2-0 in the play-off for third place. The Swedish side failed to qualify for the final stages of the 1954 World Cup but was guaranteed a place in the 1958 Finals with Sweden as host nation. Since 1958, the performances of the national team have been erratic, reaching the quarter-finals of the European Nations' Cup in 1964 and qualifying for the World Cup Finals of 1970, 1974 and 1978. Thereafter, Sweden failed to reach the Finals again until 1990 when poor performances in Italy resulted in defeats in each of the three opening group matches. In 1992, Sweden hosted the European Championships and performed creditably in the competition, losing at the semi-final stage to Germany. The Germans themselves lost in the Final to Denmark who had only been invited to take part in the Championships after the expulsion of Yugoslavia as part of an international boycott of Serbia.

Overall, then, particularly in view of the size of the country and the fact that until the late 1960s the game was still being played on an amateur basis and remains largely semi-professional even today (with the only full-time professional club being Malmö FF), Sweden has performed well at the highest levels of international football. In addition, Swedish club sides have enjoyed modest success in European competitions, with Malmö reaching the European Cup Final of 1979, only to lose to English league champions Nottingham Forest, and IFK Göteborg winning the UEFA Cup in 1982 and 1987, beating Hamburg SV and Dundee United respectively. These performances were all the more remarkable since football is essentially a summer sport in Sweden, with domestic competitions starting in the spring and continuing until the autumn. To make progress in European competitions, therefore, involves Swedish clubs playing the later rounds at a time when they are denied competitive matches at home.

In general, Swedish football has had three, or perhaps four, periods of marked success (Sund, 1991:124). According to Bill Sund, these are (1) the late 1940s during which the Swedish team won the Olympic Gold Medal; (2) 1958 when Sweden reached the World Cup Final; and (3) the 1970s when Swedish sides played in all three World Cup Final tournaments contested in that decade. As a fourth possibility, Sund adds the late 1970s and 1980s when Swedish club football rather than the international team took pride of place.

It is of course the players who illuminate successful periods in football history. In the 1940s, for example, Sweden possessed one of the most celebrated forward lines in the history of the game, including Gunnar

Gren, Gunnar Nordahl and Nils Liedholm, the famous Gre-no-li trio as they were christened in Italy where they had joined AC Milan after helping Sweden to win the Olympic Gold Medal in 1948. Gren, nicknamed 'The Professor' by his Italian admirers was a skilful ball player who played for Fiorentina and Genoa in addition to Milan and returned to Sweden late in his career and led a young Örgryte team to a league title. He scored 33 goals in 57 games for Sweden, played his last Allsvenskan match at the age of 44 and was still playing in Division Three when he was 50. Gunnar Nordahl was a powerful striker, arguably the greatest goalscorer in the history of Swedish football. He scored 58 goals in 77 games for Degerfors, 93 goals in 92 games for IFK Norrköping (with whom he won four league championship medals) and, before joining Milan, 44 goals in 33 games for the national side. He won Italian league title awards in 1951 and 1955 with Milan for whom he scored 176 goals in six seasons, his 35 goals in season 1949-50 being an Italian league record. He later joined Roma and then Pisa and, in total, scored 225 goals in Italian football. His four brothers were also Allsvenskan players, three of them receiving international honours and two following his example by playing in Italy. Nils Liedholm was a mid-field strategist who stayed with Milan until 1961. He captained the team for a number of seasons, won four Italian championship medals, captained the Swedish team in the 1958 World Cup Finals, when foreign-based professionals were finally permitted to play in the national side, and went on to coach at Fiorentina, Roma and Milan.

Another celebrated player who emerged shortly after the 1948 Olympic victory was Lennart 'Nacka' Skoglund, a magical entertainer and perhaps the most popular Swedish player of his time. After the 1950 World Cup Finals, Skoglund was transferred to Inter Milan with whom he won two Italian league medals. He later played for Sampdoria and Palermo and finished his career back in Sweden with his original club, Hammarby, his appearances for whom attracted large crowds. Gren, Liedholm and Skoglund all played in the 1958 World Cup team and they were joined in the forward line by Kurt Hamrin and Agne Simonsson. Hamrin was a small, tricky forward who had scored 54 goals in 62 games for AIK. In Italy, he played for Juventus, Padua, Fiorentina and Milan. He won European Cup Winners' Cup medals with Fiorentina in 1961 and Milan in 1967 and, in 1969, played in Milan's European Cup winning side. He finished his career in Italy with Napoli. He had scored 190 goals in Italian football as well as 17 goals in 32 appearances for Sweden. Simonsson replaced Nordahl as centre forward in the national team. He played 51 times for his country and scored 27 goals, including two against England at Wembley in 1959 when he contributed massively to a 3-2 victory for Sweden. He was signed by Real Madrid shortly afterwards but soon returned to Sweden where he joined Örgryte for whom he scored 106 goals in 162 games.

The stars of the 1970s included Ralf Edström and Ove Kindvall, both of whom played in Dutch football, and goalkeeper Ronnie Hellström who was based for a time in West Germany. In addition, there was defender Björn Nordqvist who also played briefly in Holland and who made a record number of appearances for his country between 1963 and 1978, winning 115 caps, a figure which became a new world record at the time, beating that of England's Bobby Moore, although later to be overtaken by Pat Jennings of Northern Ireland.

In the 1990s, the Swedish national team contains a large number of foreign-based, full time professionals, amongst them Jonas Thern and Tomas Brolin who play their club football in Italy, Stefan Schwarz based in Portugal, Martin Dahlin in Germany, Klas Ingesson in Belgium and Anders Limpar, Patrik Andersson and Roland Nilsson who play in England. Although this is by no means an uncommon phenomenon in the game world-wide, it has been a constant factor in Swedish international selection since the late 1950s. The problem for the national coach in Sweden, as elsewhere, is to combine the talents of players who on a daily basis are adapting their skills to what are often radically different football contexts. In addition, through the years, foreign coaches have exercised a considerable degree of influence on Swedish football which, in the past, affected the style of play adopted by the national team selected only from amongst home-based players.

Particularly influential in the 1920s and 1930s, for example, were coaches from Austria and Hungary, including Kalman Konrad, Lajos Czeisler, Istvan Wampetis and Josef Nagy who trained the Swedish Olympic squad in 1924 and the 1938 World Cup team. Another major foreign figure in the history of Swedish football was Englishman George Raynor, who had played for Aldershot and Rotherham United in the English League and who was chief coach of the Swedish national team from 1946-61. After the 1958 World Cup Finals, Raynor was decorated by the King for his services to Swedish football and, in 1961, he returned to his native Yorkshire where he became manager of Doncaster Rovers in the English Fourth Division.

It is with the related issues of foreign-based players in the international team and, in particular, the influence of foreign coaches in Swedish domestic football, that the debate about the Swedish approach to the game really begins. It becomes especially heated when it is felt by some that the Swedish style of the national team is under threat even though it is generally accepted that one cannot expect a small country like Sweden to be able to create its own unique style of play which is, in some sense, quintessentially Swedish. As Bill Sund suggests, "one can hardly speak of any specifically Swedish football culture" (Sund, 1991:117). He prefers to attempt to locate Swedish football within the context of three distinctive football cultures, latin, continental (by which is meant central and northern European) and British. Sund adds the development by the Dutch of a separate football style involving 'total football' and one might suggest that the South American approach to the game represents a distinctive model rather than merely a sub-section of the European Latin culture. Historically, of these, the continental and British cultures have been the major influences on the Swedish approach to football. However, as early as the 1930s there was a debate as to which of those cultures was more appropriate to the Swedish approach. By the late 1970s this debate had intensified and it threatened to boil over completely as the recriminations began following Sweden's disastrous campaign in the 1990 World Cup Finals.

According to Tomas Peterson, from the mid 1970s, "Swedish football divided into two camps, which followed a long drawn-out struggle concerning how football should be played in the future" (Peterson, 1993:19). In particular, discussions centred around the playing system which had been introduced to domestic football by two English coaches, Bob Houghton at Malmö FF and Roy Hodgson at Halmstads BK. Houghton arrived at Malmö in 1973 and, according to Peterson:

> his football philosophy came to influence a whole football nation and gave birth to the most extensive ideological conflict within the Swedish sports movement in modern times (Peterson, 1993:11).

The 'English' style of play promoted by Houghton and Hodgson was adopted by other clubs, especially those in western and south-western

Sweden and was widely regarded as being the major factor in the successes of Malmö and IFK Göteborg in European competitions (Sund, 1991:126). Certainly Houghton and Hodgson did not lack supporters. Amongst these was Tomas Peterson who points out that "Swedish football has historically mainly been English-influenced"(Peterson, 1993:267). Indeed, according to him those who seek to invoke the idea of 'a Swedish model' in football do so only in negative terms: the Swedish style of play is distinguished only by the fact that it is not English (Peterson, 1993:266).

Nevertheless, critics of what they regarded as 'the English model' were equally vociferous, particularly when it was felt that the national team, during Olle Nordin's period as coach, was adopting the English style of play. Somewhat disarmed by the European success of Malmö and IFK Göteborg, these critics felt vindicated by the poor performance of the national side in the 1990 World Cup Finals. As early as 1981, Lars Arnesson, then Sweden's national coach, had made his feelings known:

> The British style of hitting the long ball does not suit us. Our inspiration should come from the short passing game which is popular in other parts of Europe (Aitken, 1981).

In 1990, Arnesson was in the forefront of those who criticised the national team's performance under Nordin who was subsequently replaced as national coach by Tommy Svensson. Critics of 'the English model' now hope that it has been jettisoned in favour of a continental approach which combines "a Lutheran sense of duty" with individual flair (Sund, 1991:123).

To say the least, this entire debate about playing styles is problematic. In the first place, it is difficult to identify a specifically English, let alone British, approach. Those English clubs which enjoyed great success in European competitions during the 1970s and early 1980s used a variety of styles of play and English club football in the 1990s is characterised by a variation in approach which flies in the face of the widely held but simplistic belief that the English game is universally based on the tactics of quickly closing down opponents and pumping long balls into the opposition's half of the field. Furthermore, despite the fact that Houghton and Hodgson brought English ideas to the clubs which they coached and to Swedish domestic football more generally, the players with whom they worked were predominantly Swedish. To that extent, Peterson's description of the style of play which resulted as 'Swenglish' seems justified (Peterson, 1993). Finally, the link between domestic football and the style adopted by the national team, on which critics of Houghton and Hodgson concentrated much of their attention, is difficult to establish, particularly when, as in the case of the Swedish national side, so few of its members play in domestic football. Indeed, the perennial complaint of many national coaches is that, whereas club trainers have sufficient time to inculcate a certain style of play in their players, they themselves find it difficult to do so given the limited time spent with their squad and the fact that the players are deeply influenced by their experiences at club level.

As the debate in Sweden on rival football styles intensified, it may even have become indicative of ideological shifts in Swedish society as a whole. According to Peterson, criticism of the English coaches' influence came from two, otherwise mutually opposed, sources (Peterson, 1993:268). On one side were the traditionalists, like Gunnar Gren who, ironically given his own professional career in Italy, expressed nostalgia for the more carefree days of amateur football. On the other side, there were those, like Lars Arnesson, who supported the increased professionalisation of Swedish football but were unhappy about the growth in Sweden of what they understood to be the 'English' way of playing. The impact of these different viewpoints is difficult to assess. Although the ideas of the traditionalists will do nothing to prevent Swedes from pursuing full time careers in football, it is worth noticing that there is little immediate likelihood that clubs in Sweden will be tempted to follow the example of Malmö FF and recruit players on a full time professional basis. For their part, advocates of the 'continental' approach seem reasonably happy with the progress of the national team under the guidance of Tommy Svensson. No doubt they have also derived some satisfaction from the fact that almost as many Swedes are now watching television coverage of Italy's Serie A as regularly watch 'live' games from England. Whether the influence of Italian instead of English football will make the game in Sweden more Swedish is, of course, an altogether different matter and it is almost certain that the debate about the respective merits of different styles of play will carry on well beyond the 1994 World Cup Finals.

However, even though we cannot speak of a quintessentially Swedish style of play, it is still possible to identify certain aspects of the Swedish approach to football which are characteristic of Swedish identity more generally. Two are worthy of special mention. First, there is the discipline of

Swedish footballers who are adept, for the most part, at obeying team instructions and performing the duties assigned to them. Second, at the highest level, there exists an unswerving commitment to the interests of the national side. Only one player, Torbjörn Nilsson, a highly successful forward with IFK Göteborg, has asked to be excused from international duties and his request was prompted by his belief that he did not perform well enough when chosen to represent his country. The first of these aspects of the Swedish approach to football — the discipline of Swedish players — is scarcely surprising and can be recognised as consistent with a sense of collective responsibility which has long permeated Swedish society. In view of the historic weakness of political nationalism in Sweden, however, the commitment to the national football cause might seem somewhat incongruous. It can be explained, however, in ways which take us closer to an understanding of Swedish identity.

One must first take account of the concept of *Jantelagen* an unwritten law which operates throughout Scandinavia and demands modesty and humility. The application of the Jante law to Swedish football has had the rather unfortunate effect of preventing former star players from acquiring the status accorded to their contemporaries in other countries. On the positive side, however, *Jantelagen* ensures that no Swedish player would regard his own personal interests as superseding those of the national team and so the full-time professional who plies his trade in Italy's Serie A happily lines up with the part-timer who spends most of his working day in a Gothenburg bank; to refuse to do so would be to break the unwritten law.

Next it is important to look more closely at the principle of sporting nationalism as it operates in Sweden. For a number of reasons, this phenomenon, like political nationalism in general, has traditionally been less apparent in Sweden than in most other European countries. A policy of neutrality in international relations has meant that Sweden has no 'enemies' of recent memory. A position of strength within the Nordic region has ensured that Swedes have been less concerned to safeguard their national identity than some of their close neighbours. A commitment by the Swedish Sports Confederation to the idea of 'sport for all' has prevented the sort of emphasis on elite performance upon which sporting nationalism normally thrives. Finally, whilst other Scandinavians tend to regard the Swedes as their main rivals in a range of sports, the Swedes themselves have been more selective in the choice of sporting rivals — Denmark in football, for example, Norway in skiing, Finland in athletics and Canada, the Soviet Union (now Russia), the United States and Czechoslovakia (now the Czech Republic) in ice hockey. For these different reasons, the development of sporting nationalism has been hindered but it has never been completely eradicated. Indeed, as Billy Ehn suggests, sport has often provided Swedes with the best opportunities to express their national allegiance and such opportunities will assume even greater significance if Swedes come to feel that their identity is under threat either from EC membership or any other source (Ehn et al., 1993:206). An explanation of why Swedish sporting nationalism has so far avoided the type of jingoism which accompanies it elsewhere again helps us to acquire a fuller appreciation of Swedish identity.

A word frequently used in analyses of Swedish politics and society is *lagom* which can be roughly translated into English as meaning 'in moderation' or 'just right' (Milner, 1990:49). Although writing with the benefit of hindsight and no doubt bitterly disappointed at the time, Orvar Bergmark's comments on the 1958 World Cup Final exemplify the idea of *lagom*. According to Bergmark, "the Swedish team had done more than people had wished for: it had got to the World Cup Final" (Nilsson, 1979:191). *Lagom* ensured that Swedes were satisfied by the achievement of reaching the Final instead of being devastated by the ultimate defeat. Certainly, Sweden's Brazilian opponents that day were pleasantly surprised by the reception which their victory received. According to Guy Oliver, "they won the admiration of all the Swedes in the stadium and as a gesture paraded a huge Swedish flag around the stadium at the end" (Oliver, 1992:19). Even in the more chivalrous 1950s, few other home crowds would have been so charitable to the conquerors of their own national team in a World Cup Final. Thus, *lagom* too militates against a certain type of sporting nationalism in favour of a sense of realism and a willingness to appreciate the achievements of others. At the same time, however, it demands from Swedes not the passivity that one might expect but a willingness to participate in common activities to make sure that acceptable standards are reached (Milner, 1990:49). This aspect of *lagom* helps to explain the other, more pronounced aspect of Swedish sporting nationalism, namely a commitment to playing an active part in the administration of international sport.

Not only have Swedes willingly participated in common activities at home, they have also engaged themselves, to a disproportionately large degree, in a wide variety of international organisations. Swedish footballers, coaches and administrators have been no exception to this general rule. In their various roles, they have carried the Swedish flag metaphorically and their achievements have reflected well on their native country. In 1990, for example, Lennart Johansson was elected President of UEFA, European football's ruling body and, in that role, he has made his considerable presence felt. It is by no means frivolous to compare Johansson's involvement with world football with the commitment of fellow Swedes to a variety of international bodies, including that of Dag Hammarskjöld who was Secretary-General of the United Nations from 1953-61. Despite, or more probably because of, their country's declared neutrality, Swedes have been willing and able to play important roles on the world stage and, in a curious way, their internationalism can be seen as a form of nationalism, an expression of their belief that Sweden and the Swedes have something to offer the world in terms of selfless leadership and an appreciation of excellence. A further example of this is provided by Sweden's eagerness to host international gatherings, including sporting events.

Playing host to the 1958 World Cup Finals assumed an importance above and beyond any success achieved on the field of play by the Swedish players. It gave Swedes the opportunity to show how well they could organise a major international competition. Similarly, the European Championships of 1992 were a source of pride not only to SFF but also to wider sections of the Swedish population who were provided with further evidence of what their small country can achieve. For football supporters, of course, the performance of the Swedish team was important but more generally the image created by the tournament was what really mattered. Swedish football's commitment to international involvement will be taken a stage further in 1995 when Sweden plays host to the Women's World Cup Finals. Although there will be realistic expectations of a Swedish victory on home soil, once again the successful organisation of the competition and the way in which that reflects on Sweden as a whole will be of major importance.

In a number of different ways, therefore, the Swedes have developed a distinctive approach to football if not a distinctive style of play. What remains to be discussed is the extent to which football in Sweden reflects and is bound up with developments in modern Swedish society.

In the post-war era, Sweden has acquired a well deserved reputation for egalitarianism in relation both to social differentiation and to gender. The drive for equality is reflected in the world of Swedish football. At the turn of the century when the game began to establish its roots in Sweden, it was dominated by men, just like the wider society in which it operated. In addition, it was essentially a working-class pastime at a time when class divisions ran deeply through Swedish society. Indeed:

> the growth of football and the workers' movement went hand in hand for the most part, and in organisational terms one can assert that most football clubs were supported by the same sort of people as supported, for example, trade unions... (Peterson, 1993:15-16).

As Swedish society changed, however, largely, if by no means exclusively, as a consequence of the policies adopted by a succession of Social Democratic governments, so football responded to a new set of social relations. As class differences softened, so the likelihood that football would be regarded as an exclusively working-class sport diminished. As women secured a greater say in the general running of Swedish society, so their demand for equal treatment in the world of sport grew. As a consequence, women's football in Sweden, as in other Scandinavian countries, is well developed although this is not reflected in attendance figures for women's games and there is evidence of a widespread belief that sports like football remain essentially male dominated (Riksidrottsförbundet Informations-avdelningen, 1993). Whilst this is almost certainly true, a further explanation of the disquiet which is expressed is that in gender relations, as in many other areas, the Swedes have set themselves higher standards than exist in other countries. Although problems can be identified, the situation in Sweden is considerably better than in many other countries. SFF has a woman member of its Board, Susanne Erlandsson, and the future of the women's game looks assured. In general terms, indeed, the evolution of Swedish society would appear to have provided an ideal context for the widest possible dissemination of football's message. Swedish society is changing, however, resulting in a less favourable environment for football and much else besides.

Swedish football today faces three major problems — hooliganism, racism and what might be called public relations — all of which are illustrative of rapid social change. It is all too easy to exaggerate the scale of football hooliganism in Sweden. Not only have the media, especially the tabloid newspapers, *Aftonbladet* and *Expressen,* given it excessive publicity but arguably any hooliganism will appear significant in a society which for so long had a reputation for extremely low levels of anti-social behaviour. However, a problem exists and is often cited by people as their reason for staying away from football games. There have been numerous incidents in recent seasons involving gangs of rival fans as well as the police and much of the blame has been attached to supporters of major clubs, particularly those from Stockholm. Those include Hammarby's 'Bajen Fans' and the 'Blue Saints' who follow Djurgården. By far the biggest supporters' club in Sweden, and certainly the most notorious, is AIK's 'Black Army', which has around 3,500 members, many of whom are willing to travel regularly to watch their team play in other parts of the country (Tamas and Blombäck, 1993). Although the Black Army has been linked with a series of serious disturbances, its members' devotion to football and, above all, to AIK is undeniable. The anti-social excesses of some of its members scarcely represent a threat to the fabric of Swedish society although they may be inchoate responses to new social problems, in particular youth unemployment. Certainly AIK officials and the police have reached the conclusion that it is important to work with the Black Army in an attempt to minimise the hooligan problem.

More serious, however, is the accusation that the Black Army, together with other groups of Swedish football fans, is overtly racist. This charge assumes great significance when one realises that race relations present a major challenge to Swedish society.

Despite the relative homogeneity of the Swedish population before the modern era, it has been shown that "for several centuries Sweden had been a multi-ethnic and multi-lingual country" (Hammar, 1991:190). However, a change, both quantitative and qualitative, began to take place in the 1950s with increased demand for foreign labour and immigration grew rapidly until the end of the 1960s. At present, more than one million people of immigrant descent live in Sweden, with a majority already in possession of Swedish citizenship (Hammar, 1991:189). Despite, or arguably because of, their attempts to control immigration, the Swedish authorities have been confronted by many serious incidents prompted by anti-immigrant feeling (Westin, 1991:1). Furthermore, there is evidence to suggest that young Swedes who were once relatively well disposed towards immigrants are now moving towards a less tolerant attitude (Westin, 192:8). In such circumstances, it is easy to see how groups of young football supporters could become the source of anti-immigrant rhetoric, if not actual violence.

In the case of the Black Army, however, there is little evidence of more racist feeling than exists in the Stockholm population as a whole. Many of its members dislike immigrants, but so too do many other Stockholmers. Furthermore, the Black Army contains immigrant members although this can scarcely be interpreted as evidence of a desire for racial integration. Whether the game of football in Sweden more generally can contribute to better race relations is another matter.

Scattered throughout the Swedish football leagues are numerous clubs which serve the needs of the various ethnic communities which make up the country's immigrant population. At times, there is tension between these 'immigrant' teams. For example, in the 1970s in the southern province of Skåne it was necessary to keep Croation and Serbian teams apart to prevent violent incidents on and off the pitch. Increasingly, there are also reports of incidents in games between 'Swedish' teams and immigrants (Zachrison, 1993). One wonders if the situation is helped when a prestigious newspaper, *Dagens Nyheter,* decides to publish figures showing that 'immigrant' teams are the dirtiest in the Stockholm League (Grimlund, 1993). At present, the greatest challenge to the football authorities comes from the presence in the Swedish League's Division One (North) of Assyriska FF, a club formed by the Turkish Christian community in Södertälje near Stockholm. The team itself contains 'Swedish' players but is supported almost exclusively by 'immigrants' and fears were expressed when promotion meant fixtures with Hammarby and Djurgården, whose 'Blue Saints' have acquired a reputation for racism which exceeds that of the Black Army. So far, however, games between the Stockholm clubs and Assyriska have been played without incident. Moreover it is widely accepted that Assyriska's followers have brought atmosphere and excitement to Swedish football stadia. It remains to be seen, however, whether separate 'mmigrant' teams rather than complete integration will serve the interests of race relations in the years ahead.

Hooliganism and racism, then, are problems in contemporary Swedish society which are clearly reflected in the world of Swedish football. As in other countries, their links with the game create difficulties for those whose job it is to sell football to potential spectators and sponsors. But Swedish football faces other problems as far as public relations are concerned.

As an essentially summer sport, football is obliged to compete with a large number of alternative activities for support. Through the years, numerous suggestions have been made that a policy similar to that in other European countries should be adopted so that football would be played from the autumn until the spring with a winter break. The problem is the length and severity of the Swedish winter particularly in the north of the country. Any change to the existing situation would make it difficult, if not impossible, for northern teams to take part in national competitions and, although there are few major clubs in that area, it would be unthinkable that SFF as a national governing body could even contemplate such a development.

Another problem for football, and indeed for all Swedish sports, is the sheer size of the country. In area, it covers almost 450,000 square kilometers, a little larger than California and almost twice the size of Britain. This makes it difficult and expensive for clubs to take part in national leagues and explains why apart from Allsvenskan the rest of Swedish football is organised on a regional basis.

The Swedish Cup competition also presents problems for the football authorities. It has never captured the imagination of the Swedish public in the way that the Football Association Cup excites English football followers. Indeed, the FA Cup receives as much, if not more, publicity in Sweden than its Swedish counterpart. From the mid 1950s until the late 1960s, the competition was abandoned completely and it may be some time yet before it attains the status to be expected of a national tournament.

Swedish football also faces the problem of changing attitudes towards sport. Many young Swedes appear to want the instant gratification and well-packaged entertainment which one associates more with American sport than with football. In this respect, another very popular sport in Sweden, ice hockey, has greater potential to attract large audiences. Furthermore, it can also be regarded as being as important as football in terms of establishing Sweden's international reputation. Although a

Swedish victory in football's World Cup is not impossible, it is at best improbable. In ice hockey, however, the Swedish national team has won the World Championship on six occasions and the European Championship ten times. In addition, Swedish ice hockey players, like their footballing counterparts, consistently make their mark as professionals in other countries. In season 1992-93, for example, seventeen Swedes played for clubs in the North American National Hockey League. Ice hockey does not compete directly with football for support in Sweden. Indeed, since many clubs contain both football and hockey sections, many Swedes follow both games with equal enthusiasm. Nevertheless, no doubt the football authorities will keep a watchful eye on the way that other sports, particularly hockey, present themselves.

Despite these various problems, however, 1993 witnessed a slight increase in attendance at Allsvenskan matches due largely to the positive impression created by the organisation of the 1992 European Championships and the Swedish team's performance but also to the promotion of a well supported club, Helsingborgs IF, to Allsvenskan after an absence of 25 years (Danielsson, 1993). Furthermore the financial situation of most Allsvenskan clubs, with AIK being a notable exception, is relatively sound and overall the future of Swedish football looks bright (Persson, 1993).

In conclusion, whilst the Swedes have never developed their own distinctive style of playing football, their general approach to the game has been essentially Swedish — well organised, socially responsible and internationalist in outlook. Furthermore, Swedish football has been clearly affected by developments, good and bad, in Swedish society, such as the pursuit of equality or the problems of a multiracial society. It is unlikely that Sweden will ever win the World Cup, perhaps not even the European Championship, and Swedish clubs will find it difficult to repeat the successes of IFK Göteborg in European competitions as the elite clubs in Europe put even greater distance between themselves and the rest. Nevertheless, a significant Swedish presence will continue to exist at the highest levels of the game both on and off the field. In response to challenges to national identity, support for Swedish sport, football included, may become more stridently jingoistic but almost certainly more traditional Swedish values will ensure that the game is not disfigured to any great extent. After all, a great many Swedes agree with the statement made by their countryman, Gabriel Jönsson, that there is "a bit of poetry about football" (Jönsson, 1991:13). What will happen to the Swedes? They will be around for a long time to come bringing organisational skills, a sense of fair play and a quiet self-esteem not only to the game of football but to many other walks of life.

Acknowledgements

The author wishes to express his gratitude to the Research Committee of the Faculty of Humanities at the University of Ulster for funding his research visit to Stockholm in June 1993. He also wants to thank the following people for their invaluable assistance: Tommy Bäckman, Tomas Hammar, Tomas Johansson, Jan Lindroth, Lars-Christer Olsson and Lars Röhne.

References

Aitken, M. (1981), Interview with Lars Arnesson. Scotland versus Sweden, Official Programme, 9 September.

Danielsson, S. (1993) 'Degerfors defy the gloom', *World Soccer,* 33 (11), August.

Daun, Å. (1992), *Den europeiska identiteten,* Stockholm: Rabén och Sjögren.

Ehn, B., Frykman, J. and Löfgren, O. (1993), *Försvenskningen av Sverige,* Stockholm: Natur och Kultur.

Elklit, J and Tonsgaard, O. (1992), 'The Absence of Nationalistic Movements: the Case of the Nordic Area', in J. Coakley (ed.), *The Social Origins of Nationalist Movements. The Contemporary West European Experience,* London: Sage: pp. 81-98.

Grimlund, L. (1993) 'Invandrarlag busigast', *Dagens Nyheter,* 22 June.

Hammar, T. (1992), '"Cradle of Freedom on Earth"': Refugee Immigration and Ethnic Pluralism', in J-E. Lane (ed.)., *Understanding the Swedish Model,* London: Frank Cass: pp. 182-197.

Jarvie, G. (1993), 'Sport, nationalism and cultural identity', in L. Allison (ed.)., *The Changing Politics of Sport*, Manchester and New York, Manchester University Press: pp. 58-83.

Jönsson, Å. (1991), *Fotboll är också poesi. Gabriel Jönsson som idrottskåsör*, Lund: Wiken.

Milner, H. (1990), *Sweden: Social Democracy in Practice*, Oxford: Oxford University Press.

Nilsson, T. (1979), *Fotbollens kval och lycka. En läsebok om fotboll*,Uddevalla, Semic Förlags.

Oliver, G. (1992), *The Guinness Record of World Soccer*, Enfield: Guinness Publishing.

Persson, J. (1993), 'Äntligen går Allsvenskan med vinst', *Fotboll Magasinet*, 4, May.

Peterson, T. (1993), *Den svengelska modellen*, Lund: Arkiv Förlag.

Riksidrottsförbundet Informationsavdelning, (1993), IMU Testologen. IMU-undersökning om vad "svenska folket' tycker om Svensk Idrott.

Strindberg, A. (1967), *The Red Room. Scenes of Artistic & Literary Life*, London: Dent.

Sund, B. (1991), 'Fotbollskultur -några utvecklingstendenser', *Idrott Historia och Samhälle*: pp. 117-127.

Svenska Fotbollförbundet, (1992), *Sverige.Sweden — A Presentation*, Stockholm.

Tamas, G and Blombäck, R. (1993), 'På marsch med Black Army', *Magazine Café*, 3.

Westin, C. (1992), 'Changes in Attitudes Towards Immigrants', *Current Sweden*, 388, Stockholm: Swedish Institute.

Zachrison, G. (1993), 'Rasism på plan? Rött kort!', *Aftonbladet*, 17 June.

12 USA and the World Cup: American nativism and the rejection of the people's game

John Sugden

Why is it that the game which has been the world's most popular for almost a century has yet to become established in the world's most ethnically diverse nation? The confirmation of the United States as the host for the 1994 World Cup has given this question added significance. It is highly likely that USA 94 will be a huge success both as an entertainment spectacle and a commercial endeavour. That this can be the case in a country which does not even have a nation wide professional soccer league warrants some investigation. Indeed, the award of the World Cup to the USA by FIFA, was made conditional upon the setting up of a professional soccer league there prior to the staging of the finals in 1994. Since that agreement the United States Soccer Federation (USSF) has been forced to re negotiate its position, arguing that the establishment of a professional league would be better achieved once the soccer consciousness of the American public had been raised through the hosting of the game's greatest showcase. However, despite the guarded optimism of domestic soccer enthusiasts, there is little confidence among the global soccer fraternity that, in the wake of USA 94, soccer will seriously challenge the 'big 3', of basketball, football (American) and baseball, as the dominant American professional sports ('big 4' in certain northern and eastern regions where ice hockey has a large following).

In terms of longevity and international competition soccer is the elder statesman of American sport. Organised versions of the kicking game have been played in the United States since the 1860s. The domestic governing body, the United States Football Association (USFA) was established in

1913 and became affiliated to FIFA the same year. However, long before then the USA had played international football. In 1885 and 1886 a representative USA Xl played a series of games against Canada. While these matches have yet to be recognised by FIFA, they were the first recorded international fixtures to take place other than those between the countries which make up the United Kingdom. The USA's official international debut came in Scandinavia in 1916 when they beat Sweden 3 -2 and drew 1-1 with Norway. With the exception of 1938 the USFA has participated in every World Cup since 1930 and has made the final stages on four occasions (1930; 1934;1950; and 1990). In Brazil in 1950, the USA shocked the rest of the world by defeating a star studded England 1-0 and yet, as we shall see, this had little impact on the audience back home. Likewise their progress towards and during Italia '90 was largely ignored in the United States. Despite respectable losses to Italy (0-1) and Austria (1-2) the national soccer team's performance in Italy received scant coverage in the press and none of the games were broadcast live by any of the major television networks. In the 1960s and 1970s there were several attempts to establish soccer as a coast to coast professional sport in the United States and Canada. The North American Soccer League (NASL) which was set up in 1968, came closest to challenging the monopoly of the 'big 3', but even with the recruitment of world soccer stars such Pelé, Beckenbauer and Cruyff, the league could not capture and retain a sufficiently large audience to make it viable as a long term prospect. In 1984 the NASL went out of business and since then, with the exception of an indoor league, there has been no professional soccer played in the United States.

A conspiracy to exclude soccer?

There are a variety of overlapping explanations offered by America's soccer converts for their sport's inability to establish itself in the mainstream of American popular culture. The most popular explanations of soccer's under development can be loosely gathered under the heading of the conspiracy theory. In summary, this argument suggests that soccer has failed to take root because there is a finite limit to the American sports public's interest in invasive team sports. An increase in soccer's share of this limited pool of team sport affiliation can only be achieved at the expense of one or more of the 'big 3'. Likewise, the emergence of another extensive network for the recruitment and training of ball playing athletes is perceived as a threat to existing farm systems for the development of talent for football, basketball and baseball. Therefore, a coincidence of interests exists among America's established sports to resist the growth of soccer as a big time alternative to themselves and, from little leagues, through interscholastic, intercollegiate and up to professional sports, the American sports order is structured in such a way as to contain the expansion of the world's most popular game.

Another element of the conspiracy theory concerns the relationship between a cartel of established American sports and the American sports media. The financial success of professional sports in America is heavily dependent upon their ability to attract and sustain the interest of the media, particularly television. Once more, there is a fear that soccer can only succeed as a media sport at the expense of one or more of the 'big 3'. Over the years, as the influence of the media has increased, at intercollegiate and professional levels, the 'big 3' have tailored their games and schedules to suit the requirements of terrestrial and extra terrestrial, prime time television. Soccer in its traditional guise does not easily accommodate the commercial needs of the US television networks. It is a seamless sport which is more likely to produce a 0-0 draw as a 5-4 goal feast and the outcome of the game is by no means assured by good play and territorial dominance. This makes soccer difficult to sell to a sports viewing public who have been weaned on the stop–start diet of high scoring and statistics associated with baseball, basketball and football. Moreover, historically, the 'big 3' have accommodated the US media and viewing public by changing their format. Soccer is a world sport with regional and world governing bodies which are far less amenable to changing rules to suit media schedules or excite the casual interest of the armchair American audience. Thus, soccer represents hard work for the US media and it becomes mutually advantageous for the 'big 3' and the US media industry to work together to ensure that soccer continues to be marginalised as a profess-ional sport.

The conspiracy theory may accurately describe soccer's relationship with America's sports establishment and its media allies, but it fails to explain why the majority of the American public have been willing partners to the sport's exclusion. I intend to argue that the reason why the 'big 3' and their media allies have been able to successfully keep soccer out of the mainstream of American professional sport is because it has been and continues to be viewed by the mass of the American public as an essentially foreign game. I further intend to argue that this state of affairs currently suits the interests of the largely white middle class following which at youth and intercollegiate levels maintains soccer as an elite amateur sport in the United States. Before addressing these issues directly, though, it is necessary to consider several aspects relating to the socio-historical development of America's professional sports culture in general.

The imperial legacy and the development of modern sport in America

To begin with, the inability of soccer to develop as a mainstream sport in the United States has to be viewed as by-product of the struggle of a relatively new nation to construct a national identity which could be recognised as distinctive both from within and without. There are several facets to this struggle which are relevant to our argument. That the United States should be influenced by British sporting traditions is not surprising given the fact that most of North America, at one time or another was part of the British Empire. However, the fact that the USA did not adopt the sporting traditions of the former colonial master wholesale, as did many other former colonies, needs some explanation.

Modern sports are the product of modern societies, the institutional foundations of which were laid in the the nineteenth century on both sides of the Atlantic. Broadly speaking, the various codes of football which are played throughout the world today, including soccer and American football, share common ancestors. One ancestral line can be traced back to the rough and tumble folk games which existed throughout mediaeval Europe. In terms of structure another ancestral line is rooted the rhythms, disciplines and organisational acumen which accompanied the emergence of industrial capitalism throughout the developing world. Finally, there is the moral and spiritual dimension which emerged as an ideological complement to rational business methods. These traditions merge in the English public schools during the first half of the nineteenth century wherein codified forms of ball games and other athletic disciplines were introduced in an attempt to displace traditional rowdy, rough and tumble pastimes which generally disrupted the educational timetable and which were believed to be morally reprehensible (Holt, 1989).

The innovative approach towards sports adopted by English public schools in the nineteenth century was itself part and parcel of an complex value system which accompanied the expansion of the British Empire and British led development of industrial capitalism as a world economic order during the nineteenth and early twentieth centuries. Wherever the British waged war, administered, preached, worked or settled they played their games and, in some cases, encouraged the local population to do likewise. Hierarchy, order, discipline, self-denial, punctuality, obedience and honest toil were central to a creed which guided behaviour on the playing fields, at the war front and in the work place. At its high point more than a quarter of the habitable globe lived under the shadow of the Union Jack and those countries which were not directly subject to British rule were subject to British influence through trade, commerce and industrial development.

Nations which were part of or were touched by the British Empire were influenced by the British approach to sports in different ways. It is interesting to note that while as a world game soccer is almost certainly a British product, it has developed as the national game in very few of the former British colonies. It is the national game of many nations, such as Germany, Italy and Argentina, who were subject to British industrial and commercial influence, but who were never directly ruled by Britain. Most of the former colonies, on the other hand, either took on the more elitist British sports as their own (rugby and cricket) or invented or reconstructed their own national sports, such as rules football in Australia, Gaelic football and hurling in Ireland, ice hockey and lacrosse in Canada and baseball and American football in the United States.

Harold Perkin (1989) argues persuasively that the main reason why so many former colonies adopted elitist British sports as their own was that most of the government officials, senior military men, civil servants, educators and missionaries who recreated and administered little Englands from Johannesburg to Perth, were themselves drawn from the upper echelons of British society. As such they had been influenced both by the principles of Muscular Christianity and had come to recognise the value of sport as an agency for social bonding. Not surprisingly, the sports which they introduced were the ones with which they were familiar:

> Further afield, wherever they went throughout the world, they took their games and their social attitudes with them. Team games like cricket and rugby were ideal for keeping fit and holding the white community together in distant climes, and even where the white rulers were few and far between, tennis, golf, squash and five's were happily substituted (ibid: 148).

Clearly, in this context British sports where introduced by and for a ruling class. In places such as Australia and South Africa which had relatively large numbers of white settlers there was little overt attention paid to the sporting interests of the native population. In colonies in the West Indies and the Indian sub continent locals were encouraged to play the white man's game, particularly cricket, if only to make up the numbers. Where Britain ruled more or less directly in the second half of the nineteenth century we see a pattern through which elitist British sports and games are adopted, primarily by an émigré ruling class and subsequently by a sizable proportion of the local population, particularly the white middle classes and the educated professional elements within the indigenous population.

Meanwhile at home in Britain, well educated reformers began to introduce soccer into industrial towns and cities as part of a broader programme of "good works" designed to off-set some of the worst effects of pre-welfare, industrial capitalism. These reformers were particularly concerned with the health, moral fortitude and spiritual well being of the urban work force. Organised sports in general, and soccer in particular, were introduced in an attempt to off-set youthful idleness and channel energies outside of working hours towards activities which were deemed healthy and socially constructive (Clarke and Critcher,1985). An unintended consequence of this was that the gentleman-amateur soccer player lost control of his own game as it became massively popular among the working class and, by 1885, openly professional. Instead the educated classes turned to rugby union, which, for obvious reasons, had not proven to be as popular as soccer in the unyielding cobbled streets of Victorian England. As such, rugby union was untarnished by the lower orders and, being strictly amateur, was deemed to be more appropriate than soccer as the winter sport for young English gentlemen (Holt, 1989).

Consequently, in the second half of the nineteenth century soccer did not feature very highly in the games playing curriculum of the official British Empire. However, the unofficial Empire, the one constructed around British influence in trade, commerce and industry, extended far beyond the boundaries of the Crown Colonies. People from all sectors of British society spread throughout the trading and developing world in search of their fortunes and bringing with them the habits and customs of home:

> The British were everywhere: running cotton mills in Russia, railways and banks in South America, cattle ranches and gold mines in the American Far West, plantations in Ceylon and West Africa, farms in Kenya and Rhodesia, mines in the Transvaal, Malaya and the Andes, and banks and warehouses and factories all over Europe. And wherever two or three Britons were gathered together, to keep fit and while away the time they played the games of home (Perkin, 1989: 149).

Unlike those directly involved with the administration of the Empire, many of these commercial immigrants were not drawn from the British middle and upper classes and so had not been subject to the influences of elite education and its exclusive sporting ethos, which dwelt upon the distinction between the gentleman amateur and the artisan professional. The games they chose to play were the ones with which they were most familiar and enjoyed most. While rugby, cricket and tennis were played in almost all expatriate communities, by far the most popular sport among this group of people was association football. Moreover, because it was a simpler game and less culturally embedded than, for instance, rugby or cricket, soccer rapidly gained ground as a popular sport within the host community:

> It (soccer) was much less attractive to the public school men who went out to build the Empire. The merchants, engineers and bank clerks who went out to the rest of the world were less commonly public school boys and rarely Oxbridge graduates, and had less objection to the plebeian and less expensive game. Soccer was easier to organise and much easier to teach to the locals who took it up with enthusiasm (ibid: 151).

The existence of soccer clubs throughout the world which have retained their original English names (such as Young Boys of Bern in Switzerland, Newell's Old Boys of Argentina and several clubs in the Italian Serie A) testifies to the influence which this strata of society had on the global development of the game. Walvin (1975), Marsh (1986) and Guttman (1993) provide evidence which suggests that by the end of the nineteenth century itinerant British bankers, military personnel, railway engineers and textile workers had been instrumental in laying the foundations of soccer in Brazil, Hungary, Italy, France, Denmark, Belgium, Argentina, Russia, Uruguay, and Spain. Soccer became popular among those with whom British migrant workers and industrialists had closest contact: the local work force. That this often took place in face of stern resistance from indigenous middle and upper classes, who saw the emergence of the English game as a threat to their national cultural heritage, demonstrates the simple appeal which the game had and continues to have.

The special relationship and the development of American sports

During the same period, at least on the surface, the United States appeared to possess all of the conditions which proved to be so conducive to the development of soccer in other parts of the world. However, as Walvin (1975) explains the fact that by this time America had already developed its own national pastimes was a great impediment to soccer's growth:

> The USA with its great cities housing social groups similar to those that had monopolised football in Europe appeared to be the most likely society to adopt the new game. But the football which America adopted was not the Association game, but the native variety which had begun to emerge in the same years as the distinctive national winter game, just as baseball parallelled cricket as the American summer sport (108-109).

The same social forces which stimulated the emergence of baseball and American football as dominant sports in the United States had a considerable bearing upon soccer's failure to do likewise. First of all it is important to remember that until 1776 the United States was a significant part of the British Empire and that the vast majority of the first wave of white settlers to colonise this part of the New World were ethnically British and English speaking. The founding fathers and the architects of the American constitution were likewise white, Anglo Saxon and English speaking. As such it is not surprising that many of the country's economic, political and cultural institutions, at least in part, lean towards their British counter parts. However, it is equally important to remember that independence came only after a bitter and bloody war, in the aftermath of which many of the institutional practices of the former colonial master were rejected. It was during the nineteenth century that the United States came of age and emerged to challenge Great Britain's economic, political and cultural authority on the world stage. In this regard, the fabled special relationship between Britain and the United States is based both on mutual respect and mutual hostility. The often quoted remark that the United States and Britain are two nations divided by a common language, captures the way that the Americans have adopted and then adapted, sometimes quite radically, aspects of English culture. Markovits (1988) observes how this special relationship helped to determine the shape of the institutional network for sports in the United States:

> This strong ambivalence towards Great Britain, manifesting itself in a clear affinity fostered by a common language and a disdain for the old colonial master, whose very presence threatened the "new world's" identity formation, greatly influenced the development of public discourse in the United States in the latter half of the nineteenth century. This "special relationship" marked by both admiration and rejection, proved particularly significant in the realm of sports (130).

It is also important to remember that the United States' athletic revolution took place at a time when British sports were yet to be fully established as the dominant world model. In this respect it was easier to come up with alternative designs for sport which departed from a fledgling British orthodoxy. However, there were element of the British model which were appealing to Americans.

What they most admired was the way English sports were organised and the values which were associated with them. This rational and moralistic approach to recreation was perfectly suited to North America which was likewise experiencing unprecedented expansion in its industrial and commercial sectors. Like Britain, it too had a burgeoning industrial work force to keep fit and healthy and a rapidly expanding urban population to control and entertain during non working hours. Sports' proven capacity to operate both as an agency for social reform and social control in Britain made it appear ideally suited to the needs of modern America.

At the same time in the wake of the Civil War there was a pressing need to provide the cultural cement to reinforce the new political boundaries of the United States. The use of sport as a tool for national integration and for the enhancement of national consciousness was being demonstrated throughout the developed world, usually through employing sports of English origin. But which sports to choose to perform this function in the United States? The significant influence which the Puritans had on Yankee culture prior to the Civil War ensured that there was little in the way of sporting traditions to draw upon. The celebration of things physical outside of the context of labour had no place in a regime which stressed the relationship between physical denial and spiritual elevation (Guttman, 1988). In the latter half of the nineteenth century, however, once religion became separated from state craft and commerce, the nation turned its attention to more secular concerns including the development of an indigenous sporting culture. Unlike in the north east, the antebellum southern states were famous for their rich sporting heritage, but this was one based on the hedonistic excesses of the English aristocracy and included pastimes such as horse racing, cock fighting and fox hunting, often accompanied by gambling, womanising and bouts of heavy drinking. Such activities were associated with a regime which the Union had fought to overcome and in victory there was no way that the dilettante sporting ethos of the Confederacy would be allowed to form the basis of a new national sports culture (Oriard, 1991).

Baseball, American football and the "crowding out" of soccer in America

It was in this context that America turned its gaze towards Great Britain. While the Americans admired the Victorian values of modern British sports and games the hostile dimension of the special relationship demanded that the form of these games be radically adapted to become more characteristically American. The development of baseball provides a clear illustration of the process through which sports of the old world were adopted and adapted to meet the needs of the new. It also sheds some light upon why soccer failed to take hold in the United States during the period of its greatest growth in other parts of the world. Baseball has become so much part of the American national consciousness it functions as a totem and, as such, is surrounded by myths, the biggest of which is that it is an all-American invention. It is generally agreed by historians that while in form baseball was an adapted form of the English children's game of rounders (Guttman, 1988), in function, at least initially, it was developed as an alternative to cricket.

Cricket had been introduced into the United States by British merchants, bankers and land owners in the eighteenth century and by the middle of the nineteenth century had a strong foothold, particularly in the north east and especially around Philadelphia. On and off the field cricket was organised in such a way that it maintained the English flavour of patronage and class hierarchy. According to Bowen (1970), Cricket's "golden age" in America, which lasted from 1864 until the outbreak of the Great War in 1914 and which saw club sides in Philadelphia taking on the might of English and Australian test teams, was, to a certain extent, stimulated by the rise in popularity of baseball, which many well-to-do Anglo-Philadelphians considered to be vulgar, professional and populist.

Not that baseball began as a game for the masses. For many of American intellectuals and leaders of style, the fact that cricket was so redolent of colony and empire made it unacceptable for adoption as a national sport (Oriard, 1991). The formation of the New York Knickerbockers by a group New York business men in the 1840s formally confirmed the arrival of an home made alternative to cricket for America's upper middle classes. However, what began as a game for America's parvenu elite was rapidly taken over by people from all walks of life. It was a combination of social reform and the American Civil War which did most to develop baseball as a national pastime in America. Just as British social reformers sought to alleviate the miserable social conditions imposed by industrialism in their country, so too in the United States did a loose alliance of clerics, educators, medical professionals and like-minded philanthropists introduce rational recreation to the urban poor (Ingham and Beamish, 1993). Baseball rather than soccer was deemed to be the most appropriate game for physical and moral development of the American working class and, because of its relative simplicity and egalitarian structure, the sport proved to be very popular. As Markovits (1988) points out:

> in an interesting and lasting parallel to soccer, baseballs success was in part based on the fact that virtually no equipment or special physical attributes were necessary to enjoy or excel at the game (140).

The more popular the game became the less control the middle classes had over its development. In this sense, "baseball, like soccer, began as the invention of the middle class and was taken over by society's less privileged members"(Guttman,1988: 57).

During the American Civil War, in their spare time soldiers from both armies played a variety of simple stick and ball games akin to baseball. All that was required for a rudimentary game of baseball were a few knapsacks, a ball, a whittled spar and an open field (Swanton and Woodstock, 1980). Versions of the game could also be played in the streets and sand lots of Americas urban landscape. Moreover, the structure of the game, its division of labour and the statistics associated with it, were perfectly suited to broader principles of social organisation characteristic of the times. As Guttman observes, baseball offered:

> a unique combination of pastoral and modern elements... Playing and watching the game allowed nineteenth-century Americans to experience the comfortably familiar and the thrillingly novel, the bucolic sounds of summer and the drive and push and rush and struggle of raging, tearing, booming nineteenth century (1988: 55).

After the Civil War, in a wounded and divided nation searching for common ground upon which to build a shared cultural identity, baseball captured the popular imagination like no other aspect of everyday life:

> Throughout the 1850s, baseball caught the fancy of people from all walks in of life leading to a proliferation of clubs along occupational lines. Policemen, barkeepers, school teachers, doctors, lawyers and even clergymen had their own team. This rapid downward dissemination led to baseball's development first as New York's game, then the Northeast's game and ultimately America's game following the conclusion of the Civil War (ibid: 141).

In this way baseball spread rapidly to occupy the urban industrial recreational space which in other parts of the world was being claimed by soccer. Had baseball not already established itself in America's industrial heartland, soccer may have stood a better chance of capturing the imagination of the wider American public, particularly the working class. As it turned out, the successful dissemination of baseball "crowded out" soccer from the popular consciousness of American sports fans. However, before the introduction of floodlights and artificial turf, baseball was essentially a summer game. There should have been room for soccer to grow in the winter season, as it had done in other parts of the world. This may have happened if it had not been for the invention and spread of American football.

As was the case in England, it was the round ball which first captured the imagination of games playing gentlemen in the north east United States. The first soccer club outside of England was formed in 1862 in Boston and the game rapidly found favour among the east coast college community. Using the 1863 English Football Association rules as a guide, Yale, Princeton, Columbia and Rutgers Universities came together in 1873 to codify intercollegiate soccer. However, Harvard University, the principal academic and cultural rival to Yale, resisted moves to develop soccer as the major Ivy League game. Instead the oval ball and a version of the running game were persevered with. The game of rugby had been introduced into America's east coast campuses by students and teachers with English public school backgrounds. It seems certain that rugby was favoured over soccer because, as we have seen, during the final quarter of the nineteenth century, in England and other parts of the world, soccer had been appropriated by the working class and was rapidly developing as a professional sport. As such, soccer was deemed to be an inappropriate activity for young gentlemen who in increasing numbers turned their attention to sports which cherished the amateur ideal and remained relatively socially exclusive. Ever conscious of the social predilections of the English, America's young Brahmins followed the lead of their Oxbridge counter parts and rejected soccer in favour of rugby.

Once rugby had been adopted by the Ivy League other social and ideological forces acted to change the form and organisational structure of the game. It was a series of "international" rugby-like matches between

Harvard and their Canadian counterparts, McGill University, in 1874 which established the running game as a serious rival to soccer. As Markovits argues, "Yale's well established rivalry with Harvard proved stronger than its membership in a loose association playing the kicking game" (1988:136). With the two leading purveyors of ideas and style committed to the running and handling game, it was not long before the rest of the nation's elite colleges dropped soccer in favour of rugby.

Ironically, in the long run, it was Yale rather than Harvard, which did most to effect the transformation of rugby into American football. According to Reisman and Denney (1951), while American college athletes found the principles of rugby appealing, they were less sure about the rules of the game and the culturally located nuances through which these rules were interpreted. As the father of American football, Yale coach Walter Camp, explained:

> The American players found in this code (English Rugby Rules) many uncertain and knotty points which caused much trouble in their game, especially as they had no traditions, or older and more experienced players to whom they could turn for necessary explanations (ibid: 309).

In the absence of an indigenous Rugby tradition American players and coaches, led by Walter Camp, began to interpret and adapt the rules of the game in ways which reflected their own cultural frame of reference. Each modification contributed to a chain reaction through which additional changes to the game were proposed and implemented. Initially these rule changes were made at the behest of and for the benefit of players, but as the game increased in popularity more and more rule changes were introduced by coaches and administrators to improve the game's appeal as a spectacle. In this way, slowly but surely, a game which had been amateur, player controlled and characteristically English, became management dominated, commercially oriented and, in the bigger colleges, in all but name, professional (Sack, 1974).

However, it was more than just a problem with the rules which led Camp and his followers to reject soccer, select rugby and change it into American football. Similar social forces to those which led to the rejection of cricket and the reformation of rounders into baseball worked to ensure that neither soccer nor rugby would be suitable for adoption as a majority game for young, middle class Americans. The period in question was when the wilderness was all but tamed and the Wild West was recreated as a romantic fiction for the consumption of urban, industrial America. The notion of the physically tough, heroic and ruggedly handsome frontiers-man became part and parcel of an emergent, American national identity. As Oriard observes, the frontier image was incorporated into the ideology which drove the development of modern sports in America:

> The West disappeared as a real place to become entirely a state of mind. In that fantasy world sportsmanship and gamesmanship, despite their contradictory assumptions and implications, merged into a single sporting code that reconciled individualism with community interests, personal liberty with law, competition with fairness, violence with moral stability (Oriard, 1991: 81).

In this sense sport , in part, was to develop as a modern metaphor for the romanticised old West in America. Because rugby relied less on athletic dexterity and more on vainglorious attributes such as manliness, physical prowess and bravery it offered far more potential than soccer to act as the surrogate frontier sport. American football went a stage further than rugby by making physical prowess, heroic individualism and the triumph of good against evil central to the whole performance. This helps to explain why several teams playing in the National Football League (NFL) today, such as the Dallas Cowboys, the Washington Red Skins, the San Francisco Forty Niners and the Kansas City Chiefs, have names which are associated with the Wild West.

Stearns (1987) observes that in a parallel development, social Darwin-ism gained ground as a legitimating philosophy for sport. He argues that sport became a sphere within which Darwinism could be acted out and masculine angst, generated by competition in economic and social circles, dissipated. In this sense, Stearns argues that soccer was less useful as a vehicle for social Darwinism than American football which he views as "more symbolically anger channelling than soccer" (85). It is more than coincidental that, at the same time, social Darwinism was also being invoked as a legitimating philosophy for commerce and industry. During the latter stages of the nineteenth century almost everything in North America was influenced by the rhythms of capitalist production and consumption and the accompanying processes of urbanisation. In this regard sport was not exceptional. As Ingham and Beamish (1993) observe of America in the late nineteenth century, "culture and sport were slowly yet progressively shaped by the industrial environment of the city and the urban market" (175).

The development of American football offers a case study of the influence which political economy had on the development of sport in the United States during the period in question. Walter Camp was himself greatly influenced by the principles of rational management and industrial organisation which underwrote America's economic success and it was these principles which he drew upon most as he led the movement to scrap rugby on the nation's college campuses and forge the raw material into American football. In doing so a stage was created upon which the rugged individualism of the West and social Darwinism could be accommodated within a corporate and rational framework which was both understood by and appealing to the wider American audience.

Unlike baseball, which had rapidly diffused downwards as a blue-collar sport with a professional leading edge, for the first forty years of its existence, American football was the preserve of the expanding American middle class and as such, at least in name, remained an amateur sport. This was because the game was developed and contained within the country's intercollegiate network which was much more extensive than anywhere else in the world and of greater cultural significance. In the first half of the twentieth century in Great Britain college education was a privilege which less than 5% of the population experienced.This contrasted with the situation in North America where it was expected that after high school most of the children of the middle classes would go to one of the thousands of colleges which had proliferated from east coast to west coast in the decades surrounding the turn of the century.

Extra curricular sports, particularly American football, proved to be very popular and not just for the students who played. Even in its earliest days in the Ivy League institutions, football had proven to be a big crowd pleaser. College administrators were happy to accept the revenues which accrued to intercollegiate competitions. Intercollegiate sport in general and football in particular were too valuable to be left in the hands of students. Campus sports were taken over by professional staffs of administrators and coaches, first at Yale and progressively at institutions throughout the nation. College football developed as a huge commercial enterprise and on campuses throughout the country large stadia were constructed to accommodate the tens of thousands of students, parents, alumni and local residents who, if only out of a strong sense of civic duty, turned out to support "their" team. In this way American football came to occupy a hugely significant place in the consciousness of the middle classes and this presented a major obstacle to the development of soccer.

In the 1920s the popularity of college football and its commercial success eventually led to the development of a full blown professional league. Professional American football was nurtured first of all in the large towns and cities in the steel and coal belt and in the industrial mid-west. In this way the professional game grew as a blue-collar relative of college football in ground which in other parts of the world had proven to be fertile for the growth of soccer. By the 1950s the two systems had effectively merged with the college circuit acting as a nursery for the professional league. With an established professional peak and extensive inter collegiate farm system, American football broke its middle class boundaries and grew to be a serious rival to baseball as the national sport. Thus, even before basketball emerged to attain the status of a third, home grown, national pastime, the working class and middle class "sport space" of the American public was already crowded. There was little or no room for another outdoor team ball game, particularly one, like soccer, which could be readily associated with anti-American traditions.

American nativism, communism and the rejection of the foreign people's game

So far the development of baseball and American football at the expense of soccer has been analysed as part of a positive process through which America came of age and constructed its own national cultural style and boundaries. However, there was a negative dimension to this process of cultural reconstruction which went beyond the dictates of the special relationship with Great Britain. During the nineteenth century American nativism was a powerful force shaping America's social and political agenda. Central to any definition of American nativism are, on the one hand, the celebration of a particular concept of American national identity and, on the other hand, an intense distaste for and suspicion of foreign subcultures and alien traditions. As Higham describes it:

while drawing upon much broader cultural antipathies, and ethnocentric judgments, nativism translates into the zeal to destroy the enemies of a distinctively American way of life (1975: 6).

In reality the "distinctively American way of life" so cherished by the nativists and the driving force behind their xenophobia was a value system which claimed hegemonic authority for Anglo-Americans. The focus of the nativists enmity were the successive waves of European immigrants which flooded into the United States during the latter half of the nineteenth and early part of the twentieth centuries. After the Civil War, fuelled by the economics of reconstruction, there was a renewed influx of immigrant labour from Great Britain, Ireland, Germany, Scandinavia, Russia, Ukraine, Poland, Italy and Jews from throughout Europe. Cyclical down swings in economic fortune, however, rendered these new comers vulnerable to discrimination. The development of self-preserving ethnic enclaves which emphasised the continuation of social and cultural practices associated with the old world, was perceived by nativists as a further threat to Anglo-American supremacy. As Rader (1988) observed, alongside language and religion, recreation was one of the more important mediums through which the various immigrant groups held onto their sense of ethnic belongingness in the New World:

> While sport should not be considered a necessary precondition for the existence of any of the nineteenth-century ethnic communities, it often helped to coalesce and preserve traditional cultural patterns (142).

Almost from the outset foreign sports and games were viewed with considerable suspicion by American nativists. The Turner movement was established in Europe in 1811 and exported to the United States in the 1840s by German immigrants, many of whom were political refugees. The Turners were a particular cause for concern for the nativists because their humanistic approach to physical education was couched in a radical, anti-establishment ideology, akin to socialism. Consequently, the Turner movement was accused of fermenting anti-American feeling and "bore the brunt of mob action in several American cities" (Rader, 1988: 141). This would not be the last time that foreign radicalism and foreign sport would be connected in the minds of American nativists.

Given their Anglo-Saxon leanings, one might think that because soccer was English by origin that it would not be perceived as a foreign game by American nativists. However, as we have seen, largely through the influence of British commercial émigrés, soccer was rapidly appropriated by lower socioeconomic groups throughout the world. It was from these groups that most of the late nineteenth and early twentieth century immigrants to the United States came, bringing with them their distinctive and alien cultural preferences, including a knowledge of and liking for soccer.

Largely outside of the public gaze, soccer in the 1920s and 1930s enjoyed a growth phase within immigrant communities from industrial and commercial centres such as New York, St Louis, Chicago, Milwaukee and Fall River. It was teams from these constituencies that dominated the small number of nation-wide competitions, including The National Open Challenge Cup and the National Amateur Cup. Both of these competitions still run today, but, as Oliver (1992) observes, the names of the victors etched into these trophies underlines the ethnic dependency of the game:

> From the New York Greek Americans to the Philadelphia Ukrainians, and the Los Angeles Armenians to the German-Hungarian Soccer Club from Brooklyn, one is left in little doubt as to the composition of these teams. This has tended to alienate Americans even further away from what they already consider as a foreign sport (789).

Furthermore, in his study of ethnic sports clubs in Milwaukee, Pooley (1982) discovered that soccer clubs functioned as integral elements of ethnic subcultures and, as such, slowed the pace of immigrant assimilation into the core society. This association between soccer and entrenched pluralism reinforced the climate of opinion that it was an inappropriate sport for native Americans.

There was a tiny germ of truth which lent a certain legitimacy to the nativist's anti-foreign propaganda. A small minority of those who crossed the Atlantic in the opening decades of the twentieth century were political refugees from Europe and they brought with them a range of ideas which challenged the laissez-faire political economy of the American state. Chief among these ideas were varieties of socialism. The success of the Bolshevik Revolution in 1917 acted as an inspiration to these foreign radicals who attempted to establish in the United States something which had never existed there, namely an effective working class political movement. Indeed, as Markovits (1988) has argued persuasively, many of the explanations for soccer's exclusion as a mainstream sport in America correspond with the reasons why there is no large, organised, working class movement led by a social-democratic party in the United States:

> I am not arguing that there exists a direct relationship between the absence of soccer and 'socialism' in the United States when compared to other industrial democracies. Rather, I will try to show that some of the same American peculiarities which led to American 'exceptionalism' regarding 'socialism' also account for the subordinate place of soccer among American sports (126).

While Markovits' analysis is generally sound, there is some evidence which suggests that there may well have been a direct relationship between the exclusion of both socialism and soccer in the United States. Writing on the relationship between the American Communist Party and sports during the 1920s and 1930s, Mark Naison highlights the role played by soccer in the establishment of a workers' sports movement. During the Great Depression the American Communist Party attempted to use sport as a means of attracting and bonding workers to a broad socialist political framework. However, the communists were deeply suspicious of indigenous American sports which they believed to be woven within the fabric of American capitalism. Moreover, the vast majority of people who joined the Party at this time were not native Americans and very few of them spoke English as their first language. Likewise they were only familiar with foreign sports and games and it was these which tended to dominate the workers sports movement, such that it was:

> Some of these immigrant Communists had strong networks of sports clubs, providing an initial basis for a workers' sports organisation, but the sports which they emphasised — soccer, gymnastics, track and field — were ones which had little attraction for native Americans or even second generation immigrants. From the very first, Communist sports strategists faced a contradiction between their desire to insulate their existing following from bourgeois influences in sport and their desire to build a left wing sports movement that attracted American born workers (Naison, 1985: 131).

By the 1930s the bulk of blue collar labour already had an entrenched interest in baseball, boxing and, to a lesser extent, American football. The dual approach of Communist sports strategists which, on the one hand, vilified mainstream American sports as bourgeois and exploitative and, on the other, organised worker's sports programmes around marginal 'foreign sports', made little impact on the hearts and minds of the American work force. It only succeeded in attracting the wrath of native Americans who were able to reaffirm the connection between radical subversion and 'foreign sports'. The fact that soccer was at the vanguard of the communist sponsored workers sport movement at the time when the spectre of the 'red menace' was first evoked as a rallying call for American nativism, confirmed its status, once and for all, as an alien sport unsuitable for the consumption of patriotic Americans.

The truth of the matter was that only a small proportion of immigrants participated in the radical political movements of the 1920s and 1930s. Having fled from poverty or been forced out through persecution or exile many immigrants were happy to shed the vestiges of their homelands. This was particularly true of the children of the immigrants who wanted to consider themselves first and foremost as Americans. One way of demonstrating this was to abandon the customs of the old world and embrace those of the new There are few areas of public activity which surpass sport as a stage for demonstrating national fidelity and in large numbers the children of the immigrants channelled their athletic skills away from the games of their fathers and devoted their energies and support to the quintessentially American games of baseball and football. Soccer was popular with immigrants, but at this time, even in Europe, it was a relatively new sport which was not so culturally embedded as language or other more traditional customs. As such it was relatively easy to give up in favour of more ostentatiously American activities. In his analysis of ethnic recruitment to baseball in the first decades of the twentieth century, Guttman (1988), clearly demonstrates the appeal which all-American sports had for Europe's diaspora:

> Baseball was unquestionably a vehicle for Americanisation. Because it was perceived as the archetypically American game, baseball won the allegiance of immigrants who wished to cast their lot with their new homeland. Indeed, the children of the immigrants,

at home in America and eager to demonstrate their loyalty, became the most enthusiastic fans of all (56).

Thus, not only was soccer "crowded out" of the mainstream sports space of America by a cross-play of indigenous social forces, so too was it abandoned by large sections of the émigré community in their avid quest for assimilation into the American way of life.

Larry who? America's forgotten sporting hero

The high water mark of red and foreign phobia in the United States came after the Second World War. A series of espionage trials in the late 1940s, the outbreak of the Korean War in June 1950 and the rise of power of Senator Joseph McCarthy in 1952 exaggerated the paranoia of the American public who became suspicious of all things which were not stamped "made in America". The fear of communism proved to be the most durable of American national phobias. It is likely that the fact that soccer was adopted as the national game in most of the countries behind the Iron Curtain did little to improve its chances of being accepted as a mainstream sport in the United States.

This also may help to account for the fact that, hitherto, the United States' greatest achievement in the sport, the 1-0 defeat of England in Brazil in the 1950 World Cup, passed virtually unnoticed in the home country. So unthinkable was the result for the English that one newspaper, the Daily Express, assumed that there had been a mistake on the teleprinter and reported the result as a 10-1 victory for England! Once the result was confirmed, while the British press headlined the result as a national disaster, in the United States the event passed virtually unreported. It was as if it was perfidious to dwell on American participation in a foreign game at a time when American troops were on their way to challenge the communist menace at the front in Korea. US sports coverage was dominated by domestic achievements in baseball, golf and horse racing. The national team's World Cup win was given scant coverage in the New York Times which reported the news on the last page of its sports section. The latest tennis results from Wimbledon received more attention than the historic 1-0 defeat of England.

In the *New York Times*' report, the winning goal was wrongly attributed to Ed Souza of Fall River Mass. In fact it was Haitian born Larry Gaetjens who headed the ball past Bert Williams into the English net. There is little doubt that because the match winner was scored by a Haitian the achievement of the US team was devalued in the eyes of the American public. As Widows observes, despite the Bello Horizonte result, in the United States soccer continued to be treated as a marginal sport and viewed as memento of the old world:

> Although the rest of the world marvelled at the triumph over England, the event passed almost without record in the States. To the American sports fan soccer was still merely a game played in parks and sandlots by immigrants, as part of the culture that had been left behind, like going to the appropriate church on Sundays (Widows, 1980: 124).

Moreover, for a country so wedded to single minded pursuit of victory, the fact that the national team lost the next five international games, scoring only 6 goals and conceding 24, did little to promote the idea that the result against England represented a turning point in the fortunes of the American game.

As for the forgotten hero of Bello Horezonte, Larry Geatjens left the United States to finish his playing career in France with Paris Saint Germain. After retiring from soccer he returned to his native Haiti where it is widely believed that he met his death prematurely at the hands of Papa Doc Duvalier's secret police (ibid). Needless to say this tragic event likewise escaped the attention of the American public. Today virtually nobody in the United States, including soccer enthusiasts, has ever heard of Larry Geatjens.

The NASL : a spectacular professional failure

Against considerable odds there were several attempts during the 1960s and 1970s to develop soccer as a national, major league, professional sport. The International Soccer League was created in the early 1960s and used as a vehicle for importing wholesale big name teams from Europe during their close season. Everton, West Ham, United, Dukla Prague, Monaco and Gornik Zabre were among many who were enticed to the United States for lucrative preseason tournaments (ibid). Crowds of up to 20,000 were attracted to these games and this encouraged the business community to support the setting up of a full-time professional league.

In 1966, in the after-glow of England's World Cup victory at Wembley, which had been transmitted live on American network television, no fewer than three separate groups approached the USSF with proposals for a national league. Two were persuaded to merge to form the United Soccer Association (USA).

Approved by the USSF, the USA began operation in 1967 with 12 teams. The third consortium, the National Professional Soccer League (NPSL), was snubbed by the USSF, but began operations anyway with 10 teams. As Widows points out, "there were now 22 franchises hoping to cash in on a market that had never before guaranteed success" (ibid: 124).

Neither organisation believed that the domestic farm system could support a major league soccer programme. They also knew, at least in the short term, that the bulk of the soccer audience would come from America's ethnic enclaves. The USA imitated the ISL by scheduling its league to coincide with the European close season and inviting entire teams from Europe and Latin America to represent American Cities. For example, Shamrock Rovers (Ireland) represented Boston, Cagliari (Italy) became Chicago, Stoke City (England) were Cleveland, Dundee United (Scotland) represented Dallas, Glentoran (Northern Ireland) became Detroit, Bangu (Brazil) were Houston, Cerro (Uruguay) became New York and Ado Den Haag (Holland) represented San Francisco. For their part the NPSL recruited individual players from abroad. Many of these players had been internationals who were now past their peak, but who could be expected to draw a crowd on the strength of their past exploits for club and country. However, these reputations were only meaningful to a minority, ethnic audience. Neither strategy had a chance of enticing home grown Americans away from the 'big 3'. On the contrary, by recruiting extensively from abroad, the USA and NPSL reaffirmed the foreign status of soccer in the eyes of the very people who had to be courted as paying customers if the professional game were to survive.

In their first year of operation neither league attracted sufficient numbers of spectators to be independently viable. Houston were the only team to have a home gate average over 10,000. After a chaotic first season, during which 5 franchises went out of business, the USA and the NPSL were forced to merge to become the NASL. The NASL adopted the recruitment model of the NPSL and brought in many players from overseas. Initially the new league fared worse than its two predecessors. Attendances continued to decline as ethnic audiences, who were schooled in soccer to the highest European and Latin American standards, became disillusioned with the second rate competition which was on offer. At the end of the NASL's first season 12 teams folded and, with only 5 teams remaining to start the 1969 season, CBS cancelled its contract to provide network television coverage of professional soccer.

The fact that rather than folding the league grew in the 1970s to pose a serious, if fleeting, threat to the dominance of the 'big 3' can be attributed to two factors. Firstly, large numbers of middle class parents were becoming unhappy with the expense, risk, specialist physical demands, and violence associated with American football. Also their off-spring were being squeezed out of top-class college football through the recruitment of talented athletes from poorer sections of America. In addition, by the 1960s American football, both on and off campus, had grown into a giant multi-billion dollar entertainment industry for mass consumption. The vulgarisation of American football rendered it less suitable as a vehicle to help the children of the middle classes to develop the physical, social and moral qualities which were deemed important in their later lives as doctors, lawyers, business executives and so forth.

In increasing numbers indigenous middle class parents and physical educators began to experiment with soccer as an alternative autumn/winter sport for their children. In 1962 less than 2% of American high schools played competitive soccer. By 1988 more than 35% featured soccer as a interscholastic sport (National Federation of State High School Associations, 1988). This boom in popularity at a high school level was matched by the soccer's elevated status as an intercollegiate sport. Soccer now had a youth caucus which was not so obviously dependent on immigrant and ethnic involvement. In particular the growing strength of soccer as an intercollegiate sport gave the NASL an alternative and more obviously 'American' domestic farm system to recruit from. College sports have long played a crucial role in the selecting and training of athletes for professional sport in America. Basketball and American football are almost totally dependent on the National Collegiate Athletic Association (NCAA) for recruits. Previously, any home grown talent for one or other of the professional soccer leagues or for the national team came largely from ethnic leagues. However, while the NCAA could provide clean cut Americans who looked the part for the NASL, in terms of actually playing the game, the intercollegiate network could not match European and South America standards. In this regard the NASL faced a dilemma. On the one hand, by recruiting college graduates the NASL stood a better chance of attracting a wider American audience. On the other hand, Americans are not used to substandard sports. It was unlikely that native Americans would turn out in numbers to watch soccer if the quality was inferior. Furthermore, the soccer-educated, ethnic audiences would almost certainly turn their backs on Americanised soccer if it was of low quality.

In the short term the NASL solved this problem by recruiting it's journeymen players from the NCAA and at the same bringing in foreign stars to fill the pivotal roles. In its first few struggling seasons the NASL had relied heavily on "lower division British players-some of whom did their profession less than justice by treating the experience as a paid holiday" (Widows, 1980:128-129). In the mid-1970s the NASL began to entice bigger names into American soccer. Most notable among these was Pelé who joined New York Cosmos on June 11th 1975. At 34, Pelé was still reckoned to be the greatest soccer player in the world. He was the one soccer player who was widely known in the United States. Almost over night Pelé's presence transformed the fortunes of the league.

In playing in the NASL, Pelé gave the league legitimacy, not just in the eyes of the American audience, but also in the eyes of other world famous foreign players who became eager to extend their playing careers in the United States. From Britain came players such as Bobby Moore, George Best, Rodney Marsh and Dennis Tueart. Eusebio joined from Portugal, Carlos Alberto came from Brazil, Giorgio Chinaglia defected from Italy, Franz Beckenbauer left West Germany and perhaps the second greatest player in the world at the time, Johan Cruyff left Holland at the peak of his powers to play in the NASL. Initially this star-studded strategy proved to be a great success. For instance, in the late 1970s the New York Cosmos regularly attracted crowds in excess of 50,000 to their home games at Giants Stadium in New Jersey.

However, in the longer term, the presence of so many fading world stars in the NASL and the fact that they so brilliantly outshone the best of

America's home grown youth only served to underline the fact that the United States was a second class soccer nation. The more successful the league became the more it became dominated by foreigners. In the 'win at all costs' atmosphere of American sport, NASL coaches, the majority of whom were themselves from overseas, tended to rely more and more on imported talent at the expense of graduates from the NCAA. Furthermore, as the stakes were raised in intercollegiate, soccer more and more college coaches recruited players on scholarships from overseas (Bale, 1991). Consequently, many of the best players produced by the NCAA for the NASL draft were themselves foreigners.

Despite the introduction of rules designed to augment the numbers of native Americans on each team, the NASL continued to be dominated by overseas players. In 1979 the Vancouver Whitecaps won the championship in a play-off against the Cosmos with no less than 10 British players in the team. For their part Cosmos roster "read like a gathering of the United Nations" (Widows, 1980:131). By the early 1980s the novelty of the NASL began to wear off. Unable to identify with the teams and lacking a full appreciation for the finer points of the game crowds began to dwindle. At the same time the League became mired in a damaging litigation battle with the NFL over the issue of cross-ownership (Barnes, 1988). As attendances fell and litigation dragged on, the sponsors and the media abandoned the professional soccer experiment. Under such circumstances, as Oliver (1992) explains, the eventual demise of the league in 1984 was inevitable:

> The major problem was that the game was built up on an artificial basis. Clubs will only survive and even thrive if they have a history that supporters and owners can identify with. None of the NASL clubs had that, and so from the very start the idea was doomed to failure. Football was simply not allowed to grow naturally, and no matter how much money was thrown at it the conditions were not right (790).

Youth and college soccer: a minority sport, but not for minorities?

While the top-down approach to establishing soccer as a big-time professional sport in the United States was a spectacular failure, the game's growth at youth level is unabated. It is suggested that because of soccer's increasing popularity at a grass roots level, it is only a matter of time before it flourishes, naturally as a professional game. However, a closer look at the demographic structure of the game's youthful underpinnings suggest otherwise. Geographically, youth soccer remains a minority sport. It is played extensively along the eastern seaboard and has gained ground in the north east corner of the mid-west. Soccer is also very popular along the west coast, particularly in California. But, apart from in metropolitan areas of Texas and Georgia, soccer remains under-developed within the macho-sports culture of the southern states and in the cowboy states of the plains and mountain west. There are still large areas of the United States where people neither know nor care about the round ball unless it is one to be propelled into a basket.

Even in regions where youth soccer is relatively strong it has failed to have a serious impact in the inner cities. In American cities soccer is played either in the middle class suburbs by middle class youngsters who are overwhelmingly white, or in the city centre public parks by recent expat-riates from countries such as Haiti, Jamaica and Costa Rica. The ethnic dominated leagues still exist in and around cities such as St Louis, San Francisco, Philadelphia, New York, Hartford and Fall River, but there is little relationship between this dimension of the American game and the white, middle class, high school and college versions. Unless they happen to be recent immigrants from countries with a soccer tradition, very few ethnic minorities play the game and soccer is virtually ignored by the Afro-American community. There are some signs that the game is becoming popular among Hispanic youth along the west coast, but this ground-swell is yet to have an impact on the game at a senior level.Whether it be from the cobbled streets of east Belfast or from the shanty towns surrounding Rio de Jeneiro, throughout the soccer-playing world the most prodigious talent has emerged out of the social conditions imposed by urban poverty. This reservoir of sporting ambition remains virtually closed to soccer in America.

There are obvious reasons for this. Apart from being something to be enjoyed for its own sake, throughout the world, success in sport is seen as a potential escape from urban poverty. This has been particularly true of sport in the United States. It terms of their numbers relative to the overall population, the contribution of Afro-Americans and other minorities to the farm systems of established professional sports has been disproportion-ately high. Boxing, basketball, American football and, to a slightly lesser extent, baseball are all heavily dependent on Afro-American athletes. Fame and fortune accompany these sports at the highest levels and it is towards them that the energies and aspirations of the best minority and inner-city athletes are directed. Relative to the numbers of blacks in America, this creates a high proportion of successful black sports performers who serve as role models for up and coming generations of minority, inner-city youngsters. In this way a recruitment cycle is initiated through which the most physically literate children of the lower classes are both guided and self-driven towards established, big-time sports to the exclusion of soccer. There is little room in this scenario for a sport which lacks a professional peak, has only a slender base in the inner-cities and which has no tradition within the Afro-American community. Unless soccer can break this cycle and persuade sufficient numbers of physically gifted, minority and inner-city youngsters to take up soccer as their number one sport, it is highly unlikely that the United States will ever develop as a global soccer power.

However, within the middle class soccer subculture there is no great desire to see the game diffused to the inner-cities. In a curious reversal of what had happened more than a hundred years earlier, since the 1970s the round ball and kicking game have begun to challenge American football for preeminence as the appropriate game for middle class children. Parents and coaches highlight soccer's practical advantages in comparison to grid iron: its safety record; its inclusiveness of a wide range of physical types; its low cost; and so forth. But behind such rationalisations there may be deeper seated motivations. As Mark Lawson observes, belying its social location as a working class sport in the rest of the world, involvement with soccer has become an Anglo-Saxon status symbol for affluent Americans:

> Improbably to those who were familiar with the game in its English version, soccer became a minor snob prop, like pet alligators and Tuscan extra virgin olive oil (1993: 27).

It is no coincidence that the most significant overseas contribution to the development of soccer as a youth and intercollegiate sport has come from Great Britain. Bale (1991) estimates that the British Isles contribute almost 25% of foreign soccer players recruited on scholarships to American universities. This does not account for the many coaches working at

American colleges who likewise come from England, Scotland, Wales and both halves of Ireland. Neither does it evaluate the influence of the large number of British coaches who are employed in seasonal soccer camps which cater for a largely white middle class clientele. This Anglo involvement suits white, middle class America which no longer views British hegemony as a threat. On the contrary, in increasing numbers they view their Anglo-Saxon heritage as a refuge in the face of an increasing Afro-American, Latin and Asian cultural invasion. While basketball, American football, track and field and, to some extent, baseball have become increasingly dominated by Afro-Americans, middle class soccer remains a largely white, Anglo Saxon preserve.

But soccer at this level in America is not a male preserve. In focusing on the failure of men's soccer to gain acceptance as a full blooded American sport there is a tendency to neglect soccer's real success story in the United States. The United States women's team became world champions in 1991 when they beat Norway 5-2 in the women's World Cup final in China. This reflects the fact that nowhere in the world is women's soccer more developed than in North America. The burgeoning of the men's game in schools and colleges has been matched every step of the way by advances in women's and girl's soccer. In many countries, where women do not enjoy equal status to men and where soccer is the national sport, there is a strong bias against women playing the game. In Britain, for instance, girls soccer does not feature in the school's curriculum and while there are some women's soccer leagues they are regarded with a mixture of curiosity, ridicule and contempt by a wider, male dominated, sports audience. Because soccer in America does not have the status of a national game and, outside of the ethnic leagues, has no tradition of male preeminence, it has been relatively easy for American females to take up the game. If in significant numbers women turned their attentions to American football it is likely that they would face the same resistance which impedes the growth of women's soccer in other parts of the world. However, in the absence of such resistance, American women have been able to enter soccer free of stigma and have excelled at it. Ironically, however, the very success of the women's game in America provides sure confirmation that the men's game is a marginal sport in the United States. Furthermore, the fact that American women play the game so well and in such large numbers is used as propaganda to support the view that men's soccer is a game for second-rate athletes who are unable to contend with the masculine rigours of the home grown variety of football.

Conclusion

To reiterate the question which opened this chapter, why is it that the game which has been the world's most popular for almost a century has yet to become established in the world's most ethnically diverse nation? As we have discovered the answer lies within the complex webbing of social processes which accompanied America's break away from the British Empire and its subsequent development in the nineteenth and twentieth centuries as one of the most powerful and self sufficient nations in the world. It has something to do with the manner in which bourgeois America transformed middle class English games into sports which were more characteristically American. It has a lot to do with the way these Americanised games spread downwards and outwards and were appropriated by the lower classes, leaving little space for the cultivation of another team ball game. Soccer's rejection by the indigenous population was assisted by the game's association with foreigners at a time when the American nativist movement was as its height. This was not helped by the American Communist Party in the 1920s and 1930s which attempted to use soccer to mobilise working class support for socialism. Finally, soccer's exclusion was made complete by the millions of immigrants who, hungry with desire for assimilation into the United States, turned their backs on the customs and traditions of the old world.

All of these tendencies remain deep seated within the American psyche. This helps to explain why since the Second World War, even with the world's top soccer stars playing there in the 1970s, and the national team having some notable performances in the World Cup, professional soccer has failed to take hold in the United States. The current popularity of the game at youth and intercollegiate levels belies the fact that soccer has gained little ground in blue-collar America, is all but ignored by Afro-Americans and, outside of recent émigré enclaves, has a very low profile in the inner cities. The fact that the game has been so successfully appropriated by women only serves to confirm, both in the mind of the dispassionate observer and in the mind of the average American sports fan, that soccer is an inappropriate sport for healthy American males. Mark

249

Lawson (1993) compares the award of the World Cup to the United States with the American movie "Indecent Proposal" in which a millionaire offers a married woman $1 million to sleep with him:

> The American admirers of Association football have, metaphorically, paid FIFA to get into bed with them. Now, as in the film, the problem is to persuade others of the logic of the arrangement (30).

The weight of the arguments outlined in this chapter suggests that no matter of how well the 1994 World Cup is organised, and regardless of how many tickets are sold, so long as soccer in America continues to be viewed as a game for foreigners, rich white kids and women, its chances of becoming established as a mainstream professional sport there are minimal.

References

Bale, J. (1991), *The Brawn Drain,* Chicago: University of Illinois Press.

Barnes, J. (1988), *Sports and the Law in Canada,* Toronto: Butterworths.

Bowen, R. (1970), *Cricket: a History,* London: Eyre and Spottiswoode.

Guttman, A. (1988), *A Whole New Ball Game,* Chapel Hill: University of North Carolina Press.

Guttman, A. (1993), 'The Diffusion of Sports and the Problem of Cultural Imperialism' in E. Dunning, J. Maguire and R. Pearton (eds.), *The Sports Process,* Champaign, IL : Human Kinetics Publishers: pp.125-135.

Ingham, A. and Beamish, B. (1993), 'The Diffusion of Sports and the Problem of Cultural Imperialism' in E. Dunning, J. Maguire and R. Pearton (eds.), *The Sports Process,* Champaign, IL: Human Kinetics Publishers: pp. 169-206.

Higham, J. (1975), *Strangers in the Land,* New York: Antheum.

Holt, R. (1989), *Sport and the British,* Oxford: Clarendon.

Lawson M. (1993), 'Moving the Goalposts', in *The Independent Magazine,* Issue 246, May 29: pp. 26-30.

Markovitz, A. (1988), 'The other American exceptionalism — why there is no soccer in the United States', *Praxis International*, 8:2 July: pp.125-154.

Mason, T. (1984),'Some Englishmen and Scotsmen Abroad: the Spread of World Football', in A. Tomlinson and G. Whannel (eds.), *Off the Ball*, London: Pluto: pp. 67-82.

Naison, M. (1985), 'Lefties and Righties: the communist party and sport during the great depression', in D. Spivey, (ed.), *Sport in America*, Westport: Greenwood Press: pp. 129-144.

Oliver, G. (1992), *The Guinness Record of World Soccer*, Enfield: Guinness Publishers.

Oriard, M. (1991), *Sporting with the Gods*, Cambridge: Cambridge University Press.

Pooley, J. (1981), 'Ethnic soccer clubs in Milwaukee: a study in assimilation', in M. Hart and S, Birrell (eds.) *Sport in the Socio-Cultural Process*, Dubuque: William Brown: pp. 430-447.

Perkin, H. (1989),'Teaching the nations how to play: sport and society in the British Empire and the Commonwealth', in *The International Journal of the History of Sport*, Volume 6, Number 2, September: pp.145-155.

Rader, B. (1988), 'The quest for sub communities and the rise of American sport', in P. Zingg (ed.), *The Sporting Image*, New York: University Press of America: pp. 139-151.

Reisman, D. and Denny, R. (1951), 'Football in America: a study in culture diffusion', in *American Quarterly*, 3: pp. 309-325.

Stearns, P. (1987), 'Men, boys and anger in American society', in J. A. Mangan and J. Walvin (eds.), *Manliness and Morality:* pp. 75-91.

Sack, A. (1974), The Commercialization and Rationalisation of Intercollegiate Football. Unpublished PhD. dissertation, Penn. State University.

Swanton, E. and Woodstock J. (198), *Barclays World of Cricket*, London: Collins.

Walvin, J. (1975), *The People's Game: A Social History of British Football*, London: Macmillan.

Widows, R. (1980), *The Encyclopaedia of World Football*, London: Marshall Cavendish.

13 USSR/Russia and the World Cup: Come on you Reds!

Bob Edelman and Jim Riordan

Until its demise the Soviet Union vied with the USA for the position of top sporting nation in the world. Since entering the modern Olympics, for instance, its medal count placed the Soviet Union at the top of any official ranking of global sporting super power. The 1980 Olympic Games were held in Moscow and, in the absence of many western nations who boycotted those games, the Soviet Union became both host and "champions". The Soviets were never slow in recognising the political and ideological value of success in international sport. It seemed that few opportunities were missed to showcase Soviet achievements in world sport. It is surprising, therefore, that the USSR's performances in soccer, a game with a long history of huge popularity in Russia and its allied states were, in comparison with its Olympic success, modest.

Soccer began to take on an organised form in the 1890s, partly encouraged by the success of cycling in attracting paying spectators. The most important agents in popularising the game in Russia were British residents — primarily owners of local factories and mills, their managers and technicians, and the British diplomatic corps. Their dominance over soccer in Russia lasted until about 1908, when Russian clubs were numerous and strong enough to beat — and usurp the positions of — their former instructors.

Oddly enough, the first football game started by the British in Russia appears to have been rugby; the bold pioneer was a Mr. Hopper, a Scotsman who worked in Moscow. His efforts to launch rugby football were soon cut short however. In 1886, the game was stopped by the police authorities who considered it brutal and liable to incite riots and demonstrations.

In the early days of soccer in Russia, the game was played, first, by the British among themselves and, a little later, by mixed teams of British and Russians, the latter being mainly students, cadets and clerks in business houses. In 1894, however, Harry Charnock, general manager of the vast Morozov mills (and one of four soccer-playing brothers — from Bolton — in Moscow) introduced soccer to his workers. This step was said to be an attempt to woo them away from vodka-drinking on Sunday, the only free day of the week.

The first recorded soccer match among Russians was played in the interval between cycling races at the Semyonov Hippodrome in St. Petersburg in 1892. The rules of this 'kick-and-rush' game were primitive, and there was no referee — since nobody knew exactly how the game was played. It took a Russian-born Frenchman, Georges Duperont (later to become President of the All-Russia Football Association and, in Soviet times, Chairman of the Petrograd Football League) a member of the St. Petersburg Circle of Amateur Athletes, to translate literature on the game and to arrange the first Russian match to be played, in 1896, roughly according to the rules adopted by the English FA. The next year, Duperont's team was challenged by the Petersburg Sports Circle, which played on the parade ground of the First Cadet Corps. This is regarded as the birth of organised Russian soccer. A section of the St. Petersburg Circle of Amateur Athletes branched off to form a soccer club under the name of Sport in 1897, but it was two years before a second Russian soccer club was formed.

A printed code was forthcoming in 1900 and paved the way for the first football league in Russia, the St. Petersburg Football League (the Moscow Football League was not formed until 1910) being formed in 1901 by three foreign residents' clubs (Nevka, Nevsky and Victoria) which contested the first football championships in 1901, to the winners of which an English entrepreneur, T. M. Aspden, awarded the Aspden cup, contested until 1917.

By 1910 the popularity of soccer almost certainly exceeded that of any other sport in terms of both participants and spectators. The British diplomat, Robert Bruce Lockhart, who played for the Moscow Morozovtsy team, reports that "at a league match the average attendance was about twelve thousand people, and the women must have contributed thirty percent of the total".[1] The proliferation of teams, the uncertain interpretation of the rules and manner of play, especially between Russian and English residents' teams, along with the desire and need for regular organised competition on a nationwide level led, in January 1912, to the holding of the first conference of the All-Russia Football Association, set up for the purpose of "of uniting all Russian sports organisations involved in soccer, working out uniform laws of play and affiliating to FIFA"[2]. The Russian FA, then, came into existence 49 years after the English FA, but only twelve years after the German.

In 1912, the newly-formed Russian FA sent the first team of Russian nationals abroad to represent their country, in the Stockholm Olympic Games. It lost to Finland and, distrastrously, to Germany (0-16) — a defeat that dented Russian national pride. That was the first and last time that a Russian national team competed abroad in Tsarist times.

Post 1917

In the circumstances of Civil War that followed the Russian Revolution of October 1917, the military was put in charge of all sports amenities; it set about requisitioning all sports equipment and clubs. So all soccer clubs were more or less 'nationalised'. Nonetheless, soccer, like a few other team games, was particularly encouraged: city championships continued after 1917, despite the chaotic conditions. The authorities also organised a national festival of physical culture timed to coincide with the Second Congress of the Third International (19 July-17 August 1920). In honour of the latter event, a sports programme was put on in the new Red Stadium (formerly the Moscow River Yacht Club and later to become the foundation of the Lenin Stadium) the star feature of which was an 'international' soccer match between a Russian team and foreign delegates at the Congress. A young Scottish Temperance Society delegate, William Gallagher (later to become Chairman of the British Communist Party), captained the foreign delegates' team, which included a Canadian, Dick Beech; an Irishman, Paddy Murphy; an Englishman, Tom Quelch; five Americans, Joe Chaplin, Joe Fineberg, Eddie McAlpine, David Ramsey and the writer (and ex-Harvard soccer player) John Reed (of *Ten Days That Shook the World* fame) and two Dutchmen. The International XI lost by a heavy margin, the winners receiving the valuable prizes of one jar of fruit and one bag of flour each!

Another state initiative was to take soccer from town to village and to outlying parts of the old Russian Empire (as in the first-ever Central Asian Games held in 1920). It was later recognised that, in their haste to use organised sports like soccer as a cohesive agent to bring peoples of the Soviet land together, some officials had tried to import into Central Asia European games for which their existed no real popular (or urban) basis. Soccer was said to have been used by local religious leaders as anti-Russian propaganda. "Addressing the local population, the mullahs would say, 'See, the Russians have brought you the head of the devil; see how it jumps and brings you misfortune'".[3] It is perhaps natural that the primitive origins of the game should be harked back to by pre-industrial people unaccustomed to games that were highly controlled and circumscribed by rules which ensured that the excitement of the struggle did not carry the players too far.

During the 1920s, the period known as NEP — the New Economic Policy — doubts were cast on the social value of competitive sports like soccer. Competitive sport, it was said, distorted the 'eternal ideals' of physical culture; instead of being universal, it led to narrow specialisation that was detrimental to health; it encouraged commercialism, professionalisation and demoralisation. Competitive sport diverted attention from the basic socialist aim of providing recreation for the masses; it turned them into passive spectators.

It was a period decisive for the future of Soviet society, with the death of Lenin and an acute struggle in many spheres of life, culminating in the defeat of the Trotskyist tendency, the development of bureaucratisation, the forcible collectivisation of agriculture and the start of the 'revolution from above'. By the end of the period, Stalin's preeminence was unchallenged and the whole country may be described as having been thrust into the straightjacket of industrialisation.

The modern era of Soviet spectator sports really began with the 1930s (the First Five Year Plan had been launched in October 1928, and the forced collectivisation of agriculture had begun in 1929). The previously haphazard and inconsistent structure of soccer, the most popular of all sports, would now come to an end. Instead of the occasional tournament, an All-Union league was established, in which permanently organised club teams, representing various sports societies, played each other on a regular seasonal basis. The organisers of Soviet sport chose to establish a truly national league in order to accommodate the growing demand for sports entertainment. This model had been developed by the highly successful soccer enterprises in the West, and it was the path now chosen by both soccer professionals and government organisers as the best way to promote the sport in the Soviet Union. It was also thought that by forming a nationwide soccer league, it would be possible to create yet another institution that could reinforce the sense of cohesion in the farflung multinational state that the USSR had become.

By the mid-1930s, the country had weathered the most wrenching phases of the industrialisation drive. Millions of peasants had been uprooted from the countryside and thrown into factories, construction sites and mines. Tens of thousands of workers had moved from the factory floor to positions of management and power. The society of the 1930s differed from that of the preceding period, therefore, in seeing the flourishing of all manner of competitive sports (soccer, basketball, volleyball) with mass spectator appeal and the official encouragement of leagues, stadiums, cups, championships, popularity polls, cults of sporting heroes — all the appendages of a sub-system consciously designed to provide general recreation for the fast-growing urban populace. The new sporting spectacles helped also distract the masses from the hard and exacting life beyond the stadia. The many sports parades and pageants which constituted a background to the sports competitions were intended, too, to create and reinforce this group feeling and demonstrate to people (abroad as well as at home) how happy and carefree life was under socialism in the Soviet Union — "under the sun of the Stalin Constitution", as it was said after 1936. It is significant that important soccer matches (cup final, international fixtures) often accompanied a major political events (May Day, Constitution Day, Anniversary of the October Revolution). In this way, soccer, and sport generally, became a means of linking members of the public with politics, the Party and, of course, Stalin (his portrait, in hundreds of copies, deputising for his person — since he preferred to cultivate the image of himself as a remote godhead).

The old format of soccer competition was no longer suitable. Instead the authorities organised a league similar to those operating in the West. The championship would now be contested by club teams sponsored by the various sports societies in the major cities. The season would stretch over the summer, as teams played each other in a regularly scheduled pattern. This change would provide a stimulus for the players and entertainment for the public.

In addition to the first league season in 1936, limited to seven top club teams, a cup competition was arranged in the same year. While the league afforded an opportunity for the best players to polish their skills, the cup competition played an important part in expanding the mass base of the sport. Despite the hope engendered by the new form, soccer's organisers would constantly struggle to find an optimum structure and schedule. The number of teams permitted to compete at the Group A (first division) level changed each year, and there were constant disputes about fair ways to arrange the schedule. In the vast land, with a still-inadequate railway network, it was by no means certain that teams would show up for scheduled games, and when both teams appeared the referees were often missing.

Soccer in the late 1930s was dominated by the rivalry of the two great Moscow sides, Dinamo and Spartak. Sponsored and financed by the Ministry of the Interior, Dinamo was known for its precise and technical game, featuring constant running and long passing. Spartak, sponsored by the wealthy industrial cooperatives, featured a more improvisatory style that stressed ball control and precision passing. These images — Dinamo's rationalism/discipline, and Spartak's romanticism/improvisation — heightened the rivalry. Whether true or not, Soviet fans continued to hold to these images throughout the history of both clubs.

Among the Moscow teams, only the Central House of the Red Army (later renamed the Central Sports Club of the Army) could challenge the Big Two. The Lokomotiv Society, representing transport workers; the Torpedo Society, sponsored by the ZIS motor works; the Krylya sovetov (Wings of the Soviets) from the aviation industry also fielded respectable teams that attracted smaller but loyal followings of Moscow fans. Outside the capital, Dinamo Tbilisi in Georgia's capital city established itself as a power, as did Dinamo Kiev in the Ukraine's capital.

Both the league and the cup competitions proved attractive to the public and soccer quickly acquired an even more sizeable mass following. In 1938, first division games averaged crowds of 19,000 and the next year ten million attended soccer at all levels of competition. Cup finals and meetings between Spartak and Dinamo could overflow Moscow's largest stadium, the Dinamo Stadium, but as few as five thousand Muscovites might watch Central Army take on Torpedo. Odessa, Leningrad, Kiev and Tbilisi were hotbeds of soccer interest, and each city had a large stadium with a capacity of between 20,000 and 40,000.[4]

While domestic competition had established a fairly big audience, international matches proved to be the biggest attraction. In 1936, Turkish teams made their last appearance in Moscow before the war, and Dinamo Moscow played several games in Czechoslovakia. But the turning point for Soviet soccer came the next summer. At the height of the Spanish Civil War, an all-star team of Basque players drawn from the leading clubs of Spain toured Europe to raise funds for the Republican cause. The Basques arrived in Moscow on 16 June 1937 to huge acclaim. They won all their initial matches, including a 2-1 defeat of Dinamo Moscow before over 90,000 fans in the Dinamo Stadium. Finally, Spartak Moscow won a much disputed victory 6-2 against an extremely tired team that had played a dozen matches in almost as many days. This was the first defeat of a first class professional team by any Soviet side. This honour had gone to Spartak and not Dinamo, a fact that did not sit well with Dinamo's new President, Lavrenty Beria, Stalin's chief of Secret Police.

The next year Spartak defeated Beria's favourite team, Dinamo Tbilisi, 1-0 — on a disputed goal in the cup semi-final. Two weeks later, Spartak won the final 3-1 against Stalinets of Leningrad, before 70,000 fans. Almost immediately the Party Central Committee ordered Spartak to replay the semi-final against Dinamo Tbilisi. So the first semi-final game in soccer history to be held after a final actually took place. Despite the machinations, Spartak managed to win 3-2 and keep the cup.

Everyone connected with Spartak was to pay dearly for this affront to Beria (who had in his youth been a mediocre and, according to Nikolai Starostin who played against him, extremely crude and dirty player). During the purges of the late 1930s, the head of Spartak's sponsor, the Industrial Cooperatives — Kazimir Vasilievsky — was arrested in 1939, as was Alexander Kosarev, head of the Komsomol which had initially been instrumental in establishing Spartak; Kosarev, then a member of the Politburo of the Communist Party, was executed. Then came the arrest of Spartak's best players, including the four Starostin brothers — of whom Nikolai was both Spartak and the Soviet national team captain; they were only released from labour camps after Stalin's death, in 1955.

Political interference in soccer was nothing new. Every Soviet stadium had its 'government box' and clubs knew they had to cater to the politically privileged and powerful. Spartak regularly gave out a thousand tickets a game — to members of the Party Central Committee and the Moscow City Council. For some members of the apparat, good seats were not enough. They named and dismissed coaches and sought to dictate team line-ups, actions that were deeply resented by soccer professionals.

In the mid-1930s soccer became fully professionalised. As a former Dinamo Moscow player in the late 1930s, Yevgeny Yeliseyev writes:

> With the very first league season among club teams, players became professionals. They received a wage for their work. When I played for Moscow Dinamo, I was registered as a PE instructor for Dinamo, and for the first time in my life began to receive money for playing soccer. This system existed in both army and trade union teams as well.[4]

Teams also came to spend as much as two months in the south for pre-season training. The demands of soccer now made the holding of a regular job, at best, a formality.

Sports 'businessmen' now began to roam the country in search of soccer talent. Players moved from team to team looking for better deals, and the sports societies developed their own talent in special schools. The hypocrisy of professionalism in this era was of a very different order than it would assume after 1945. The various fig-leaves used to disguise the practices gave something of a tinge of semi-professionalism rather than complete professionalism to big time soccer.

The rise in playing standards and attendances at matches did not, however, have a positive effect on behaviour. If anything, the greater importance of soccer led to a decline in sportsmanship. After the first two months of the inaugural 1936 season, the Football Section's disciplinary committee was required to deal with 43 separate incidents of 'hooliganism'. It was not uncommon for players to kick an injured opponent lying on the ground in pain, and cursing referees was widespread. It has to be said that refereeing standards were far from uniformly high and it sometimes happened that referees lost control of matches; often the referees themselves received suspensions. Teams were allowed to object to the naming of a particular referee; before one game in 1939, Spartak v. Central Army, eight candidates were rejected before the teams could agree on a referee.

It became common for the press and sports officials to attribute poor behaviour to lack of 'political education'. Insufficient political training evidently contributed to the low results on the field, as well as misbehaviour off it. Most teams had Komsomol cells, and one player was designated as the 'political leader' (politruk). Spartak's captain, Nikolai Starostin, later claimed that Spartak's disciplined behaviour was the result of cultural education, including attendance at plays, lectures and museums. In fact, Spartak's players were as liable as any others to indulge in dirty play; one can only speculate that this political and cultural training was mere window dressing and lip service to political overseers.

If the players did not always approach the task of playing soccer with official values in mind, the same may be said of the fans who watched the matches. Their love of the sport and the way they consumed it closely paralleled the experience of their counterparts in the West. Fans came to adopt favourite teams. Stars emerged who were heroes to the public. Fathers took their sons to matches as the sport became an important form of male socialisation. More and more matches were broadcast over the radio as millions listened. In the increasingly anomic and crowded world of the new Soviet cities, with so many recent immigrants, a fan could attend a match and find an immediate sense of community.

The cramped conditions and surly service at soccer stadiums did not, of course, contribute to public order. Fans often threw bottles (vodka drinking being a traditional pastime at soccer matches) and other objects on the pitch. At other times, they invaded the pitch. Full scale riots were rare, but some did occur. After one particularly violent disorder at a 1937 match in Leningrad, the authorities instituted the practice of ringing the pitch with soldiers. This approach to crowd control continued to the end of the Soviet period in 1991 despite the fact that at many matches soldiers outnumbered spectators.

By the end of the 1930s, soccer in the USSR had taken on may of the characteristics of professional sports in the West. It was something that the Soviet public very much wanted and the authorities knew it had to provide, but in consuming this particular spectator sport, Soviet citizens ascribed to it very different meanings than did those who produced and supported it.

In the war years, it is an indication of the popularity that soccer had achieved that the sport was used often to boost morale. For example, soccer matches took place in besieged Leningrad; a commentary on some of the matches was broadcast throughout the Soviet Union and all along the battlefront. A far more deadly match was played in Kiev between Dinamo Kiev and officers from the Luftwaffe — the famous 'match of death', won 5-3 by Dinamo even though the players knew that victory would mean their execution. In the wake of the bloody Battle of Stalingrad, a hastily reassembled Spartak team played a side of local stars before 10,000 fans in a makeshift stadium. The larger lesson associated with these games was that the popular love of soccer was so strong that even in the most tragic of circumstances people still played and watched it. To do so was to snatch some small piece of humanity in the midst of misery.

Postwar football in the Soviet Union

Although the war had brought German invasion and extensive damage to the Soviet Union (not to mention some 25 million war deaths) it also brought Soviet power and influence into the heart of Europe — a source of seemingly interminable friction with the Western powers. In these conditions of international conflict and economic devastation, the Soviet people had to turn to the task of reconstruction, which, once again, had to be accomplished largely from the country's own resources. Peace brought no relenting in either economic tempos or political pressures (and purges, including athletes and all involved in sport).

Soviet soccer received its biggest boost in mass popularity at the end of the 1945 season. Dinamo Moscow took up an invitation to tour Scandinavia and the United Kingdom. For the Soviet soccer following, Britain had remained the centre of the soccer world, so matches against British clubs would be the ultimate test. When Dinamo left Moscow on 4 November 1945, they took with them Vsevolod Bobrov of the Central Army team and two members of Dinamo Leningrad — following the well established practice of strengthening touring clubs with stars from other teams (contemporary British accounts show no awareness of this 'reinforcement'). The matches attracted huge attendances — for example, the first match against Chelsea had over 85,000, with spectators on the roof tops and along the touchline. The 3-3 draw did not reflect the run of play, which was heavily in favour of Dinamo. The match was broadcast live to the Soviet Union by the first of the great sports broadcasters, Vadim Sinyavsky. Four days later, Dinamo beat Cardiff in Wales 10-1. The crucial match, however, followed four days later in London when Arsenal entertained Dinamo. Arsenal had strengthened its team by inviting several players from other teams; Dinamo protested (though no one mentioned that eight of Dinamo's 13 goals had so far been scored by non-Dinamo players) — to no avail. The match was played in the most bizarre of conditions: a London pea soup fog. Under normal circumstances, the game would have been postponed, but so great was the anticipation that huge crowds massed early in the morning outside the Tottenham Hotspur ground where the match was held owing to bomb damage at Arsenal's ground. The police decided to admit a crowd of no more than 50,000 at ten thirty, four hours before kick off. By the kick off time it was hard to call the match off. Dinamo won 4-3 (despite Stanley Mortenson of Blackpool scoring a hat trick for Arsenal). The reaction back home was ecstatic; Dinamo's victory won a huge audience for soccer in the USSR, as millions listened to the broadcasts and read the extensive press coverage. Fans now had an excellent reason to believe that Soviet soccer was as good as any in the world. One week after defeating Arsenal, Dinamo drew 2-2 with Glasgow Rangers before 90,000 at Ibrox Park.

As much as any single event, Dinamo's tour demonstrated sport's international political potential to the Party leadership. Soviet athletes were to be carriers of 'peace and friendship', and their successes could be seen as proof of the superiority of the society that bred them. This took an additional significance after the Party launched its policy in 1949 of "winning world supremacy in all the major sports in the immediate future"[6].

The postwar period witnessed a boom in soccer attendance. Important matches between Moscow's leading teams and against top provincial contenders such as Dinamo Tbilisi and Kiev regularly packed Dinamo Stadium with crowds of between seventy and ninety thousand. In the first two years of postwar soccer, an estimated twelve million attended first division matches; with a twelve team league, this meant an average gate of 45,000. Even allowing for the relative cheapness of tickets, this was an impressive figure, and large crowds were no longer limited to the capital.

After the war, soccer moved to a new level of popular culture. Soccer was no longer simply one of the many products of the mass culture industry. It now had a broad and committed audience, and that audience followed the sport on its own terms rather than on those of the authorities

— a 'negotiated' rather than 'dominated' response to the state's attempt to control mass culture. Soccer became a regular daily concern, even passion, for many Soviet males. While they may have accepted the fundamental legitimacy of the political and sports systems, they did not always respond unquestioningly to the particular set of messages the Party and state attached to the sporting events that were made available.

Increased international competition, it was now thought, would give Soviet soccer many more opportunities to tests its coaching methods. In 1946, the USSR joined FIFA, which meant that soccer officials could now schedule matches with foreign professionals, though considerable care was taken in selecting opponents. Teams from Eastern Europe provided the bulk of the competition, and no team the calibre of Dinamo's British opponents would be faced until after Stalin's death (1953). By 1948, however, international competition became much less frequent under the impact of the Cold War and the increasingly xenophobic internal atmosphere. Between 1948 and 1950 Soviet teams ceased to play any foreign opponents, and an attempt was made to find Russian language equivalents for the many English words that had come into the sports vocabulary, such as the following prescriptions:

futbol → *nozhnoi myach*		*offsaid* → *vne igry*	
golkeeper → *vratar*		*korner* → *uglovoi*	
pass → *podacha*		*forvard* → *napadayushchy*	
bootsy → *botinki*		*shorty* → *trusiki*	
referee → *sudya*		*khafbek* → *poluzashchitnik*	

The most ridiculous was changing '*penalty*' to '*shtrafnoi*' (from the German '*Straf*'). It is interesting to note that at a Soviet soccer match in the 1950s onwards, one could hear a mixture of these terms (often from the same person) although *nozhnoi myach* for *futbol* never caught on (unlike *ruchnoi myach* which competed equally for modern usage with "*gandbol*").

In the immediate postwar period, the accent on political-ideological work increased. Success was explained by the high level of such training. All players were exhorted to read Stalin's biography and study his works, as well as the history of the Communist Party and Marxism-Leninism. One can easily imagine that many players took this all with a pinch of salt —

probably as seriously as some modern American college athletes tackle their academic studies. Certainly, if political ideological education had been as effective as its proponents had wished, there would have been far fewer problems that it was supposed to combat. The problems of dirty play, attacks on referees, disobeying of coaches, missing training, and the 'star syndrome' continued unabated. The same applied to the fans. Postwar fans acted much like their counterparts in other countries. The fundamental difference was in the minds of the organisers of Soviet sports events. Those who presented Western sports spectacles were far less concerned than were Soviet officials with the moral, cultural and political lessons of the spectacles they were presenting.

An example of gross interference of the political authorities in soccer centred on the Central Army team. In the postwar years, soccer was dominated by the team representing the Central House of the Red Army which won five of the seven league championships between 1945 and 1951 (Dinamo Moscow won the other two). In the wake of victory over the Nazis the army had come to enjoy unparalleled popularity in society, and its sports organisations were able to translate this support into strength on the pitch. The army was, of course, always able to draft promising young players from other clubs. Moreover, with the USSR about to join the Olympic movement, it had to show that its athletes received no remuneration from sport and did not pursue sport as a career. No better model could be found than the 'soldier athlete'. Despite their lack of military training the players of the Central Army team had the rank of lieutenant — hence their nickname, the 'team of lieutenants'.

In making their debut at the 1952 Olympics, the Soviet soccer team was optimistic of a gold medal against the amateur teams of the West and the fairly weak teams of Eastern Europe, all of which had been beaten by Soviet teams, with the exception of that of Yugoslavia (following Tito's split with Stalin). In the first match against Yugoslavia, the Soviet team recovered from 1-5 to draw 5-5; but in the replay, lost 3-1. The Olympics had received extensive coverage in Soviet newspapers but the defeat at the hands of the 'soviet-fascist Tito clique' was deemed so shameful that it was not reported at all. Only after Stalin's death could it be mentioned. In the September following the Olympics, the daily sports paper *Sovetsky Sport* ran the league standings. Central Army was missing. The team had been disbanded, as had been the Air Force team, with their players distributed to other teams (they had formed the nucleus of the Soviet Olympic team). In addition, several players and coaches lost their 'Honoured Master of Sport' or 'Master of Sport' titles. The punishments stopped there however. No one was arrested or exiled. But it would be two years before any team from the armed forces appeared in the Soviet first division. In the interim, Stalin died. The fate of the 'team of lieutenants' remains the quintessential case of political meddling in sport during the Stalin period. It was never to be repeated.

Post-Stalin soccer

When Stalin died in 1953, relations with the West had deteriorated to a state of dangerous confrontation. In the next decade, however, the tone of Soviet foreign policy became less strident. A policy of 'peaceful coexistence' would evolve, as Nikita Khrushchev consolidated his power. In this new situation, communism and capitalism were still in contention, but not necessarily on a collision course. The Olympic Games soon became one element of that competition; in a way they became a surrogate for the Cold War. In the light of these developments, the Party sought to portray Soviet dominance of the Olympics as proof of the superiority of the communist system, not only in sport, but in other areas of human endeavour too. It has to be pointed out that sport — apart from initial space conquest — was the only tangible and visible area in which the Soviet communist system was able to demonstrate its superiority.

Soviet (and other communist nations') superiority at the Olympic Games has been well documented. However, when the Soviet Union came to play Western professionals in the more popular spectator sports of soccer, basketball, tennis and ice hockey, the overall record was far less impressive than it was in the Olympics. When Soviet athletes ventured outside the officially amateur ranks, they lost almost as often as they won, and this mixture of success and failure, as opposed to nearly total Olympic domination, more accurately reflects the limited place sport came to assume in postwar Soviet society.

In the postwar period there was no question more intractable than the ongoing failure of the national soccer team to live up to the hopes and expectations of its millions of fans. The country faced three huge handicaps in seeking international soccer success. The first problem was the climate.

In most of Europe, the soccer season starts in late summer and continues through the relatively mild winter until May. The harsh Russian winter has made such a domestic schedule impossible. Because most international competitions culminate in the late spring or early summer, a time when Soviet players are only just getting into form, they have enormous difficulties with opponents whose schedules have led up to these decisive moments.

The second factor hampering Soviet soccer was that, as far as the sports authorities were concerned, it was only one of several sports in the Olympic programme. The insistence on across the board (in Olympic sports) excellence, important for dominating the medal table, restricted soccer's capacity to attract the nation's best athletes. Until the late 1980s, the rewards in soccer were not that much greater than those in other sports; as a result, the talent pool was spread more thinly over a wider range of sports than was the case in Western countries like Italy, Britain, France, Spain and Germany (and South America especially). In other parts of the world, the most remunerative sports tended to attract the best athletes, but in the Soviet Union the popular dream of soccer glory was undermined by the official emphasis on Olympic victory.

The third reason for Soviet soccer's relative failures internationally is that for a long time it was the only sport in which Soviet teams played against other professionals — from the earliest days of the postwar era (even previously). This was not the case for most other sports in the Olympic programme. The best athletes in the West were always professionals; but by claiming to be amateurs, Soviet athletes were able, in many sports, to limit the talent pool available to their opponents. This would never be the case in soccer.

The Soviet Union did not enter the World Cup until 1958. Before then, the national team and several of the leading clubs played numerous 'friendlies' against a carefully chosen list of opponents, picked for the often contradictory concerns of their prestige and defeatability. In 1953, however, Soviet club teams again began to play foreign opponents, at home and abroad. These matches took place in late summer before the opening of the European season and in the autumn after the end of the Soviet season. The opponents included Ujpest Dosza of Budapest and Rapid Vienna.

The 1954 international calendar was also dominated by club teams. Arsenal returned Dinamo's 1945 visit with an October game in Moscow, won 5-0 by Dinamo. A month later, Spartak played Arsenal in London, winning 2-1. Just two weeks earlier they had beaten Anderlecht in Brussels by the stunning 7-0 margin. That summer the national team was finally assembled for the first time since the 1952 Olympic defeat; led by their new coach Gavril Kachalin, they drew 1-1 in Moscow against the powerful Hungarian team led by Puskas and Kocsis.

The peak of pre-World Cup international activity came in 1955. Dinamo Moscow and Spartak toured England and Italy where they took on Wolverhampton Wanderers, AC Milan and Fiorentina, but the highlight of the year came that summer when the national team beat the recently crowned world champions West Germany in Moscow. In 1956, at the Melbourne Olympics, the USSR, with eight players from Spartak, defeated Yugoslavia 1-0 in the final to take the gold medal. The Olympics, however, were far from the ultimate test. The World Cup now beckoned.

The first Soviet appearance in the World Cup began a series of frustrations that were relieved only by occasional good results in the less prestigious, but still important, European Cup. This extremely limited record of international success was not for the want of trying. In the inevitable tensions between the demands of the national team and the needs of the clubs, the national team was always given preference. League schedules were continually being disrupted, and the clubs had no choice but to release their players for international events. Coaches of the national team came and went at a dizzying pace, with 31 changes between 1952 and 1983. In all 15 men held the job, with Kachalin and Beskov each having four turns at the helm. The press was filled with analysis, criticism and recrimination, but aside from the European title in 1960 and a semi-final World Cup appearance in 1966, there was little to show for all the effort.

It was a source of continuing frustration that so large a nation with so much sporting success should not be able to achieve equally good results in its most popular sport. But this record should not be seen as anomalous. The failures were as much a reflection of the weaknesses of the Soviet sports system as Olympic victories were signs of its strengths. When competing against professional athletes who enjoyed the support and resources of powerful Western nations, Soviet teams had difficulty winning consistently. In the World Cup, the team would make the final stages of the competition in the host country and play well in the opening rounds. They would then advance to the quarter-finals, where they would be eliminated, often in bizarre circumstances. Only in 1966 did they get as far as the semi-finals, where they lost 2-1 to West Germany (having had their left winger, Igor Chislenko, sent off controversially in the first half).

After that success in England, expectations were high for the 1968 European Cup, but the team would draw with Italy in the semi-finals, only to be eliminated by the toss of a coin. They then lost third place to England. Kachalin was back in charge of the team that went to Mexico in 1970. A new generation of players was recruited, but yet another fiasco occurred. The team played brilliantly in the first round games, despite the problems of heat and altitude. Then they met Uruguay in the quarter finals. Again controversially, they had a goal disallowed in extra time, then conceded a hotly disputed goal three minutes from time.

The criticism this time was louder and longer than ever before. *Izvestia* said it received almost 300,000 letters about the team's performance; the outpouring was a reflection of soccer's huge popularity, and it is hard to imagine such hand wringing in any other sport. After the Mexican 'disaster' of 1970, the Soviet national team did not appear in another World Cup until 1982. The only bright spot during these years was a European Cup Championship appearance in 1972, where they lost to the powerful West Germans. In 1974, their refusal to play Chile cost them a place in the finals, and in 1978 the team did not even qualify to go to Argentina. This last disaster marked the failure of the great experiment in which the highly successful Dinamo Kiev side of the mid-1970s served as the basis for the national team. Under the hyper-rational coaching of Valery Lobanovsky, Dinamo Kiev had become one of the strongest teams in Europe, winning the Cup Winners Cup and then the Super Cup in 1975. But the use of Kiev as the national team required them to play league games, national cup games, European club games, elmination games for the World and European cups, and Olympic Games as well. The inevitable result was exhaustion and defeat.

In 1982 and 1986, the Soviet team made it to the final stage, but the old pattern was repeated. Fine play in the first round only created anticipation that turned to disappointment with later defeats. In 1982, they lost in Spain to Poland; in 1986 in Mexico they lost a strange match in the quarter final to Belgium 4-3.

In other international competitions, the record was also less than brilliant. In the three European club tournaments, Soviet teams won a total of three times. Dinamo Kiev took the less competitive Cup Winners Cup twice, whilst Dinamo Tbilisi won it once. In 1970, Dinamo Moscow played in the Cup Winners final only to lose to Glasgow Rangers. The summer schedule, the cause of so many of Soviet soccer's problems, had a particularly adverse effect in these tournaments, which begin in the autumn and resume in early spring. In the autumn, Soviet teams were quite successful. After playing an entire season they were in good physical condition and the level of team play was relatively high. Few Soviet teams, however, managed to clear the hurdle erected by the resumption of the tournaments in early March when the Russian weather was still harsh and teams were coming off their winter lay-off.

Olympic victories also became harder to achieve after the triumph of 1956. FIFA attempted to minimise the advantage of the officially amateur teams from Eastern Europe. No player, professional or amateur, who had taken part in any World Cup game could now take part in the Olympics. While this change hurt the Soviet Union, it did not have the predicted effect of preventing the other East European teams from dominating Olympic competition in the interim. In 1976, the Soviet Union sent a particularly strong team precisely because they had not taken part in the 1974 World Cup. The top Soviet striker, Oleg Blokhin, would lead many of his Dinamo Kiev team mates into Montreal, but they could do no more than bring home the bronze.

The contrast between Olympic victory in so many sports and international defeat in soccer troubled Soviet fans, players, coaches, journalists and bureaucrats. Sports officials had to learn the painful lesson that they could not have it all. The same might be said for the larger needs of Soviet society, which were always subordinated to the military and geopolitical concerns of the state. If Olympic sports were a correlation of the heavy industry long favoured by the Party, then soccer can be said to represent the long suffering and neglected consumer sector.

As soccer became a truly nationwide, rather than simply Russian, pastime, provincial teams came to challenge the clubs from Moscow. Throughout the 1950s, Moscow remained the centre of Soviet soccer and, in 1954, what had been the city's strongest team, Central Army, was re-established. Its players came back into the army fold. But it was to be only in 1970 that it recovered its former glory and won the championship, its first title since the 'team of lieutenants' and its last until Soviet soccer's final season in 1991. With the return of Nikolai Starostin from exile in 1955, Spartak again assumed a position at the highest level of soccer and, in 1956, Spartak made up the base of the national team that won the Olympic title in Melbourne.

As provincial cities grew, their capacity to support big time soccer teams increased. More and more towns built large stadiums, and more and more local and Republican institutions were able to devote resources to the game. TV helped promote soccer in all corners of the land. A team in the first division was an important status symbol for a city and its leaders. It became fashionable for various powerful 'patrons' of the game to attract players and coaches to provincial centres with substantial rewards of apart- ments, cars and money. In the past, Moscow's teams had been able to summon virtually any of the nation's best players, but from the 1960s they faced stiff competition for talent.

One of the first signs of the shift in the balance of power came in 1961 when Dinamo Kiev won the title. Using all the considerable resources of the Ukrainian Communist Party, along with innovatory coaching of Victor Maslov, Dinamo Kiev was eventually able to assemble not just a strong team, but a powerful organisation that would remain at the fore- front of Soviet soccer thereafter, winning eleven more championships and contending for the title nearly every year. Other teams from the periphery would follow their example: Zarya Voroshilovgrad (1972), Ararat Yerevan (1973), Dinamo Tbilisi (1978), Dinamo Minsk (1982), Dnepr Dnepropetrovsk (1983 and 1988), and Zenit Leningrad (1984) all won championships. During this same period Spartak took four titles, but in the mid-1970s its fortunes fell so low that it was briefly relegated to the second division. Of the other Moscow teams, Torpedo and TSKA won twice, while Dinamo won once.

Throughout this period familiar problems dogged soccer: arranging match results, 'buying off' referees, dirty play and misbehaviour off the field. These and other difficulties in the sport were often caused by the growing influence of the 'patrons' (*metsenaty* — Mycenaeans). These men were usually local Party bosses, plant managers, trade union officials, and KGB or army generals, all of whom were leaders of various organisations that sponsored teams. Like the meddling owners of Western professional teams the patrons sought to dismiss coaches at a whim, dictate team selec- tion and tactics, buy players, bribe referees and fix games.

The acquisition of players was the commonest area of patron involvement. The use of apartments, cars, money and gifts to entice players became a big shady business that was extensively discussed in the press. Player movement, one of the most salient indicators of professionalism, had been common in Soviet soccer from its earliest days, but in the post-Stalin period the practice became even more widespread and blatant. The always murky rules on player movement were constantly being rewritten to control it, but no sooner were new regulations in force than the patrons found ways to circumvent them. Formally, players had to submit applications to the Sports Technical Committee of the Football Federation; and the Federation Board could overrule any decision of the Committee. Unlike in the West, the team losing a player received neither money nor other players in compensation. Since a player could not be the property of a team and no contracts were signed, Soviet players actually had more freedom within the Soviet market than did contemporary Western players in theirs. In 1972, new rules were introduced to restrict the number of players a club could invite and the number of times a player could move in his career. In principle, the only transfers that were looked on favourably were those from a lower division to a higher.

Rigged matches, bribed referees, bought players, cynical tactics and all the tricks of the patrons meant that soccer came to reflect the ways the broader society actually operated. Formal structures were supplemented by a wide range of informal practices. Soccer became a true phenomenon of popular culture. Its usual practices were not simply imposed from above but were the result of interaction between those who produced and those who consumed the game.

The perestroika period: 1985-1991

When Mikhail Gorbachov came to power in 1985, he initiated a long overdue but ultimately unsuccessful attempt to overhaul and reform the whole society. By the end of the 1970s, the time had come to satisfy the long suffering consumer sector of Soviet society, but the old structures just could not respond to this new need; this was the whole crux of the problem and Gorbachov's failure.

Soviet sports spectators, even at the height of Stalinism, had always been able to make choices in the way they patronised sports events, and these 'consumer options' took on added significance with the launching of perestroika. The ultimately unsuccessful attempt to graft some form of capitalism on to the economic practices of what was called the 'command administrative system' gave those choices a special importance. Heavily subsidised institutions and enterprises were left to their own devices after 1985, as the state could no longer afford to do everything. The many pressing needs of the perestroika process, not to mention the crisis it eventually provoked, once again pushed state support for sports to the background. With the economy grinding to a halt in 1990, the government was unable to divert new resources to any leisure activity, and the sports world increasingly found itself thrown back on its own devices, forced to generate its own support.

Many firms and institutions had to become self financing as the USSR lurched towards the establishment of market relations. Goskomsport and the various sports federations lost much of their government funding, and eventually the Sports Committee would cease to exist with the breakup of the USSR in 1991. The various clubs, however, would continue to exist even after the end of the Union, and they had long been required to make their own money even before perestroika began. Nevertheless, after 1985, self financing required teams to re-examine the once scorned practices of commercialism, but this change would prove less dramatic and unprecedented in the sphere of spectator sports than it seemed at first glance.

The new emphasis on making money, in turn, led to a search for an updated version of the partial professionalism of the pre-war period. The possibility of organising spectator sports on what was called an openly professional basis challenged the bureaucratic approach followed for decades by the various versions of the state Sports Committee. Between 1985 and 1991, a variety of independent forces sought new ways to organise the production of spectator sports, as players, coaches and club officials attempted to wrest power from state functionaries.

Yet the debates on the subject were not about professionalisation; a struggle was taking place between state appointed bureaucrats and professional specialists for the control of big time sports. The issue was commercialisation rather than professionalisation. Would sports like soccer now become money making enterprises? And who would control the profits?

But there were problems ahead. Soccer, the best attended sport, drew an average first division crowd of 20,000 in the early 1980s, an entirely respect-able figure that put the USSR fourth among European nations. In the wake of the national team's attractive play in the 1986 World Cup, attendances rose in the 1987 season to 27,000 a game, but by 1988 the average first division crowd fell to 23,000. In 1989 it declined to well below 20,000 and, in 1990, under the impact of the economic crisis and that year's unexpected World Cup failure, only an average of 16,000 came to each match. The next year, as the crisis worsened, only 12,000 attended.

The combination of poor facilities and half empty stands clearly indicated one absolutely central fact about soccer in the Soviet Union. Neither the Party nor the public could be described as 'soccer (or any sport) crazy'. The metaphors of sport rarely extended to other spheres of life. While there was always considerable interest in sport, even passion for soccer, it would hardly be right to argue that either state or society was obsessed with watching soccer. The resources available for sports activities generally and the time devoted to them were always limited compared to the other needs of society. Sport played a decidedly secondary role in Soviet life. Loyalties may have run deep, but few fans defined their own happiness in terms of the success or failure of their favourite teams.

Nevertheless, there was always the potential for passion-driven disorder when large numbers of people gathered at any spectacle, especially in such a multi-national country as the USSR. And the problem grew far more acute during perestroika, mirroring the rising ethnic tensions as the 'empire' was riven apart: Armenians v. Azerbaidzhanis, Armenians v. Russians, Georgians v. Russians, Central Asians v. Europeans, etc. All such tensions were reflected in riots or near riots on the soccer field after 1985.

Those involved in much of the non-ethnic soccer violence were young, disaffected teenagers and workers. Their social profile was roughly similar to that of soccer hooligans elsewhere, and in many cases they displayed similar levels of informal organisation. Bored, disaffected, relatively nihilistic young workers dominated the newspaper accounts of fan violence. Much of the discussion revealed a generation split. One regular theme was that young hooligans were not particularly interested in soccer. Spectator sports generally became a vehicle through which broader forms of youthful alienation were expressed. Instead of operating as a spectacle for instilling certain desirable values, soccer became a medium for expressing anger and boredom — an arena for seizing a sense of strength and power that otherwise many young people did not feel.

If sports entertainments were to stand on their own, the process had to start with the most watched sports; but given the attendance problems, this change was not a simple process. Accordingly, the first experiments were in soccer, and the first team to declare itself to be fully professionalised was Dnepr of Dnepropetrovsk, champions in 1983 and a leading contender for the title after that. In order to survive financially, the team proposed to make the bulk of its money from the sale of tickets. Funds also were to come from membership of its supporters club, along with the sale of souvenirs, programmes and other club associated items. While the team was to be formally independent from its long standing patron, the vast Southern Engineering Works, it continued to look at this enterprise for financial support, which now was to be given in the form of commercial sponsorship. Additionally, the soccer team became part of an ensemble of other enterprises, some of them private (called 'co-operative' at that time). Players and coaches signed three year contracts, and a larger portion of their earnings was to come from performance bonuses. The club also took the unprecedented step of officially rewarding players differently, based on individual performance.

As it turned out, the 1988 season was extremely successful for Dnepr on the field. They won the championship, partly because their leading rivals, Spartak and Dinamo Kiev, were weakened by having to sell their best players in the middle of the season to foreign clubs. But Dnepr's success on the field did not lead to an increased attendance, and it just about broke even by the end of the season. After the 1989 season, the Dnepr experiment proved to be a failure. Even so, other clubs followed suit: Spartak, Ararat, Dinamo Tbilisi, Shakhtyor and Zenit.

Faced with mounting financial difficulties, many clubs sought to raise hard currency through a variety of sponsorship deals with foreign firms. A separate body, Sovintersport, was set up in 1987 to handle all sports contacts with foreign agencies, and Soviet national teams began to carry advertising for Western companies on their kit. Soccer clubs taking part in the European Cup competitions had already been wearing the names of foreign firms, and an Italian company put its logo on the shirts of several teams during domestic league games as well. By far the largest source of hard currency, however, was earned by the selling of Soviet players to foreign teams. Initially, several soccer stars over thirty were signed on less than lucrative contracts to Finland and Austria. They included Dinamo

Kiev's Oleg Blokhin, who played in 1987 and 1988 for an Austrian second division team.

By the summer of 1988, the situation would change dramatically. The 1986 player of the year, Alexander Zavarov of Dinamo Kiev, was sold to Juventus for five million dollars, while Spartak's defender Khidiatulin went to Toulouse for somewhat less. Soon after Spartak's Rinat Dasayev, voted the best goalkeeper in the world in 1988, was sold to Seville for more than two million dollars. In the years after those first deals, dozens of Soviet players went to Britain, Spain, France, Germany, Greece and Sweden, as well as to Italy, Austria and Finland. Initially, only those who had passed their twenty eighth birthday were permitted to leave but, as the financial crisis deepened, this barrier was dropped. Players still at the peak of their careers, like Protasov, Litovchenko and Kanchelskis signed with European teams for substantial sums.

The exodus of the country's best players certainly helped erode interest in domestic competition. The poor performance in the 1990 World Cup and the worsening economic crisis also combined to reduce attendance to 14,000 a game in 1990. The first of the 'foreigners' (Zavarov, Dasayev and Khidiatulin) all performed poorly at the World Cup, confirming fears about the impact of a 'football diaspora'. But with attendances dwindling and no near prospect of increased TV revenues, many clubs came to survive entirely by the sale of players and by foreign tours. Even Spartak found itself in this situation. In fact, however, much of the money received for foreign sales did not find its way back into the clubs — often going to dubious business ventures unrelated to soccer.

In 1989 the first legal and above board transfer fee in the history of Soviet sport occurred — 37,000 rubles for the sale of Leningrad Zenit's Oleg Salenko to Dinamo Kiev. It seemed that one of the iron laws of Western sport had been established. Rich teams succeeded and poor ones failed. By 1991 though the contract system seemed to have taken effect, and many transfers were blocked because the contracts of the players in question had not expired. All the changes that came with open professionalisation forced teams to raise ticket prices; but the sluggish market for spectator sports was not able to support such developments. Professional sport in the West had historically been promoted by the public's enormous appetite for this form of entertainment. While there remained a latent desire for soccer among Soviet citizens, it was far from clear that such a desire was sufficient to support a free standing professional soccer system, especially in the context of the economic crisis, which robbed spectators of the leisure time they needed to get out of the bread queues and into the stadium.

Some conclusions

During perestroika, self financing was supposed to diminish state control of spectator sports like soccer, and reorganise them on a self sustaining basis. But the arguments over professionalisation, fostered by the campaign for autonomy, were not about paying athletes, nor were they about making soccer events more 'fun' for the fans. Rather, the battle over professionalisation was a struggle for the control of the production of soccer spectacles. Specialists who earned their living from soccer sought to take control away from bureaucrats. These attempts to change the nature of soviet soccer, and sport generally, were only partially successful during perestroika. But for the fan, concerned with the entertainment value of his or her favourite sport, little changed. Soviet spectators had always regarded big time soccer as a 'professional' sport. Thus, fans were indifferent to the issue of which group would control the game. The reorganisation of soccer did nothing to halt the decline in attendance, and by the final season, the average crowd at first division matches had fallen to 12,000.

Soviet entry into the global economy after 1988 also had an adverse effect on domestic sports. In the world market for top flight athletes, particularly soccer players, a poorer USSR had difficulty retaining its best talents, and a 'brawn drain' soon developed. The top stars of soccer went to work in Europe, not at home. They became part, along with stars of basketball, ice hockey, volleyball, handball, tennis, cycling and athletics, of a global monoculture of high performance sport tied to increasingly sophisticated international networks of advertising and promotion that were themselves arms of a wide range of multinational companies.

The possibility of soccer inside the USSR being organised as an enterprise threatened the teams that had historically received the highest level of state support — the army and Dinamo clubs. These most traditional elements feared that civilian teams sponsored by commercial firms would have enhanced opportunities for generating wealth and for using that money to increase their success on the field. This trend also had the potential of changing the political and ideological role of Soviet soccer heroes. They would no longer be soldiers or policemen. Instead, the new stars would be civilians who were far less likely to be models for official values.

By 1988, official amateurism had been abandoned. Curiously, jettisoning the myth of the amateur was itself an adjustment to Western complaints about the original communist invention of the state professional. Soviet sports authorities, in turn accepted the need to compete with outsiders under conditions dictated by the international market for sports spectacles. Soviet soccer authorities recognised that the success of their players contributed to the appeal of the game, and they were eager to enjoy the commercial advantages generated by soccer competitions.

Whether the change in the fans' refrain from 'Come on you Reds' to 'Come on you Blues' (the new national team colour) will bring greater joy to Russian/Ukranian/Georgian and a score of other national soccer fans, or success to their teams at home and abroad, remains to be seen. Having performed so strongly in the qualifying competition it will be fascinating to observe the progress of the soccer representatives of the new nation state of Russia in their first visit to the United States in a post-Cold War climate.[7]

Notes and references

[1] Lockhart, R. B. (1958), *Giants Cast Long Shadows*, London: Putnam, p. 175.

[2] Kiselev, N. Y. (1970), *70 futbolnykh let*, Leningrad: p. 39.

[3] Yeschin, A. (1938), *Nationalny vapros v fizkulturnom dvizhenil*, Moscow-Leningrad: p. 76.

[4] This was the era of the design of giant stadia in the form of vast amphitheatres — e.g. the Kirov Stadium in Leningrad, with seating for 15,000 spectators, the Bagirov Stadium in Baku for 80,000 and the projected Stalin Izmailovsky Stadium in Moscow for 250,000 spectators (which was never completed).

[5] Yevgeny Yeliseyev, (July, 1990), 'Futbolom spressovannye god', *Sportivnye igry:* p. 7.

[6] *Kultura i zhizn*, 11 January, 1949.

[7] The scholarship and sources upon which this case study is based can be found in Robert Edelman (1993) *Serious Fun. A History of Spectator Sports in the USSR*, New York: Oxford University Press; and James Riordan (1977) *Sport in Soviet Society*, Cambridge: Cambridge University Press.

Section III
Understanding the World Cup in the global culture and system: Theoretical overviews

14 Football passion and the World Cup: Why so much sound and fury?*

Christian Bromberger

> You wouldn't go to see Macbeth to learn about Scottish history; but you do go to learn about how a man feels when he has won a kingdom but lost his soul.[1]

Can we really credit a football match with the worth and allegorical depth of a great piece of theatre? Is it possible to put forward the argument that if we today (the men amongst us, at least) love these events, it is not just to know the final result or what sort of game it was, but because a profoundly significant game is being played out on the field which intensifies and enacts the fundamental values of life.

These are quite iconoclastic premises which contradict the more generally accepted judgement of sporting events. A well established tradition in philosophy and sociology treats these mass gatherings with great caution, defining their primary function not as something which expresses the essential matter but which deflects attention away from it. We are told that we are dealing with the opium of the people, popular entertainment which helps blur people's perception of their place in society and of their everyday problems both as individuals and as a group, manipulation of the masses, compensatory fantasies and an entertainment which promotes a fleeting and illusory sense of unanimity which masks the tensions and conflicts of everyday life. There is no end to the restrictive labels which

* Translated by Christopher Young, Department of German, Faculty of Modern and Mediaeval Languages, University of Cambridge and Pembroke College, from "Le football comme vision du monde", *Le Monde diplomatique*, June 1992.

281

high-handedly dismiss these surges of collective passion.

This critical and disenchanted view is not devoid of arguments in its favour: in Italy under the fascists as in Argentina under the military junta, the national team's successes were exploited as propaganda; there is any number of provincial moguls or captains of industry (Achille Lauro in Naples, the Agnelli family in Turin, the Peugeots in Sochaux, Bernard Tapie in Marseilles, for instance) who have been able to use their role at the head of a club either directly or indirectly to promote their own public image or consolidate their power base. Moreover, in support of this view one might also note that it is often those towns which have fallen on bad times and lost their esteem which, in their nostalgic yearning for past glories, are most passionate about the clubs that represent them, as if the team's exploits will dress and make up for their current wounds.

However, extending the argument that mobilising forces of football lie exclusively in the hands of the powerful and of states to create an illusion soon brings us full circle to its contradiction, i.e. situations where clubs, stadia, competitions have acted as powerful catalysts for protest and demand by exciting rather than anaesthetising political consciousness: 1958 saw the team of the Algerian National Liberation Front (Front de Libération Nationale), made up of famous players who had walked out of the French league, take part in a world wide tour — a forerunner to the birth of a nation; 1984 brought iron and steel workers from Lorraine (supporters of FC Metz) - protesting their anger — onto the streets of Paris after their club had won in the French Cup. On another level, the magazine *Napulissimo*, which is published by the young fans, is concerned as much with the latest exploits of the stars as with social problems in that city of the Italian South. Beyond these individual cases one hardly need emphasise how football acted as an agent of revelation and formed the cultural and symbolic cement which held the working classes of Northern Europe together in the first half of this century. Quite simply, when one attempts to trace football's latent functions one finds multivalent, fluent and contradictory processes which defy any single or reductive interpretation.

But, you could say, what will we say about the crowds? These are certainly anonymous united hordes in which communal fervour, the mirthful pleasure of being together and one consensual mobilisation against the opposition at least temporarily anaesthetise any awareness of individual differences. Here again this observation needs to be refined. By their very form as compartmentalised rings where hierarchies are established and flaunted (from the terraces to the stands), stadia can be understood as one of those rare spaces where, in the image of modern times, society gives itself a perceptible image not only of unity but also of the contrasts which mould it. This partitioning does not escape the notice of the supporters. Those on the terraces, aware that they are where they belong, sometimes jeer other supporters of the same club seated in the stand, whom they consider over-formal and more than a shade too unenthusiastic. This is one observation among many others concerning the heterogenous nature of the supporters and the rivalries between groups of fans at the same club, which strongly counterbalances judgements on the mystifying functions of sporting events and on unanimity in crowd behaviour.

Football fanatics are no different from anyone else in that they are neither culturally illiterate nor locked by their passions into an illusion, incapable of maintaining a critical distance *vis-à-vis* the world around them. If the match is neither a seductive fiction nor a pernicious mirage, what then is the meaning of the sudden surges of passion to which it gives rise?

Football in its current organisational format — from local and regional leagues to a world championship — provides a forum for the expression of affirmed collective identities and local or regional antagonisms. It is certainly in this ability to mobilise and display loyalties that one must seek an explanation for the remarkable popularity of this team sport which relies on physical contact and open competitiveness. Every match between rival towns, regions and countries takes the form of a ritualised war complete with anthems, military fanfares and banners wielded by fans who form the support divisions and who even call themselves "brigades", "commandos", "legions" and "assault troops"[2]. But this celebratory function of supporters' group loyalty cannot in itself explain the tension which weighs upon a match and the manifestations of violent behaviour.

In order to do this phenomenon justice and avoid misinterpretation we must first of all ask ourselves what constitutes such a dramatic spectacle in which the narrative develops before a watching public who can - or believe they can — influence and even change the dénouement. Players themselves can sense this dynamic interplay of actor and audience. The French star Eric Cantona, darling of the English soccer Premier League in the early 1990s, fed off the emotions of this dynamic: "There is ... room for love between the crowd and the players. The crowd vibrates with the game"[3].

During a match the partisan behaviour of the crowd is certainly a noisy affirmation of a specific identity but also a natural result of the vast breadth of emotion collected together at one place and at one time. There is nothing less satisfying than a match where there is nothing at stake at which one cannot feel involved as an actor in the scene and the transition from "them" to "us" is not made. The explosion of verbal and gestural expression, the emblems wielded and the insults that are hurled are all part of the confrontational nature of the spectacle and it would be wrong to overinterpret them. Is that to say, however, that these phenomena lack any sense? Definitely not. A football stadium is one of those rare spaces where collective emotions are unbridled (in the words of Norbert Elias, a "controlled decontrolling of emotions"[4]), where socially taboo values are allowed to be expressed (the crude affirmation of one's dislike of The Other, for instance).

In other words, the rhetoric of the fans is to be sought both within and outside the logic of the game. When the *tifosi* chant "Devi morire" ("You must die") at an opposition player who has gone down injured, they do not actually want him to die but the tone of their curse is not devoid of meaning. When Milan supporters call the Neapolitans "Africans" it is not an innocent insult but the impact can be rationalised when one recalls that the same Milan fans got behind Cameroon in the 1990 World Cup against an Argentinian team which included a Naples player: Diego Maradona. It would therefore be equally imprudent to claim the arbitrary nature of fans' language as it would be to attribute to it excessive depths of motivation.

But do such emotions work themselves out completely in terms of the confrontation with The Other and in a mimetic participation in the game?

Football fascinates us not just because of its ability to mobilise or its emotive rhetoric but because, like a caricatural melodrama, it lays bare the major symbolic axes of our societies. Its deep structure (the laws of the genre rather than the rules of the game) represents the uncertain fate of man in the world of today.

What exactly does it tell us? As in other sports, it celebrates merit, performance and competition among equals; in stark and brutal fashion it holds up the uncertainty and changing nature of individual and collective status for our inspection. This is symbolised by the emblematic figures of players on the substitutes' bench, the recurrent rise and fall of the stars, the promotion and relegation of teams, a set ranking system — this golden rule of all modern societies founded on the evaluation of ability. As clearly shown by Alain Ehrenberg[5], the popularity of sport lies in its ability to embody the ideals of democratic societies by showing us via the heroes that "anyone can become someone", that status is not given at birth but won in the course of a lifetime. It is after all significant that competitive sport took form in those societies built on the ideal of democracy (ancient Greece, 19th century England) and in places where social competition and a change in hierarchical structures were conceivable. There could be nothing more different from football, on the other hand, than *tlatchtli*, the ball game played by Aztecs which has several formal similarities with today's sport. In a society where a man's fate was fixed from birth and no room was left for chance, success and defeat were endowed with an equal symbolic value: it was inconceivable - even in the game - to have a change of position[6].

Nonetheless, can one reduce the fictionalising process of the imaginary at work in football to the simple celebration of merit where success would be directly proportional to each individual's qualities? This sport — and undoubtedly this is one of its special attractions — presents a more complex and contradictory picture of life.

As well as individual performance, football stresses the value of team work, solidarity, division of labour and collective planning — very much in the image of the industrial world which originally produced it. The mottos of many clubs (from Benfica's "E pluribus unum" to Liverpool's "You'll never walk alone") underline this necessary cooperative effort on the road to success. On the pitch each position requires the implementation of specific skills (the power of the "libero" who demands respect; the stamina of the midfield — "the lungs of the team"; the subtle skills of the wingers who can "dribble on a pocket handkerchief"; the tactical nous of the playmaker). To the same extent the different sorts of fans can find a broad spectrum of contrasting players with whom they might identify them-selves (allegiance to certain stars changes according to a complex play of affinities which more or less reflect social identities). But, if a football match gives you as much to watch as it does to think about this is because of the special place occupied by uncertainty and chance due to the complicated techniques involved in a game based on an unusual usage of the foot, head and upper body, and to the wide range of parameters which need to be mastered in order to secure victory; and also to the devastatingly powerful role of the referee who must immediately penalise offences which are often difficult to discern clearly.

The spectre of chance, which is rarely conceptualised and from which emerges a sense of destiny, hangs over these sporting encounters in such a way that it reminds us with brutal honesty that merit alone is not always enough to get you ahead, just as in those television game shows which revolve around the wheel of fortune rather than knowledge. Just as it might change the run of life, chance can change the trajectory of the ball against the run of play.

Writing for the *Observer* newspaper during the World Cup Finals in Sweden in 1958, Danny Blanchflower — Celtic bard of soccer as well as captain of the Northern Irish side which defied all probability by reaching the last eight of that tournament — put this point poetically:

> In a lifetime of chasing a football around, I have experienced these 'curiouser' fortunes. Usually the ball has responded reasonably to my desires. At times it has seemed to anticipate my every wish and flowed so smoothly that I thought it a part of me and that the whole wide world lay obediently at my feet. But there have been times when it would bounce awkwardly and I had despairing days fighting the unseen forces that bedevilled it (7 June, 1958).

It is these variables of chance which players and supporters try to ward off by means of a plethora of micro-rituals which aim to propitiate the course of fate. Football can therefore be understood as an infinite variation on the drama of fortune in this world. If the road to success depends on a mixture of merit and luck, then you also have to help yourself along with a little cheating: pretence and deception when executed opportunely, in football more so than in other sports, can prove advantageous. The black figure of the referee counteracts the many forms of trickery with the strictures of the law. Yet since most rules only punish deliberate infringements (intentionality is extremely difficult to establish — was the hand-ball deliberate, the tackle a foul or not?), a match opens itself up to a debate of theatrical proportions on the validity and arbitrariness of a flawed justice. The now notorious 1982 World Cup semi-final in Seville between West Germany and France is a case in point: minutes after coming onto the field as a substitute, the French defender, Battiston, was cruelly felled in the penalty area by the opposition goalkeeper, Schumacher. Whilst the Frenchman was stretchered off, never to kick a ball again, the referee awarded West Germany a goal-kick and Schumacher (whose name is still synonymous with that dreadful foul) went on to save the crucial penalty (in the first penalty shoot-out in World Cup competition) to seal his team's place in the final.

Justice was jeered at, too, when the organisers of USA '94 sacrificed the equality of meritocracy for the satiation of geographical and ethnic hungers and markets. In previous competitions the seedings for the draw had relied upon individual nations' objective performances in the three previous World Cup tournaments.Yet the rankings for 1994 were manipulated to cater for the partisan passions of ethnic communities within the USA. Thus Ireland may have lost the benefits of an objective 'second seed' status, yet gained (along with Italy) a significant form of home advantage on the fields of New York.

Football therefore embodies an image of today's world which is at once consistent and contradictory. It celebrates individual and collective merit in the form of a competition which aims to reward the best but it also underlines the role of luck and cheating in the achievement of success both of which in their own way laugh in the face of merit. By these elements and the particular form taken on by justice, it shows a world which is conceivable in human terms, even when success stands you up. For societies where everyone is urged on towards success both individually as well as collectively, failure and misfortune are only psychologically acceptable if they can be explained away in terms of a third party action, injustice or fate. Football holds an unimpeachable order based on pure merit in tension with its appeal to suspicion and necessary uncertainty. What would be the point of a completely transparent society or world where everyone could have rational surety of occupying the position they deserved?

If football uncovers the meanderings of our made to measure fate, it brings us equally startlingly face to face with other essential truths which everyday life conceals or renders imperceptible. It tells us loud and clear that in a world where natural possessions are in finite supply, one person's happiness is conditional on another's misfortune (*mors tua, vita mea*). The Gahuku-Gama of New Guinea grasped this cast iron law of football and of Western society so well that they were quick to get round it in order to make the game correspond more closely with their Weltanschauung.

"They play as many games on consecutive days as are necessary for each team's victories to cancel out their losses."[7] But our own notion of happiness does not only consist of our neighbour's set-back or the defeat of today's opponent. So that we can ultimately gain success, as is accurately illustrated by the mathematics of league systems, close or distant rivals, be they weak or strong, must win or lose on other fields.

Football competitions therefore display another law of modern life: the complex interdependence of individual destinies and fortunes on the road to happiness.

Against this universal backdrop, every league and international team makes its mark and leaves behind specific traditions. Competitions allow us to read in them the general values which mould our age as well as the individual styles of the opposing groups involved. This style, perceived as the emblem of a common sense of belonging is a far cry from the real-life practice of the players and often resembles the monolithic, stereotypical self-image which a collectivity projects to itself and others. The dynamics of this are dictated by how men enjoy *talking about* their team's playing style and their own existence rather than how they actually play and live. The Brazilian style of play which valorises the art of dodging therefore presents an illustration of the golden rule of a social sphere where it is important to know how to work your way out of trouble with stylish dissimulation[8]. The "Swiss Bolt" system of the thirties reflected a country in the process of retiring into itself during times of increasing conflict. The French World Cup side of 1982 (driven by the talented midfield force and panache and 'champagne soccer' of Tigana, Giresse, Genghini and Platini) continued to attack with true Gallic extravagance having taken a 3-1 lead within the first seven minutes of extra time in the semi-final, thus allowing the Germans to fight back and ultimately triumph in a display of extreme teutonic tenacity. One might also think of the *squadra azzurra*, the expressive metaphor for the Italian way of life with its combination of hard graft from the *braccianti del catenaccio* (the artisans of the defense) and the creative genius of the *artisti del contro-piede* (the artistes of the attacking midfield)[9]. Confirming territorial allegiances and particularly national and nationalistic loyalties in a more or less aggressive mode, football goes beyond the classification of senses of belonging and identity by verbalising their imagined ideological substance.

With its masculine language of reference which transcends temporal and spacial boundaries, brings the particular and the universal into dialogue and thrusts together the elements of merit and chance, justice and arbitrariness, "them" and "us", a football match can be seen as one of the profound symbolic matrices of our time. Under the guise of worthless popular entertainment, it casts a harsh light on essential matters and has become a sort of paradigm of collective activity. Members of industry, management and government have not missed the mark with their indulgence in sporting metaphors. Now, however, the direction of the comparison is being reversed: whilst once the team was compared to a business organisation, today it is the latter with the former. Such perceptions of the game vary, of course, according to context, place, class, group and age, and this flexibility of representation is possible because of the wide range of positive values the sport puts on stage: team spirit, a sense of duty, competitiveness, discipline, team work, strength and skill. But beyond these variations and the contrasting models of collective life which the football team might bring together in our imagination, the match reminds us week after week in rapier-like fashion of the fundamental truth of an uncertain world: destiny is fated to be an eternal recommencement.

November 1993 saw the French national side concede a last-gasp goal in Paris against a team of underrated Bulgarians, to lose 2-1. Just weeks earlier, they had in an uncannily similar fashion given away two goals in the concluding moments of a home tie against Israel, converting a comfortable 2-1 winning margin into a 3-2 defeat. Certainty collapsed onto uncertainty in both these acts of France's tragic drama. One point (for a draw, or tied result) from either of these fixtures would have guaranteed France's appearance in the World Cup '94 in the USA. These two defeats condemned France to omission from the '94 American Dream. In 1998 France itself will play host to the footballing dreams of the world's leading teams (thus qualifying automatically for the competition outside the meritocracy and chance of the group system), having had four years in which to endure the anguished wait for the possibility of a more fortuitous cycle of the *éternel recommencement*.

Notes and references

1   Northrop Frye, quoted by Clifford Geertz in support of his interpretation of cockfighting in Bali in terms of a *'jeu profond'* or 'deep play'. See Clifford Geertz (1973) 'Deep Play: notes on the Balinese cockfight', *The Interpretation of Cultures*, New York: Basic Books.

2   C.f. Ignacio Ramonio, 'Le Football c'est la guerre', *le Monde diplomatique*, June 1990.

3   See Mick Cleary 'Beware of a white elephant', *The Observer*, 12 December 1993.

4   Elias, N. and Dunning, E. (1986), *Quest for Excitement. Sport and Leisure in the Civilizing Process*, Oxford: Blackwell.

5   Ehrenberg, A. (1991), *Le Culte de la performance*, Paris: Calmann-Lévy.

6   C.f. Christian Duverger (1978), *L'Esprit du jeu chez les Aztèques*, Paris: Mouton.

7   Claude Lévi-Strauss (1962), *la Pensée sauvage*, Paris: Plon.

8   C.f. Roberto Da Matta, 'Notes sur le futebol brésilien', *le Débat* (19), February 1982.

9   C.f. *Catenaccio e contropiede. Materiali e immaginari del football italiano*, edited by Riccardo Grozio, A Pellicani, Rome, 1990.

15 Media culture and the World Cup: The last World Cup?

Steve Redhead

"...all gone to look for America..." Simon and Garfunkel, 'America', *Bookends* (CBS, 1968)*

This chapter critically considers the work of Jean Baudrillard on 'America' and suggests possible uses of this, and other literature, for those wishing to adopt a popular cultural studies approach to the World Cup and especially to USA '94.

Firstly, I want to set this chapter in its cultural studies context by briefly referencing a selected group of previous, mainly British, analyses of the soccer World Cup as an event over the last thirty years. Most of these have concentrated on the extent to which 'reality' has been displaced by the televisual or cinematic 'image'. Since England's home victory over West Germany in 1966 the World Cup in soccer as a global television event seems increasingly constructed by, for, and in the mass media.

Perspectives on World Cup cultures

Discussion of articles and books which were written around the subsequent World Cup Finals and which reflect this apparently incremental process of 'mediatisation' is set out in the next four sections in recent World Cup Final historical order: 1974 in West Germany; 1978 in Argentina; 1982 in Spain; 1986 in Mexico.

---

* To gain the intended 1990s effect, this line from the song should be imagined as if it was in a 'grunge' version like The Lemonheads' treatment of *Mrs Robinson* (Atlantic Records, 1992), another late 1960s Simon and Garfunkel number from the same LP.

1974 in West Germany

The first piece of work I want to refer to is a pamphlet called *Football on Television* (Buscombe, 1975) which comprised a study of television coverage of the 1974 World Cup eventually won by the hosts in the Final against the 'total football' of Holland [see Merkel's piece on Germany in this volume]. In it Edward Buscombe and his colleagues at the British Film Institute (BFI) — and elsewhere — concentrate on football on television, focusing on the debates (circa 1975) about the problem of 'mediation'. The crux of the contemporary debate in the mid-1970s — and as Garry Whannel (Whannel, 1992) has shown ever since — was the extent to which television programmes in general, and sports coverage in particular, were not so much a record of events as socially constructed phenomena. A major focus, too, was the exploration of the values and ideologies generated in the process of social construction.

1978 in Argentina

Secondly, as the venue moved to South America, I want to cite two contrasting European perspectives: an influential article in the film theory journal *Screen*, 'Television — Football — The World' (Nowell-Smith, 1978/9), and an essay by Umberto Eco before he achieved global fame as a (postmodern) novelist, 'The World Cup and Its Pomps' (in Eco, 1987). Geoffrey Nowell-Smith, focusing on Argentina 1978, explicitly built on the BFI study, theorising television as "never exactly a reproduction of" an event but "always, in some way or other, a *representation*", recognising nevertheless that "the prejudice dies hard that television is there to reproduce; that its subject is given reality" (Nowell-Smith, 1978/9: 46). He notes the irony of holding the World Cup in a country where government, and other groups', terror reigns and citizens frequently 'disappear'. Eco's piece on the World Cup in Argentina in 1978 stressed that this faraway global television event was taking place in the year of the Red Brigade's kidnapping and killing of former Prime Minister of Italy, Aldo Moro. Eco's chapter in 'Reports From the Global Village', a most appropriately named section of his collected essays *Travels in Hyperreality* (originally published as *Faith in Fakes*), is concerned as much with the wave of terrorism then sweeping late 1970s Italy as with football. It discusses the way that the "World Cup has so morbidly polarised the attention of the public and the devotion of the mass media" arguing further that "public opinion, especially in Italy, has never needed a nice international championship more than it does now" (Eco, 1987: 170). In other words, in Eco's judgment, the global televising of an event like the World Cup deflects attention from other, harsher 'realities'. This point is reinforced by Archetti in his case study of Argentina earlier in this volume.

1982 in Spain

The tournament in Spain took place against the backcloth of a recently finished war over the Falklands/Malvinas in the South Atlantic, involving three of the competitors, England, Northern Ireland and Argentina. In 'The World Cup — A Political Football', Alan Clarke and Justin Wren-Lewis (1983) develop the ideas of both the BFI study and Nowell-Smith (Eco's account, though written in 1978, was not published in English until 1986) in an article for the then recently launched journal *Theory, Culture and Society*. They examine the "ways in which political discourses did and did not intrude on to the footballing world as seen on television in June/July 1982" (Clarke and Wren-Lewis, 1983: 123) — that is, the period of the World Cup in Spain. The claim by Clarke and Wren-Lewis is that "the footballing world is a well developed site that does not easily appropriate discourses outside itself", and one which "indeed has its own politics" (Clarke and Wren-Lewis, 1983: 131).

1986 in Mexico

In an edited collection of papers which provides the model for this volume on the World Cup in USA '94, *Off the Ball* (Tomlinson and Whannel, 1986), various references to the mass media and the World Cup appear. This relationship between modern media and global soccer culture is especially evident in 'Tunnel Vision: Television's World Cup' written by Christine Geraghty and Philip Simpson (who were then connected to the BFI) with the increasingly important media and sport theorist Garry Whannel. The essay ranges across the history of the World Cup and the related history of the televising of the event. The three authors' incisive discussion shows how "television football became a global phenomenon" but also emphasises that a "western oriented view of the sport has become the norm in much of the world" (Tomlinson and Whannel, 1986: 20).

All of the essays I have briefly referenced so far reflect a concern that, incrementally every four years, the televising of the World Cup from the

1960s onwards displayed a trend more generally seen in the electronic transformation of Western culture which was producing an increasing domination of the 'image'. For some commentators, however, the (post)-modern world was fast becoming more than just a more visual culture; it was seen instead as a fully fledged post-literate culture of television images with no, or at least little, reference to something previously known as 'reality' at all. The coverage of global sport by the time of the 1990 World Cup Finals was seen by a few critics as having already reached this stage. The critical analysis made by these writers was of a qualitatively different kind to that reviewed so far. It drew on the controversial perspectives of postmodernism, even where its authors denied the definitions and assumptions assumed to be behind such a label.

1990 in Italy

The best example of such a different perspective is *All Played Out*, Pete Davies' (1991) book on Italia '90. Following on from his earlier forays into mass market fiction, *The Last Election* (Davies, 1987) and *Dollarville* (Davies, 1990) the book is a "post-modern-ish" travel/ theory journey through the World Cup Finals in Italy 1990, implying that events such as this have become part of a media saturated (hyper)reality designated by Davies as "Planet Football". Planet Football is described as "an unreality zone of media and marketing mayhem, a land of hysterical fantasy" much of which relates, as Davies skilfully shows, to ever present impending doom of soccer related violence. My own, idiosyncratic, discussion about Italia '90 is contained in a chapter called "Ninety Minute Culture: E for England Party Mix" in *Football With Attitude* (Redhead, 1991) and re-presents the hysterical media stories of English hooliganism at the World Cup Finals in Italy in such a way that it is as if the (hooligan) event which had been widely predicted in the mass media *hardly* took place, a conclusion which Davies also independently reaches. None of his analysis — or mine — suggests that there is no 'real' fan violence at World Cup finals, but it does stress the important role of news/media expectations and their often self-fulfilling prophecies. More controversially in Davies there is the hint — taken up with much postmodern theorising — that an event of, say, hooliganism which is not covered in the media has not fully occurred at all — in other words it is not 'real'. Davies' title phrase is taken up throughout his book suggesting the 'death' or 'exhaustion' of all kinds of aspects of football and media culture including the post-colonial English national football team, former winners of the Jules Rimet trophy in 1966.

In summer 1993, a year prior to the World Cup being staged in the USA in 1994, Davies (1993) published a post-Italia '90 article on America and soccer's biggest prize. Following hard on the heels of more mainstream football writers (for instance, Barclay, 1993, and Glanville, 1993) Davies takes a careful look at the implications for the development of soccer in America of the USA being the host nation. He focuses on the crucial dimensions of space and time in a country the size of America and the likely impact of the global telecommunications industry on the internal consumption of the event. The 'new' experience of having the World Cup in the USA for the first time despite the country having entered the inaugural finals in Uruguay in 1930, and qualified for more of the last stages in the intervening years, is prominent in the article giving rise to an optimistic view of both how the World Cup will be staged in '94 and the likely impact on the playing of soccer in future in the United States (see Sugden in this volume.) However, there is pessimism in Davies' account, too, as he notes the potential for the World Cup to 'disappear' when he claims:

> The baffling vastness of America presents all manner of difficulties both for organisations and for fans...So it may be that the World Cup will be huge in nine cities, and that in Kansas or Idaho they won't give a cuss. Eleven weekend games will be live on ABC and the other 41 will be on ESPN — a 24 hour sports cable network reaching 70 million homes — but whether anyone will watch outside those nine immediately concerned media markets remains to be seen...we should...be watching with some fascination to see what they do with it; but if there's one country on this earth where the World Cup can happen and a whole bunch of people not even notice or care, then this is the one.

Another writer who has cultivated the idea of 'disappearance' is the infuriating, reluctant, guru of the "post", Jean Baudrillard. Baudrillard has proclaimed the complete meaninglessness of the term postmodernism in his statement that "there is no such thing as postmodernism"[1] (Gane, 1993: 22) and denied being anything approximating to a 'postmodernist'. His own biographical trajectory, and eventual rise to academic super-stardom can be usefully compared to that of Umberto Eco (see Rojek and Turner, 1993 introduction). Both authors, interestingly, are fascinated by America and the fake/hyperreal but Eco retains a 'respectable' gravitas inside and outside the academy whereas Baudrillard provokes the most extreme hostility as well as uncritical celebration. Let us consider the commentaries of Baudrillard on the areas which I have already covered with regard to Eco.

Although he has written very little about sport, Baudrillard has mused in a collection of essays "on extreme phenomena" called *The Transparency of Evil* (Baudrillard, 1993) about the extent to which media coverage displaces the 'real' event. For Baudrillard, in the essay entitled 'The Mirror of Terrorism':

> The most striking thing about events such as those that took place at the Heysel Stadium, Brussels, in 1985, is not their violence per se but the way in which this violence was given currency by television, and in the process turned into a travesty of itself (Baudrillard, 1993: 75).

He comments further that:

> The Romans were straightforward enough to mount spectacles of this kind, complete with wild beasts and gladiators, in the full light of day. We can put on such shows only in the wings, as it were — accidentally, or illegally, all the while denouncing them on moral grounds. (Not that this prevents us from disseminating them worldwide as fodder for TV audiences: the few minutes of film from the Heysel Stadium were the most often broadcast images of the year.) Even the 1984 Olympic Games in Los Angeles were transformed into a giant parade, a worldwide show which, just like the Berlin Games of 1936, took place in an atmosphere of terrorism created by a power's need to show off its muscles: the worldwide spectacle of sport was thus turned into a Cold War strategy — an utter corruption of the Olympic ideal. Once wrenched away from its basic principle, sport can be pressed into the service of any end whatsoever: as a parade of prestige or of violence, it slips...from play founded on competition and representation to circus like play, play based on the pull of vertigo (Baudrillard, 1993: 77).

Baudrillard follows this point later in the essay by commenting on a post-Heysel European Cup tie in 1987 between Real Madrid and Napoli which was ordered by UEFA (the European Union of Football Associations) to be played behind closed doors. He writes that:

> ...the match took place at night in a completely empty stadium, without a single spectator, as a consequence of disciplinary action taken by the International Federation in response to the excesses of Madrid supporters at an earlier game. Thousands of fans besieged the stadium, but no one got in. The match was relayed in its entirety via television. A ban of this kind could never do away with the chauvinistic passions surrounding soccer, but it does perfectly exemplify the terroristic hyperrealism of our world, a world where a 'real' event occurs in a vacuum, stripped of its context and visible only from afar, televisually. Here we have a sort of surgically accurate prefiguration of the events of our future: events so minimal that they might well not need take place at all — along with their maximal enlargement on screens. No one will have directly experienced the actual course of such happenings, but everyone will have received an image of them. A pure event, in other words, devoid of any reference in nature, and readily susceptible to replacement by synthetic images. The phantom football match should obviously be seen in conjunction with the Heysel Stadium game, when the real event, football, was once again eclipsed — on this occasion by a much more dramatic form of violence. There is always the danger that this kind of transition may occur, that spectators may cease to be spectators and slip into the role of victims or murderers, that sport may cease to be sport and transformed into terrorism: that is why the public must simply be eliminated, to ensure that the only event occurring is strictly televisual in nature. Every real referent must disappear so that the event may become acceptable on television's mental screen" (Baudrillard, 1993: 79-80).

Baudrillard's various comments quoted above from *The Transparency of Evil* come in the context of the 'live' televising of the deaths of 39 Italian fans at the Heysel Stadium football disaster at the European Cup Final in May

1985[2] rather than a World Cup Finals, but any analysis of mass media presentation of the next World Cup, USA '94, will need to accommodate the extent to which the "real referent" has in fact disappeared over recent years and how far audiences, both 'live' and television, have been transformed by the increasing domination of the "mental screen".

Perspectives on USA '94 and beyond

The 1994 tournament will be held in the USA, the land of the mediascape, with Japan (see Horne and Jary in this volume) waiting in the wings to host the first Finals following the year 2000 after France, Baudrillard's home country, has staged them in 1998. The 1994 event may well mark a watershed in the mediatising of this ultimate example of global popular culture. A more 'passive', as opposed to 'participatory', audience for football is one possible outcome as soccer is globally consumed more and more through the mediation of television. American 'live' audiences for USA '94 are likely to be the least committed and knowledgeable of any World Cup held so far. There is also widespread fear that the lack of informed, technical knowledge amongst broadcasters will lead to a reduction in the generally high quality coverage of sport on TV in the USA. The commercial and media aspect to the event is assumed by large sections of football fans in Europe to be the reason for the award of the staging of the competition in a country where soccer has such a low profile compared to baseball, basketball and American football. The USA is generally perceived by commentators as an eccentric choice for the 1994 Finals. Certainly, European sports journalists reacted cynically — with a few exceptions such as Patrick Barclay (Barclay, 1993) — when the news of the USA as the venue was announced. For instance, Michael Parkinson (Parkinson, 1992) noted in the context of writing about some sporting ideas he wanted to send to the Fédération Internationale des Football Associations:

> I hope they will take my suggestions seriously in Zurich. I am hopeful. They might sound barmy but the people at FIFA are used to that. It was they after all, who gave the next World Cup to the yanks.

Nevertheless, sports journalists' sarcasm notwithstanding, the final of the 1994 World Cup will be held in the same city as hosted the 1984 Olympic

Games, itself a new moment in the globalisation and commodification of sport. It will be played in the Pasadena Rose Bowl in Los Angeles, California, where a large crowd witnessed the Olympic Soccer Final in 1984. Germany, the holders of the World Cup after defeating the 1986 winners, Argentina, in an acrimonious final in Italy in 1990, will open USA '94 at Chicago stadium at Soldier Field on Friday June 17 in a tournament of 24 finalists. The teams were put in groups of four at the final draw in Las Vegas in December 1993. Widely predicted changes to the actual on-field playing of the game of football as a consequence of the staging of the tournament in the television saturated USA have not yet been forthcoming. For instance, the president of FIFA, João Havelange, declared in November 1992 — after much previous speculation to the contrary — that his plan to split matches into four quarters would not be implemented in time for the 1994 Finals. However, the ever faster changes in new communications technologies at the end of the millennium will inevitably coincide with the televising of the 1994 World Cup and its aftermath. For instance, in early 1992 it was proclaimed that armchair British football fans would soon be able to select their own television pictures following the launch of a new cable service ("Soccer Fans Get Choice of TV Shot in Cable's 'Next Best Thing To Terraces'", headlined *The Guardian* on February 12, 1992). Interactive television was seen by the providers, the Videotron cable company, as enabling viewers to select from four cable channels all covering a match simultaneously with different facilities such as camera angles and statistical information. At the time Greg Dyke, London Weekend Television chief executive, called the Videotron experiment "a big, big message for the 21st century".

I want to argue in this essay however that we can use Baudrillard, in a more complex way than merely reproducing what he has written about the hyperreality of modern media culture, some of which is based upon his extremely controversial contention that 'TV is the world'. As a contribution to what the disciplinary field which I have elsewhere labelled as 'Popular Cultural Studies'[3] can now bring to the analysis of "USA '94", the remainder of this chapter critically appraises Jean Baudrillard's travel/theory/adventure book *America* (Baudrillard, 1988) — published originally in France in 1986 as *Amerique* by Grasset of Paris — and assesses its implications for the study of the hosting of the World Cup by a country Baudrillard describes as "(un)culture" (Baudrillard, 1993: 79) and "born modern"[4] (Baudrillard, 1993: 73) or hypermodern and, further, as "the original version of modernity" which "has no past and no founding truth" and that "lives in a perpetual present...in perpetual simulation, in a perpetual present of signs" (Baudrillard, 1988: 76). In his role as a European tourist travelling to the USA, Baudrillard proclaims that Europe has *disappeared* into America, or, more accurately, into California: in "Los Angeles, Europe has disappeared", he says (Baudrillard, 1993: 81). In a recent book of essays on Baudrillard, Barry Smart and Bryan Turner (Rojek and Turner, 1993, see especially Chapters 3 and 8) argue, legitimately, that the Europe/America couplet which Baudrillard uses is located in a more general historical critical transatlantic tradition. Baudrillard, as is his wont, merely pushes this tradition to its limit in his comparing and contrasting of 'modern' America and 'traditional' Europe, the New World and the Old World.

Apart from the contributors to the above collection of essays perhaps the scholar most critically sympathetic to Baudrillard has been Mike Gane. In Gane's book of selected interviews with Baudrillard (Gane, 1993), which contains a most revealing introduction focusing on the difference between Baudrillard's writings and his interviews, one of the sections is entitled 'America as Fiction' (Gane, 1993, pp. 131-135) and reproduces a previously little known interview with Baudrillard about his views on America at the time of the French publication of the book. Baudrillard comments in this interview that the last thing he wants to suggest "is that America is some sort of paradise. It is precisely its rawness which interests me and its primeval character, although one shouldn't confuse it with some sort of primitive society." He goes on to "specify that *America* should not be read as a realist text. Its subject matter being a fiction itself." For Baudrillard the difficulty in the book had been to "evoke this transpolitical, transhistorical reality" of an American society which "is not a society of appearances". In Baudrillard's argument it has no counterpart to the games of seduction with which he sees Europe as being so familiar. For him Americans "experience reality like a tracking shot" which is why they succeed so well with certain media, particularly television. This fascination with the object of his post-tourist inquiry (or what he did on his holidays!) does not mean that Baudrillard "likes" what he sees. He is, simultaneously, seduced and repelled. His view is that "America is hell" ("I vomit it out") and that it is, as a whole, a "matter of abjection" but "such criticisms are inconsequential" because at "every instant this object is transfigured. It is the miracle of realised utopia...America is a place where utopia was realised by a geographical displacement and conservation of the ideas of the eighteenth century."

Nevertheless, looking back a few years after the book was first published and realising that the utopia he mentions has a historical referent in *1950s* America, Baudrillard claims that the United States has "changed since I wrote *America*. It now functions only in the mode of protectionism, survival." He confesses, in a separate interview in the collection which dates from 1991, to having lost his "exaltation over America", a confession which itself perplexed some critics on the left who had thought they had perceived in *America* a Baudrillard who was "condemning the dehumanising influence of America". Nothing could be further from the truth. "It's become trivial", he says, "it finds it is being overtaken by a non-realistic model such as the Japanese model...between Japan and the rational and technicist West, there is an irreducible antagonism" (Gane, 1993: 187). Even in *America* itself there is a hint of the 'disillusionment' with even an achieved utopia when Baudrillard argues that "today the orgy is over" and that the United States, along with everybody else, "now has to face up to a soft world order, a soft situation" where "power has become impotent" and de-centred (Baudrillard, 1993: 107). Baudrillard, here at least, certainly articulates the experience of many European, and other, tourists of America as an empire at the end of its tether.

For some critics the publication of *America* was worth taking seriously (though not without a very rigorous critical reading) as an exposition of elementary errors and prejudices in Baudrillard. For many others it was a sign of how far Baudrillard's once left wing credentials had slipped around the head of just another 'lazy' French academic. For yet others, the 'panic' theorists of postmodernity, Baudrillard's vision was, if loaded in manic fashion onto other examples of French intellectual production, a paradigm case of the hyperreality of postmodernity (the idea of Disneyland being the 'real' America, for instance) and also evidence of a wider connection between Europe and America. For Arthur Kroker (Kroker, 1992) especially almost all of the leading contemporary French social and cultural theory — most explicitly Baudrillard but Lyotard, Foucault and others too — is integrally related to 'America'. Kroker asks (rhetorically):

And why the fascination with French thought? Because its discourse is a theoretical foreground to America's political background: fractal thinkers in whose central images one finds the key power configurations of the American hologram...French thought, therefore, as a violent decoding and recoding of the American way, which is to say, of all the world, since America is today the global hologram (Kroker, 1992: 1-3).

The comparative (economic) failure of Euro Disney in France may call into question such ubiquitousness of the American hologram, and also some of the wilder elements of Kroker's own 'panic' appropriation of Baudrillard, but the different versions/visions of America are there for all to see. For Baudrillard himself, *America* was:

...a book I wrote in a flash of inspiration. I loved that country. The book is talked about a lot, but there was nothing but negative reactions. On the one hand, I've been treated like the last of the Europeans, stuffed with prejudices and self satisfaction, who had understood nothing about the reality of America. It was impossible to connect that by saying that I was not presuming to judge American reality. My critics were reading the wrong book. On the other hand, some people read it another way (Gane, 1993: 189).

Baudrillard's 'astral' America is clearly distinct from the economic and social 'reality' of America and there are obviously many different Americas; as Barry Smart has pointed out "Baudrillard arrived already in possession of America, possessed by it, a colonised subject of its empire of cinematic signs" (in Rojek and Turner, 1993: 55). Personally, I am convinced that any popular cultural studies criticism of the 1994 World Cup in America (and, for that matter, beyond) needs to take Baudrillard's version of America seriously but with a good deal of caution, too. As Mike Gane (Gane, 1991b) has contended about Baudrillard's work in general:

He is not always capable of surprising and provoking us to the degree he would wish, and some of his analyses are vulnerable to the most harsh of judgments. Yet the overall impression we are left with is of a consistency and persistence of critical imagination which produces, sometimes, remarkable insights. Some of his work is utterly self defeating, even hypocritical. But there is an undeniable vitality and creativity coupled with an undying fidelity not to a utopian vision in a passive sense, but to a passionate utopian practice in theory (Gane, 1991: 1157).

This judgment by Gane, with which I concur, serves also as a useful summary of Baudrillard's writing in *America* specifically. It means, though, that when using such a text as one way into the consideration of USA '94 as a global media event the precise angle of the 'flight' to America needs elaboration.

My own 'America' is a less cinematic one than Baudrillard's. In a way some of my previous works on soccer's mediatised culture from a popular cultural studies perspective — *Sing When You're Winning* (Redhead, 1987) and *Football With Attitude* (Redhead, 1991) for instance — combine elements from what was once called the 'new journalism', the beat poetry of Jack Kerouac and several decades of American rock culture with an iconoclastic use of theories of the so-called 'postmodern condition'. A subtitle such as 'The Last[5] World Cup' has, for me at least, the distant echoes of an empire of pop culture signs including Hunter S. Thompson's *Fear and Loathing in Las Vegas* and *Fear and Loathing: The Campaign Trail '72*, Jack Kerouac's *On the Road*, Bob Dylan's *Highway 61 Revisited* and *Blonde on Blonde*, and R.E.M.'s *Automatic For The People*. In my fictional journey to 'America' and USA '94, Jean Baudrillard (with his French sidekick, Paul Virilio armed with the "aesthetics of disappearance") meet the above characters on their way to the World Cup Final in L.A. Both Baudrillard and, say, Hunter Thompson, in their very different ways, have, during the last twenty five years, provided insights into the American (or 'Western' or 'Capitalist') condition; when the spirits of these two mavericks meet up (one a visitor from the outside, one a visitor from within) the product may be something of a postmodern travelogue entitled 'Veneer and Loafing in Los Angeles' perhaps, or 'Fear and Loathing in Pontiac' as the self-styled "half decent football magazine" *When Saturday Comes* (issue for September 1993) suggested in its preview of USA '94.

A number of travelogues, besides Baudrillard's own, have in fact been written on the USA. Recently this has been done by utilising genres such as American popular music (Brown, 1993; Bull, 1993; Heath, 1993; and to some extent Davies, 1992) and popular crime fiction (Williams, 1991) as a way into American popular culture: as a journey to the heart of the contemporary American dream. I have suggested in this essay that the search also might be done through soccer, and the event of USA '94, and that a critical reading of Baudrillard's *America* might be a helpful guide. But soccer is in many ways alien to American popular culture, an originally European cultural form inserting itself into the psyche (or sign) of America. Baudrillard's series of distinctions and contrast between a modern, deculturated America and an older, more historical, 'cultured' Europe is one possible frame for analysing the media presentation which will take place in summer '94. Nevertheless, for conventional academic researchers the way to study the production, consumption and regulation of a globalised TV event like the soccer World Cup is more likely to be by 'zapping' the channels ('surfing') on as many television sets as can be found in as many countries as possible. Such research design may not necessarily even entail visiting the United States of America during the period that the event takes place at all. In this sense the methodology and theoretical apparatus which lends itself most easily to such cultural analysis is the sort exemplified by the BFI study of the televising of the 1974 Finals (Buscombe, 1975) which was referenced at the beginning of this chapter. Such an approach does resolve some difficult research problems (such as how to fund travel from other countries to the USA!) though to eschew any form of ethnography in these cases is likely to lead to only a very partial view of an event. Conventional ethnographic study could, and should, be done to supplement media and textual analysis of what occurs on television screens. For instance, the sorts of 'world cup cultures' which have been excavated so expertly in this volume have their reverberations in the various ethnic cultures in the United States itself — Hispanic, African, European, Oriental and so on. To rely simply on the semiotic analysis of TV signs in accounting for an event such as the USA '94 risks ignoring how the event is *differentially* consumed by a variegated (live and television) audience and to accept the dangerous logic of the complete disappearance of the "real referent".

What can finally be said about the coming of USA '94? Even though Havelange's plan to divide the 90 minutes of play into four quarters — to better accommodate television advertising — has been shelved, many effects of the World Cup being staged in the home of the ultimate landscape of the media are manifest even now. The World Cup '94, in many ways, could be said to have 'already taken place' in terms of its

contribution to the global media coverage of soccer, especially in Europe. The transformations of the football audience — from more participatory to more passive — are already well advanced as I have argued in other work (see Redhead, 1993). The 'disappearance' of the audience which Baudrillard toys with in the comments which I quoted earlier from *The Transparency of Evil* has not of course, literally, taken place, apart from isolated games (like the one he reviews) where indiscipline by supporters has led to governing bodies ordering the playing of matches behind closed doors. Nevertheless, it is clear that the reorganisation of the business side of many of the world's biggest soccer clubs (AC Milan, Barcelona, Manchester United, and so on) is proceeding in such a way that 'live' paying spectators will not necessarily be required in order that these entities survive in future as economically successful corporations. Television revenues, sales from various commercial exploitation of related commodities, and sponsorship already count for far more than spectator income. The drive for more passive (at the ground or at home watching television) rather than more participatory spectators risks, of course, diluting the spectacle itself, which for many critics depends on the enthusiasm generated by participatory football fans. Whether the 'resistance' movement amongst fans in many countries succeeds in fighting this modernisation and rationalisation of global soccer is at present unpredictable, but in Britain, for instance, clubs — such as Arsenal — have already experimented (albeit during ground reconstruction) with the 'simulation' of a participatory crowd. Artists' impressions of a terrace crowd, and piped chanting/cheering, were part of the simulation of a whole 'end' of terrace culture.

However, the implication of Jean Baudrillard's work for popular cultural study of the World Cup is even more fundamental than this. The problem posed by Baudrillard is how to make sense of something which is so 'mediatised' — so hyperreal — that it can be said:

> (a) to have already taken place; or
>
> (b) that it will not take place; or
>
> (c) that it will hardly take place.

For Baudrillard, the Gulf War (Baudrillard, 1991) was such an event to be analysed in these terms. For some of his harshest critics like Christopher Norris (Norris, 1991) this approach to a local/ global war was ludicrous —

and worse — politically dishonest in view of the terrible loss in Iraqi, and other populations', lives. At first, Baudrillard's position on the Gulf conflict, before any military hostilities began between Iraq and the 'allies', seemed to be a fairly straightforward prediction that there would be no war — merely *simulation* of war — but once there was fighting in early 1991 this argument had to be clarified. In the context of the aftermath of a global event such as Italia '90, I argued in a footnote on the Iraq war that "within months the world was plunged into ultra high-technological warfare in the Gulf where video games replaced dead bodies as the products of war" (Redhead, 1991: 107). As Gane (1993) points out in his analysis of Baudrillard's writings on the war once it had begun (which have still not been translated into English in their entirety) Baudrillard could have easily outlined — as I did — the "novelty of war in which computer simulation played...a major part in the technological armoury of both sides." But, Gane rightly points out, "Baudrillard went considerably further" suggesting that "everything was unreal: the war, the victory, the defeat" (Gane, 1993:7-8). Baudrillard rarely, in fact, goes this far in his varied writings and interviews — that is, implying total simulation and the complete disappearance of the event/referent — and as can be seen from his analysis of Heysel, and subsequent soccer events, the theoretical desire to do so is often limited in practice, giving way to a more balanced account of the "hyperreal". It is debilitating to follow Baudrillard at his most extreme — he sets up, as many have pointed out, his own 'disappearance' — and clearly, barring unforeseen circumstances, the World Cup *really* will take place in the USA in 1994. Nevertheless, the event, as a global media show, may well have, as I have argued, been foreshadowed in the changing face of television driven, media mogul dominated world soccer culture over the last few years. But what will be extremely interesting to watch — as well, as hopefully, at least some of the matches themselves — is the way in which the separate world cup cultures, the separate national identities formed around soccer which fill the pages of this volume, will come out in USA '94. The 1990 tournament in Italy brought howls of protest that, in playing styles, 'we are all Europeans now' and that as a result of most of the world's best players being collected into Italian league soccer difference and spontaneity were in danger of being squeezed out of the world football game. Maybe this European football culture will disappear in America as Baudrillard's tourist gaze implies. Or maybe not. Is the USA '94 set to

become a watershed of a different kind; of renewal in global *and* local soccer culture. Perhaps after USA '94 has taken place we will be able to look back on the event with an optimism for the future — the emergence of a 'new Brazil' amongst the emergent soccer nations of Africa, South America (keep an eye on Bolivia) or Asia (watch out for Japan as 2000 approaches) for instance?

Acknowledgements

I would like to thank participants at the North American Society for the Sociology of Sport Annual Meeting, University of Ottawa, Canada, November 3-7, 1993 for their helpful comments on an earlier conference paper version of this chapter, and the School of Law at the Manchester Metropolitan University for financing the trip to Canada to deliver the paper.

Notes

1   For a thorough discussion of Baudrillard's large body of work in the context of this debate about postmodernism, see also Gane, 1991(a) and Gane, 1991(b). All three of Gane's books on Baudrillard make out an extremely good case for regarding Baudrillard as anti-modernist *and* anti-postmodernist.

2   For my own satirical account of the youth cultural context of the Heysel disaster, Thatcherite politics and the mass media, see Redhead, 1987.

3   For a history and outline of the possible field designated by the label 'Popular Cultural Studies' and how it might be seen to grow out of, but also differ from, previous formulations such as 'Contemporary Cultural Studies', see Redhead, 1994, forthcoming.

4   Baudrillard's view in *America* is that "you are born modern, you do not become so". See, in contrast, for a 1990s Marxist oriented sociology of '(post) modern' America, Woodiwiss, 1993. Woodiwiss sees postmodernism (which he defines to incorporate Baudrillard) as having made a contribution to a more adequate sociology without accepting the on-set of a qualitatively different and new 'postmodern' world which has replaced a pre-existing condition of modernity. He is sceptical about the generalisation of hyperreality/postmodernity "amongst even the

advanced capitalist nations of the world" and specifically rejects "post-Marxist" contentions.

5   The idea of the 'last' is deliberately jokey. It does not suggest that I think there will literally be no new World Cup Finals after 1994 in the USA. There is, though, a serious implication of such a phrase as 'the last'. I used it in the subtitle to Redhead, 1987 (*The Last Football Book*) as I do here to draw attention both to the specific historical deterioration in the genre (either football writing or the World Cup as a spectacle) *and* the more philosophical idea of 'end of....' See Kroker and Kroker, 1993 for a similar use in the different context of sexuality.

References

Barclay, Patrick (1993), 'A Family at War in the Land of Hype and Glory', *The Observer*, June 20.

Baudrillard, Jean (1988), *America, London:* Verso.

———(1991), 'The Reality Gulf' *The Guardian*, January 11.

———(1993), *The Transparency of Evil: Essays on Extreme Phenomena*, London: Verso.

Brown, Mick (1993), *American Heartbeat*, London: Michael Joseph.

Bull, Andy (1993), *Coast to Coast*, London: Black Swan.

Buscombe, Edward (ed.) (1975), *Football On Television*, London: British Film Institute.

Clarke, Alan and Wren-Lewis, Justin (1983), 'The World Cup — A Political Football', *Theory, Culture and Society*, Volume 1, Number 3, pp.123-133.

Davies, Pete (1987), *The Last Election*, Harmondsworth, Penguin.

———(1990), *Dollarville*, London: Vintage.

———(1991), *All Played Out*, London: Heinemann.

———(1992), *Storm Country*, London: Heinemann.

———(1993), 'Tomorrow the World', *The Guardian*, June 26.

Eco, Umberto (1987), *Travels in Hyperreality*, London: Picador.

Gane, Mike (1991a), *Baudrillard: Critical and Fatal Theory*, London: Routledge.

———(1991b), *Baudrillard's Bestiary*, London: Routledge.

———(1993), *Baudrillard Live, London:* Routledge.

Glanville, Brian (1993), *The Story of the World Cup*, London: Faber and Faber.

Heath, Chris (1993), *The Pet Shop Boys Versus America*, Viking, London.

Kroker, Arthur (1992), *The Possessed Individual: Technology and Postmodernity*, London: Macmillan.

Kroker, Arthur and Kroker, Marilouise (eds.) (1993), *The Last Sex*, London: Macmillan.

Norris, Christopher (1991), *Uncritical Theory*, London: Lawrence and Wishart.

Nowell-Smith, Geoffrey (1978), 'Television — Football — The World', *Screen*, Volume 19, Number 4, 1978/9: 45-59.

Parkinson, Michael (1992), *Sporting Lives*, London: Pavilion.

Redhead, Steve (1987), *Sing When You're Winning: The Last Football Book*, London: Pluto Press.

———(1991), *Football With Attitude*, Manchester: Wordsmith.

———(1994, forthcoming), *Unpopular Cultures*, Manchester: Manchester University Press.

Redhead, Steve (ed.) (1991), *The Passion and the Fashion: Football Fandom in the New Europe*, Aldershot: Avebury.

Rojek, Chris and Turner, Bryan (eds.) (1993), *Forget Baudrillard?* London: Routledge.

Tomlinson, Alan and Whannel, Garry (eds.) (1986), *Off The Ball: The Football World Cup*, London: Pluto Press.

Whannel, Garry (1992), *Fields in Vision: Television Sport and Cultural Transformation*, London: Routledge.

Woodiwiss, Anthony (1992), *Postmodernity USA: The Crisis of Social Modernism in Postwar America*, London: Sage.

Williams, John (1991), *Into The Badlands*, London: Paladin.

Index

311

HOSTS AND CHAMPIONS

SOCCER CULTURES, NATIONAL IDENTITIES AND THE USA WORLD CUP

Hosts and Champions takes a dispassionate look at one of the world's biggest sporting events. Along with the Olympic Games, the soccer World Cup dominates the global sporting calendar of competing nations and of spectators.

In 1994 the World Cup is hosted by the USA, and the passions and dramas of the sport played at its highest level will be presented to a nation which has a traditional ambivalence to the introduction and development of soccer. How will the USA respond to this latest soccer invasion? How will the world's elite soccer-playing nations respond to the USA?

Pre-tournament polls have located soccer way down any popularity chart in the USA. But will the skills of the Brazilians, the aggression of the Argentinians, the free spirit of the Cameroons, the artistry of the Romanians, the endeavour of the Scandinavians, the volatility of the Italians, the flair of the Spanish and the industry of the Irish, lay the foundations for the real flowering of soccer in the North American continent?

Hosts and Champions gives the background to soccer's worldwide popularity and looks at where the World Cup has been played and how it has been won. It includes case-study chapters on: Argentina – Brazil – England – Germany – Ireland – Italy – Japan – Norway – Russia – Sweden – USA, and general essays on the growth of the world game, the cultural meanings of soccer and the ever-increasing role of the media in staging the sports spectacle.

The book captures the international impact of soccer and also probes the cultural distinctiveness of the game in the stories of its growth in different countries and nations. It will help the fan and the potential fan, as well as the serious scholar of sport, understand how in USA '94 soccer's World Cup offered the American public a Real World Series, featuring the globe's most popular competitive team sport.

The book's editors are two Englishmen whose interest in world sport, comparative studies and international relations has pervaded their professional lives. Dr John Sugden is Senior Lecturer in the Division of Sport and Leisure Studies at the University of Ulster, Northern Ireland. Professor Alan Tomlinson is Professor of Leisure Studies in the Chelsea School (Faculty of Education, Sport and Leisure), University of Brighton, England.

GB £14.95

arena

Gower House, Croft Road, Aldershot
Hampshire GU11 3HR, England

ISBN 1-85742-228-7

01495>

9 781857 422283